Tourism in the Age of Globalisation

Tourism in the Age of Globalisation

Dr. Binoy Srivastava

SWASTIK

SWASTIK PUBLICATIONS

DELHI–110094 (INDIA)

SWASTIK PUBLICATIONS
31 Gali No. 1, A Block, Pocket 5, CRP Water Tank,
Sonia Vihar, Delhi-110094
Cell: 9968482939, 9899462604
e-mail: swastik_books@yahoo.com

Tourism in the Age of Globalisation

First Published 2012

ISBN:- 978-93-81084-26-7

PRINTED IN INDIA

Published by Indra Mani Pandey for Swastik Publications, Delhi and Printed at Asian Offset Press, Delhi-53

PREFACE

A traveler can decide today to go to the North Pole and be there by tomorrow. Global infrastructures such as transportation and communications and global policies for free trade have created a situation where people and businesses in the global North can easily access natural resources and cultures in the global South. Until 1999, when thousands of people around the world began organising against it (*e.g.*, the Battle in Seattle), globalisation was not regarded as a danger to local economies and cultural diversity. In fact, politicians and the media tout globalisation as the path to greater wealth and success. Although globalisation may be the most primary transformation of the world's political and economic structures since the industrial revolution, its implications have yet to be fully understood and debated.

Most of the economic restructuring is in the interest of big business, not in the interest of the public. Under the banner of free trade, corporations have come to shape our lives through the consumer products we buy including technology, the media that feed us information, even the educational system that trains us. Politicians chant the mantra of privatisation and globalisation. What does that mean for individuals? This means interaction and thus the necessity of global tourism.

It is in this context this book evaluates the nature and resilience of the emerging global economy and its implications for tourism. The book presents contextual overviews of globalization, including territorial economic integration. The book looks at the globalization of tourism demand and marketing. It includes an analysis of the new tourist and consumer, and the effects of globalization on tourism promotion. It deals with globalization and competitiveness in tourism. Issues examined include inter-firm alliances, safety and national security, quality management, and tourism education in a global economy. It focuses on the globalization of tourism's approach to sustainability. It covers environmental policies, cultural identity, and sustainable development.

Author

CONTENTS

1

Tourism, Globalisation and the Competitive Advantage of Nations

TOURISM AND GLOBALISATION

A traveler can decide today to go to the North Pole and be there by tomorrow. Global infrastructures such as transportation and communications and global policies for free trade have created a situation where people and businesses in the global North can easily access natural resources and cultures in the global South.

Until 1999, when thousands of people around the world began organising against it (*e.g.*, the Battle in Seattle), globalisation was not regarded as a danger to local economies and cultural diversity. In fact, politicians and the media tout globalisation as the path to greater wealth and success. Although globalisation may be the most primary transformation of the world's political and economic structures since the industrial revolution, its implications have yet to be fully understood and debated.

Most of the economic restructuring is in the interest of big business, not in the interest of the public. Under the banner of free trade, corporations have come to shape our lives through the consumer products we buy including technology, the media that feed us information, even the educational system that trains us. Politicians chant the mantra of privatisation and globalisation. What does that mean for individuals?

According to Martin Khor, president of the non-governmental organisation (NGO) Third World Network, globalisation is a leading threat to local communities, particularly in the global South:

"Before colonial rule and the infusion of Western systems, people in the Third World lived in relatively self-sufficient communities… The modes of production and style of life were largely in harmony with the natural environment. Colonial rule… changed the social and economic structures of Third World societies. The new structures, consumption styles, and technological systems became so ingrained in Third World economies that even after the attainment of political independence, the importation of Western values, products, technologies and capital continued and expanded.

"Third World governments were loaned billions of dollars to finance expensive infrastructure projects… They were also supported by foundations, research institutions, and scientists in the industrialised countries that carried out research on new agricultural technologies that would 'modernize' the Third World that is, that would create conditions whereby the Third World would become dependent on the transnational companies for technology and inputs."

The development of vast infrastructures such as roads and other transportation routes goes hand in hand with tourism development. As more tourists seek out hard-to-reach "frontier" destinations, those areas become popularised, and soon private industry takes over.

Once an area is targeted for tourism development, the process begins with road building and displacement of the local population. Communication systems go in, as do energy-intensive and pollutive accommodations for visitors. The roads and communications in turn provide other industries with easy access to cheap labour and natural resources.

This cycle of development is occurring at alarming rates in small communities and villages throughout the world; many of these areas are considered the most important biologically diverse regions of the planet. At the same time, roads built into places like the Amazon to serve primarily as transportation routes for extractive industries such as oil, logging, and mining inevitably become new corridors for colonists, including tourists.

Tourism increases local reliance upon a global economy, leaking many economic benefits outside of the community back to the companies and countries that control most of the travel infrastructure. At the same time, tourism decreases dependence on local resources, as technologies, food, and health services are imported. Local people may also be pushed out or sell out, and local prices for commodities and services rise, as do taxes.

A number of groups and individuals are concerned about the negative impacts of economic centralisation via free trade and regional agreements such as the General Agreement on Tariffs and Trade (GATT) and the European Union. These organisations point out that the promotion of greater economic units and the expanded transport infrastructures they require result in urbanisation in the global North and South alike, placing greater pressures on wilderness areas and destroying family farms and rural communities around the world.

Proponents of free trade promise that all trading partners will be better off and that the practice will usher in a new era of global cooperation and prosperity, but according to a report by the International Society for Ecology and Culture:

The reality is far different. Increased levels of world trade will lead to a widening of the gap between rich and poor, to further environmental decline, and to the enrichment of corporations at the expense of people in both the North and South.

Small farmers and shopkeepers will be driven under by producers and marketers whose activities are undertaken at an ever larger scale, and many local economies will simply not survive. Rural communities will be hardest hit, intensifying the trend toward urbanisation. These 'free trade' agreements are fundamentally anti-democratic. The ease with which corporations will be able to transcend national boundaries – to move wherever environmental and health standards are the weakest and wages lowest will strip voters and even governments of their power to curb corporate excess...

In the new global economy, production everywhere will be focused on the needs of a single, Western monoculture, while Indigenous cultures and diverse location-specific adaptations will be steadily erased. Local self-sufficiency will become an ever more distant memory." Since September 11, 2001, the threat of global terrorism has been a key factor in government relationships and the tightening of restrictions for travelers. That day's events and aftermath have had an enormous impact on the airline industry.

Tourism plays an increasingly important role in international relations. Links exist between tourist flow and regional integration, governments, military, and economic aid. "Most nations have several policies towards foreign tourists that are based not only on anticipated length of stay, but also on the degree of international cooperation existing between the two countries." Tourism is big business for governments and private enterprise alike. Any country with still-pristine areas of forests, beaches, mountains, and parklands or with ethnic tribes and other unique rural cultures has something to market in the global economy.

Some of the largest corporations in the world are designing and carrying out policies that open up borders and allow them to operate in areas once restricted to individual country corporations. The tourist industry's entrance into and operations in China, the Middle East, the former Soviet Union, parts of the African continent, and countries with human rights abuses show that government and big business can work together despite trade restrictions and political differences.

Corporations have become dominant governing institutions, often exceeding governments in size and power. As David Korten states, "Increasingly, it is the corporate interest more than the human interest that defines the policy agendas of states and international bodies, although this reality and its implications have gone largely unnoticed and unaddressed." Nowhere is this more true than within travel and tourism.

Governmental instruments and international organisations that help shape international tourism policy encourage the growth and involvement of transnational corporations because they provide quick money and expanded trade and services. In supporting and increasing the power of such corporations, governments are ignoring the numerous inequalities, exploitation, and dislocations they foster.

Countries create lax trade environments to attract the tourism industry, lifting restrictions that are applied to other industries and offering many incentives. As Alexander Goldsmith explains:

Free trade zones (FTZs) are regions that have been fiscally or juridically redefined by their 'host country' to give them a comparative advantage over neighbouring regions and countries in luring transnational corporate activity. Most FTZs share the following characteristics: lax social, environmental, and employment regulations; a ready source of cheap labour; and fiscal and financial incentives that can take a huge variety of forms, although they generally consist of the lifting of customs duties, the removal of foreign exchange controls, tax holidays, and free land or reduced rents."

The travel industry benefits greatly from these FTZs, sometimes even performing what may be considered 'advance work' in doing away with free trade barriers for other industries.

LASTING ECONOMIC DEVELOPMENT-GLOBALISATION-ENVIRONMENTTOURISM IN THE OUTLOOK OF EUROPEAN INTEGRATION

More than enumerations, figures, interpretations, tourism is a reality that can't be ignored by anybody, from a luxuriant profession made by some persons or privileged groups, metamorphosing into a permanent necessity for more and more people.

The increasing of the incomes and free days (weekends, holidays) modernisation of the communication ways and of the transport means adding and the speed of going diversification of the improving of the tourist arrangements and destinations of all kinds and adapting them according to the people tastes and financial possibilities, stress century's disease, needs of relaxing and treatment all these factors and others too that influenced and fed this phenomenon, in order to maintain it lasting and ecological, too. In the context of Romania's recent adherence to the European Union, the tourism represents one of the real opportunities that the near future offers to our country.

Or, the gained experience, existent facilities and prices competitiveness are factors which recommend Romania as an attractive destination but, in the same time, the imperative action of all the ones involved in tourism will have to focus on the offered services considered to be of the best quality (conformable with the ones of other European countries) and on maintaining a natural environment its raw material in complete harmony being known the fact that then when the environment and tourism coexists in harmony, he environment takes benefit of the tourism (and vice versa!).

The importance of this reciprocal relation also reflects itself in the positive actions of preserving the tourism potential or rehabilitating the environment, but we must not overlook the destructive actions of some tourism activities such as: the excessive use of some environment components (water, air, soil *etc.*) in recreational purposes amplified by an irrational intervention, often brutal, of humans upon the environment and its natural resources.

In this purpose, the lasting tourism is and will remain in harmony with the environment and place population and culture, in such a way that its development will take place in their profit and not their disadvantage.

Lasting development is a topical world economy desideratum that is taking action on the fond of globalisation. In the spirit of the discussions of the Davos Summit, which will take place in the week of 21-27 of January and that from Genoa, referring to the world economical problems, the globalisation modifies the context of the local, national, regional and global environmental problems, which engraves new dimensions of lasting economical developments.

The realistic process of the globalisation leads to a development and an implementation of de environment politics, brings opportunities to promote the environment objectives through the economical politics reorientation (especially those of fiscal nature), as directly protecting the environment's qualities instruments and that need to be taken into consideration at the accomplishment of a lasting economical development from which the tourism will benefit.

Without a lasting utilisation of the resources in tourism, the ecological support that is based on this activity destroys unrecoverable, compromising the possibility of this activity itself. That is why it is imposed the searching of ways for the accomplishment of lasting economical development in this sector, too. The main aspects that are looked at are: the evaluation methods for the environmental quality directly connected to the tourist's activity.

The environment quality evaluation is important for the economical decisions and for the avoiding of irrational use of the environment's resources. The making of the decision implies a radical change of behaviour for the producers and consumers. This thing depends on the human's capacity to understand the gravity of the ecological misbalances, of them to become fully conscious that "the nature isn't made for us, and she is not at our will", that, "the time has come for some of the alliances that have been forever there, but a long time misunderstood, between the human's, the society's history and their knowledge and adventure to explore nature."

The "removal" of natural resources from their place, for the mass utilisation of wood or for the tourist "directions" is conditioned by the use of human resources, looked at as quantity, structural and as quality, for further use of the human intervention in nature. Of the quality, structure and quantity of economical resources it depends, lastly the grade in which humans and society satisfy their individual and collective needs.

Once with the economical development, the complexity and diversification of that emphasis, the human-nature relations become more ample, deeper and more contradictory. The growth and diversification of social needs attracts the increase of investing and consumable goods and the satisfying of this at a very high level, in the given production conditions, imposing the increase of economy, of the human intervention in the natural environment. That is why, the natural resources reserves decrease, the auto-regulation of nature is endangered by the comedown of the quality of the environment and the humannature relations are damaged.

This relation is characterised by a continuous exchange of substance, energy, information and work, generated by the increasing and diverse social need. The man, as an essential compound of the natural biosphere system is also the base of the social one. As a bio-psycho-social being, the human, through his work, consciously modifies the natural environment, adapting it to his needs.

The bio-physiological, cultural, psychological and psychosocial, material and spiritual evolving needs of the humans have a propelling force and are a reason for all the economical activities that took place during the historical development, from the dawns of human history, until today, are some of the constructive elements of social life, by encountering in a whole, the existence and social conscience.

The economical theory defines the concept of human needs as an ensemble of human preferences, desires and expectations to be, to know, to believe and to achieve goods that are conditioned and become effective depending on the economic-social development, as the development grade of the individual. They represent an ensemble of productive and not productive necessities, considered at a social scale, of the economic unities, the institutions and the population, including the spiritual needs education, culture, science; also the health consists an impulse of the material and spiritual production development. The human needs represent the main point in which come together material, direct and the spiritual, indirect factors of the social conscience existence, expressed through a whole system of economical, political and cultural interests.

That is why, the knowing of the volume and diversity of these human necessities and also their hierarchy because they have a decisive importance for the orientation and decision fundament regarding the social-economical development process.

We need to respect the social needs and resources system in the forest and tourist space in order to meet the eco-economical requirements taking into consideration the permanent nature-human-economy relation. The available resources for the environment improvement at a global and even at Romania's level have been and are limited. On another hand, the costs of the accomplishment of some environment objectives in the forest and tourist sectors are generally very high.

The main implementation limitations are determined by the general scarcity of financial resources and especially, by the lack of institutional capacity, more than the specific environment protection problems or possible solutions. In this context, the solving of the problems depends on the clear point-out of the objectives and the identification of the most effective ways of accomplishment.

The priority evaluation, the risks and the advantages is an essential preliminary condition to a lasting development strategy, which identifies those politics and investments that connect the social objectives and those implying the environmental protection, avoiding by this, the need of later expensive remedies. To obtain noticeable results, are promoted the "winning-winning" type investments those who justify themselves from the environmental protection point of view (for example, improvements in the efficiency of energy and other resources consume in the homing structure administration).

Priority Establishment

The priorities must reflect the urgency and importance of environmental problems with direct implication in the tourist phenomenon. The priority establishment implies a difficult selection process.

The priority establishment criteria, in their importance order are:

The harms to health: In the existing data base, the population's health is affected in the analysed sectors, mainly by:

1. Plumb in the air and soil coming from the means of transport
2. Depositing dust in the atmosphere coming from the warming of housing spaces, electrical warming stations, etc;

The Water Contamination and Aliments with Different Pollutants

1. The productivity decrease because of the physical capital and natural resources destroy.
2. The decomposing or threaten with irreversible damage to the biological diversity, generally, and also the underwater areas (natural and artificial lakes, rivers), lawns, marine and gradient ecosystems, forests and especially mountain habitats.

Also, priority is given to the rapports like "small costs-big benefits" in problems of growing importance on a medium and long term, where a long period of time is necessary for the fore seen effects to become concrete (for example, in transports). The fact that the resources are limited, mustn't lead to the reduction in investments in the environment protection. This is why are promoted the actions that turn to good account the general changing context generated by the economical transition politics, through the creation of bad combinations between the technologies, management, institutions, and the economical applied politics. The necessary flexibility for the reach of the best results with available resources is determined by the evaluation of the improvement level of the environment's quality at different costs.

The priority establishment implies a combination between the following complementary measures:

- The diminution of economical and ecological politics
- Expenses orientated harmoniously to projects or investment objectives, in order to obtain a maximum rapport between benefit and cost.
- The development of some institutions and qualification (professional training, education, exchange programs)

In the complex relation between Economy-Environment-Tourist works an optimum relational balance deployed after the application of some politics specific to the field, as in Fig.

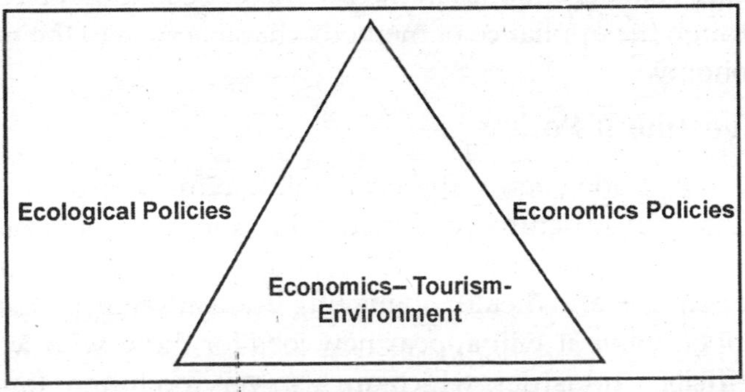

Fig. Optimum Relational triangle: Economic-Environmental tourist

Economical Policies

The transition from central planning to the market economy must not only improve the economical function on a long term, but also contribute to the environment improvement through the penalisation of the resource waste and of the pollution. Among the key factors that bring with them the improvement of economy and environment, are the restrictions for the companies' access to the budgetary state funds and take out subventions for energy, mineral and water resources.

The Ecological Policies

The accomplishment of the economic restructuring has on its base also directed for the environment protection politics, including a judicious combination between regulations and economical instruments. For example, the subvention exclusion of energy leads to a decrease of the energy consume, but at the pollution level also; the taxes for pollution have a complementary action, promoting the use of some fuels and some less polluting technologies.

The economical instruments such as taxes are applied to reach a rational utility of the resources. The existing tax systems can be developed continuously to offer an efficient instrument in the design of new healthy practices in the field of environment protection.There also exists the possibility to realise some economies in the process of ecological objectives, through the appliance of methods characteristic to the market economy.

Investment Policy

On a long term, the economical reform, especially the industry restructure combined with adequate environment protection measures, will lead to the reduction of the economical and health damaging transmissions. That will happen while it will appear new jobs for those who work in inefficient industries, which are also very polluting, to which we have to give up while the economical growth will offer them the possibility of viable companies and that of investments in new technologies.

On a short term, the public investments are orientated towards:

- The acceleration of the improvement process where there are social and economical restrictions;
- The beginning of studying the environment problems that will persist to the transaction at the market's

economy (for example, the air pollution by automobiles)

- The investments in the environment protection imply three categories of expenses:
- Dues, for functioning and maintenance (especially at local level)
- Investments with a benefic effect upon the environment (and which can be justified economically ("winning-winning" or "double-winning")

Investments for the Birth of Institutions

The functioning, maintenance, restructure and selective reorganisation of the public services for the protection of existing environments: Assuring the drinkable water, the collecting and deposit of home trash, the good functioning of the public transport systems are priorities. These need funds to cover dues, but on a short term, they mustn't claim major investments of capital.

Winning-winning investment: Are represented by small investments (often under 500 000 $) in the energy and water saving- the meter installation, the reduction of leaps-technologies with a small consume and less waste, also expenses for "good keeping" and minor improvements of the installations for the reduction of waste, leaks and material consume. All these are investments that justify themselves as such, financially and economical, but which also bring major benefits for the environment.

Lasting Policies in Tourism

The lasting tourism development policy imposes the adopting of corresponding policies for different activity domains of that sector such as:

The tourism product policy takes into consideration the stimulation of economical agents for the modernisation and growth of offer Romanian tourist quality, having as a purpose the growth of competitiveness and its activity on the intern and international market. According to the systems and quality methodologies practiced in the European Union state members (ISO 9000, ISO 14 000), quality system integrated, star classification systems, different specific quality systems- Mark Q- programme recently launched by the Tourism National Authority. Or, the Minister of Tourism will develop the following directions of action:

1. The taking over and implementation of quality indicators in tourism.
2. The grant of financial support for the tourism IMMs that implement quality systems.
3. The utilisation of the Promoting and Development of the Tourist Products Fund to improve the quality of tourist products and it implies:
   - The marketing and promotion policy
   - The work field policy

The policy regarding the role of scientific research and technological.

Development Politics in the law field:

- Policy in the fiscal field, who has as a purpose the stimulation of economical development, investments and the birth of new work places in the *private sector*;
- Policy in the field of the tourist activity and national policies correlation that is the integration of politics in the field of tourisms and in national economical policy, through the establishment of law proposals and concrete measures that facilitate the development of tourism. The accomplishment of the up-mentioned proposals presumes the realisation of national priority programmes and the adoption of measures that through their effect would put into motion the whole system of tourism development, both at the tourist national product and at each of the main tourist destinations (sea, mountain, bathing places, other destinations)

National Prior Programs

- The national tourist development program "Super-ski in the Carpathians. As a nationalinterest program for the development of mountain tourism, which in a first stage will include thePrahova Valley area with Sinaia, Busteni, Azuga, the Predeal-Rasnov area, the station Poiana Brasov, the Leaota area and Padina Cave (Ialomita Valley), Doftanei Valley area and the Upper Valley of Teleajen- the station Cheia. It will be tried to include in this program the Parang area too.
- The program for the modernisation of the Romanian seaside, through the building of the station Europe, the practice of "Continuing seaside line" project., the systematisation of the whole Black Sea seaside, the design and built of some nautical agreement areas on the principle "Aqua Land", the development of the casino activities on the seaside.
- The applying, despite the numerous failures of the tourist program "Dracula Park", designated to the revaluation of the myth, but also the historical and cultural values connected to Vlad the Empaler' epoque.
- Programmes for the rural and ecologic tourism development. The actions in this field will consist of—
    - o The improvement of the law system referring to the chase and report of tourist activity, classification of tourist structures, tourist stations and the harmonisation of those at an European level.
    - o The focusing of efforts in the form of prior programmes of the partner state system with the role to ensure the infrastructure, local public administration (which would contribute with the necessary lands to realize the projects) and the private sector, asked to finance, built, use this type of projects;

- o The making permanent of social programmes addressed to Romanian tourists like:
  Seaside for all, Tourism for health, New Year in *Romania,* who will allow the access tc tourism and vacations to some un favour categories of the population.
- o The stimulation, (as a social objective) of the development of some tourist products designated to some segments of the internal requests, with low incomes, including a web of incoming adequate structures
- o The adoption of a new tourism law

In the next period-2010- will be developed other forms of tourism too, the most important being the cultural and religious tourism, the rural and agro-tourism, the eco-tourism. In this way, there will be considered the creation of an offer for youth and adults, the extending of rural tourism and agro-tourism through the support of OMT and ONU through the "International Eco-Tourism Year" and "Mountain Year". It can be estimated that the extend of the tourist potential through a managerial activity that will have all the means of tourism, putting into light, through the homing offer and services, through the design of new various tourism programmes, developing the mountain, bathing areas, cultural, eco-tourist and rural tourist circulation, *etc.* It is therefore foreseen a tourism that will take place parallel to other activities and integrate in a complementarity's from which will benefit the production and consume.

Policies for Protecting Environment in Tourism under Globalisation

Tourism and globalisation have direct relationship with each other. Tourism has been a major source of revenue for countries, specifically in the Third world, in the past few decades. It is predicted that by 2010, one billion tourists would have traveled abroad and by 2020, this would have increased to 1.6 billion. In terms of revenue, it is predicted that by 2020, $1.5 trillion would be earned. Tourism is touted as a major source of employment worldwide.

The rise in global tourist arrivals in various countries demands an increased effective preservation. With globalisation have increased deforestation, pollution, and disruption in the ecological balance. Pollution caused by littering and improper waste disposal has now become a major problem for the community. Hotels and inns mushroomed, changing the town's landscape and straining its water resources. Commercial production of wood carvings has also affected nearby forests. Trees have been cut down to support commercial wood carving activities that cater to foreign as well as domestic tourist demand.

Revenue needs to be earned without disturbing the environment. So, a solution for this is eco-tourism. Eco-tourism is described as environment friendly, sustainable and nature-based. Currently, eco-tourism is the fastest growing sub-sector, growing at a rate of 10-15% annually. Eco-tourism now accounts for 25% of all leisure trips abroad.

TOURISM IN A GLOBAL WORLD

While "globalism" or "glocalisation" enter our personal dictionaries as a consequence of recent important changes experienced in our old globe, the two closely related developments, first the expansion of multinational and other transnational corporations, and second, the growth of information and communication technologies, including the Internet and access to it have had fundamental impacts on this global change.

In today's highly competitive business life firms try to be both local and global, big and small, centralised and decentralised, stable and dynamic; offering simultaneously standardised and customised mass-manufacturing, and individually designed goods and services, which were until recently considered to be oxymoron (Gummesson 1999).

According to Wood (1998); tourism, the world's largest industry, provides a unique vantage point for exploring globalisation, this most transformative process in the world today. "As a mode of travel, of interaction, and of visualisation and experience, tourism is not only reaching formerly isolated parts of the globe but is reshaping social life and identity at home as well. As new forms of tourism become increasingly prominent—ecotourism, ethnic tourism, "roots" and heritage tourism, *etc.*—tourism has become an integral part of all societies, eliciting active and complex responses". Including the economic, social, cultural and ecological outcomes of these processes; tourism can be considered as a "global industry", virtually operating in all countries and communities with its commercial, public-sector and non-profit players (Theobald, 1998). It "is not a clear-cut sector but an all-embracing and pervasive domain of service and industrial activities", touching on almost all spheres of service and industrial activities (Wahab and Cooper, 2001, p.5). It is indeed hard to think an aspect of tourism that is not affected by globalisation. For example, the airline and hotel sectors witness the rise of global players. Companies get increasingly involved with setting up operations in different cultural contexts (Morrison et al., 1999). Besides, more countries become generators of international tourist trips. Moreovover, the influence of an increasingly globalised media should not be ignored. With the invention and widespread use of jet airplanes and Internet, the globalisation enables profound opportunities to be exploited by tourism and hospitality organisations.

Horner and Swarbrooke (2004) also warns us about the risks for tourism coming together with the opportunities of globalisation for tourism organisations and destinations. First, the standardisation of products, which is usually implied by globalisation, seems to be extending even to cities that begin to look the same. Moreover, as driven by the developed economies, largely it seems, for their own benefit, globalisation may also increase the polarisation between rich and poor countries. On the other side, the concentration of both ownership by both horizontal and vertical integrations and power and influence by franchising and management contracts that go alongside with globalisation make medium-sized organisations mostly suffer, as they do not have the ability to fit into neither economies of scale that creates opportunities for big organisations nor niche markets for small organisations. Finally, in today's world terrorism has become an international problem, which no country is immune, including the most famous tourist destinations.

THE INTERPLAY OF LOCAL AND GLOBAL

In our discussions about globalisation, using global or local as separate terms without respecting each other, on either a cultural level or a more specific business level, seem to be troublesome, at least limited or limiting. Thus, Beynon and Durkerley (2001) discusses that the crude dichotomy between local and global has required intermediate concepts to analyze globalisation, which involves not just a top-down process but also a process of localisation. Robertson (1995) also argue that local is very much included within the global, while the process of globalisation involves 'the invention of locality'.

Besides, Naisbitt (1994) claims that the bigger and more integrated the world economy becomes the more important and powerful become the small players. Finally, Horner and Swarbrooke (2004, p.12) stress the irony that the concentration of ownership in tourism and hospitality industry, which aims to benefit from economies of scale and market power of big organisations, also "created opportunities for small organisations to succeed by exploiting niche markets with high-quality products and personalised service". One determinant and unchanging issue to point out in all the debates and interpretations of globalisation is the local and global's being together, which should hold for any debates and interpretations for localisation, too.

Theories of globalisation, nevertheless, tend to assume the existence of a global power to which the local is necessarily subordinated, deriving its meaning only from its juxtaposition to the global. This also brings the need for a new language that can suggest equal attention to the localisation of the global and the globalisation of the local (Escobar, 1999). "Glocal", as a combination of Local and Global, can be seen as a "first approximation" for this, Although it also sounds like an artificial derivation, the concept of glocal seems to be accepted by a wide audience, being used in different disciplines, and attributed different, evolving meanings. For instance, together with the technological and communicative convergences of the "cyberspace", some experts speaks of the "glocal" communication era: with local production and contents, but with a global diffusion (Wang 2000).

In the case of ecotourism and crafts, many forms of the local, as services or products of indigenous value and knowledge, are offered for global consumption, such as in tourism (Escobar, 1999). For example, according to Tsuchiko (2002), for the invaluable crafting of Japanese sword, this word of "glocal" emphasises the point that globalisation should involve harmony and recognition of differences rather than complete assimilation or homogenisation, in addition to the fact that the value of local traditions can have an international impact. On another side, the manner in which new meanings are locally attached to imported goods throw a valuable light upon cultural globalisation, and, with the careful glocal marketing of global products 'authentic' local goods seem to be under attack. In fact, a great debate goes on0whether in the world the Anglo-American popular culture is having a homogenising or hybridising effect or even resulting simultaneously in a degree of both (Beynon and Durkerley, 2001). Glocal just opens another front for the ongoing debates on the phenomenon of globalisation, and how to realize it.

EMERGENCE OF A NEW CONCEPT: LOBAL

We are still in need of better conceptualisations and terming to develop our knowledge of globalisation together with localisation, and their intermediation. The business literature basically recognises globalisation from the perspective of large international manufacturing organisations and top-down (from global to local) operations such as the tailoring of a standardised product like McDonald burger or Coca-Cola to different markets. This view affects inevitably the globalisation of the tourism and hospitality business, as well. Whereas, in other bodies of knowledge, there is the awareness of small, specific, unique local; beside the big, general, standard global; but this awareness has not yet been made explicit enough to conceptualize the bottom-up impact, from local to global, that gains pace as an equally important dynamic in globalisation: such as the offering of indigenous, local forms for global consumption, which we discussed above. "Glocal" seems to be proposed as a means to cover both of these dynamics, and is useful to capture the co-existing nature of global and local. But, it does not catch the importance of difference between these top-down and bottom-up processes and their outcomes, and this does no good, when we try to systemize and then operationalize our understandings about global and glocal. We distinguish these two from each other, and then term them accordingly, considering these two processes as two counter dynamics within a system of globalisation. The below discussion reflects this way of thinking:

If we take the original motto of glocal, "Think global, act local" that the former chairman of Sony proposed, we can benefit from this specific interpretation of glocal in international business and then re-conceptualize global, local and "lobal" with respect to this. According to that, the meanings of local and global are straightforward, representing to think and act locally and globally, respectively. Then, in addition and contrast to the original proposition of glocal, "thinking global and acting local", lobal can be defined as "thinking local and acting global." This interpretation of lobal can then contribute to the ongoing discussions about globalisation, also complementing or clarifying those of glocalisation.

This can be seen as a contribution not only to overcome some of the criticism about the understanding and use of these concepts, but also to the development of our comprehension and governance of global and local affairs. Moreover, this framework can have strategic importance especially for the sustainable development and international success of small and medium scale enterprises (SMEs) in emerging countries. The term can then be used to explain the development, production and marketing of these products and services that are indigenously or locally generated, while being offered for global commercialisation and consumption.0Putting our words about thinking and acting locally or globally into a graphical representation we can place local, global, glocal and lobal respectively in a frame of globalisation, as in the below figure:

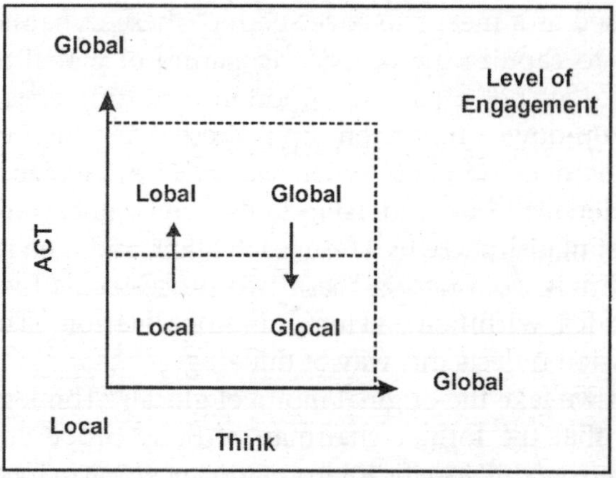

This exhibition catches the idea, which necessitates comprehending local and global together equally in the "globalisation". In addition to this, in this model we can explicitly distinguish bottom-up and top-down processes of globalisation. The model can also be further developed to exhibit interconnections among the local, lobal, global, glocal as different modes of globalisation. These interconnections and modes can then be interpreted as a pattern of development with four distinct stages, for a local organisation that goes global.

According to this conceptualisation Lobal stands as one of the stages of globalisation, making it possible that a local product, process or a group of people have significant impact on a global scale. Glocal in turn makes the global phenomena to become tailored with respect to varying localities. But then, we should discuss about the logic behind this "lobal", if it is to be both more than just another catch-phrase, and different from "glocal": The term "lobal" derives its meaning from the lobes and lobules in the body, which correspond to specialised subdivisions or units that fulfill expert functions, as important parts of a system. Within itself, the lobe governs specific designated operations, while, as a member of a very well interlinked system of organs, responds to various requests of the system. Using this metaphor from biology, in this complex system of actors and interactions we can conceptualize lobal as either a special network that consist of specialised units, or those units themselves that generate network, either of which can provide a structure, together with glocal, to bridge global and local. The importance of this lobal organisation comes from its characteristics that it can function as a local, "closed" (Maturana and Varela, 1980) individual entity, though it is still part of the bigger global system together with other lobes and organs. This approach can enable academicians and practitioners, some interesting opportunities for intra and inter levels of organisational and social analysis.

LOBAL TOURISM ORGANISATIONS

As a proposition following our discussion, we can then suggest that tourism and hospitality organisations become lobal. With the lobal tourism organisation, we propose a specialised network structure that can enable member organisations to maintain their individual indigenousness, while they can turn their unique values and knowledge into commercial products and services, benefiting from the energy and strength of a bigger tourism networks they belong. Beyond this, these organisations can become lobal international businesses, with the use of proper ICTT: Information, Communication and Transportation Technology. In support of our argument, there is already a growing literature to highlight the importance of not only networks but also ICT and knowledge management for tourism and hospitality. A network-like system is crucial for better management of knowledge, as the most important asset for sustainable competitive advantage in the knowledge socio-economy. To realize this, in U.K. it is now a government policy to develop networks and clusters for tourism entities.

In a recent article (2004) Mukherjee argues the idea of Daniel Lian that Asia should create niches of small businesses that tap wealthy consumers globally, using local ingenuity and resources. For instance, Indonesia can benefit from tourism activities like volcano trekking or pelagic sailing, which can enable thousands of small-scale businesses to employ millions of people and generate economic growth and wealth. Already, "Thailand is able to squeeze Western and Japanese tourists for more dollars by marketing health spa tourism". This kind of discussion corresponds well with arguments about sustainable competitive advantage for not only a profit making or developing organisation, but also developing industries and emerging countries or regions, all of which require a high level of organisation with network-like characteristics.

Within this proposition, we should also consider that the concept of glocal already applies the principles of product-or-service differentiation to meet different demands of international customers; however, but this kind of approach fits mainly to big multinational companies and their operations. On the other hand, lobal specifically fits well to the SMEs or organisations of SMEs that go international. Both glocal internationals and lobal SME firms tailor their operations, products and services; but in different ways.

These differences should be articulated more for a comprehension of global issues and trends in hospitality and tourism industries. The conceptualisations already available from the field of international business are concerned mostly about multi-national companies, and these do not necessarily fit into international SME. There is a need to develop modeling that can help us not only understand better about the working of SME but also integrate our understandings about multinationals and SME for a combined knowledge of the general international system. Within a system of lobal networking, individual local companies that can provide a high quality product or specialised service can come together, maintaining their localness, which gives their sustainable competitive advantage, while they can benefit from the advantages of big organisations and even become international and global with the use of technological opportunities. Finally, certainly further research is needed to assess the validity of these conceptualisations in real life situations and business circumstances.

This idea of lobal can also be applied onto a country level, specifically to countries with emerging socio-economic systems that have the potential to play leading roles in their regions, which will also determine their local and global position in return. One country should recognize its indigenous local knowledge and values, and organize lobal networks that can promote and commercialize its ingenuity, making them reputable demanded and accessible in a global scale. With its geopolitical positioning, remarkable historical and natural sources, social values and still unexploited potential Turkey can be a very good model for this.

Our proposition of lobal is not only a simple catchword that we coin to highlight and capture the importance of starting from local and small to become international and global then glocal but also it goes beyond: As a metaphoric concept it draws its origins from a real biological existence that also finds place in systems and knowledge science, which can be named as complex networks. Besides it is a good example of being able to be local while also being global, as the essence of globalisation. As still being local, while acting as a part of global, it is neither local nor global, nor glocal. As example, lobal "gastronomy" and "wine" tourisms can provide significant opportunities for a country or company to make use of its unique characteristics and turn them into a profit-making industry, making use of the advantages of globalisation while responding well to its threats like retaining and improving its authenticity against "McDonaldisation" of global dynamics.

THE POTENTIAL IMPACT OF MEDICAL TOURISM ON HEALTH WORKFORCE AND HEALTH SYSTEMS IN INDIA

"Globalisation" refers to various interrelated processes of global interconnectedness. Its two core components are economic globalisation and the associated ascendancy of deregulated markets in international trade and investment. Two other important domains are technological globalisation, especially of information and communication technologies, and cultural globalisation.

While globalisation has been a boon in most aspects, from a public-health perspective it appears to be a mixed blessing. On the one hand accelerated economic growth and technological advances have enhanced health and life expectancy in many populations. At least in the short-to-medium term, these material advances allied to social modernisation and various health-care and public health programmes have yielded gains in population health. On the other hand, aspects of globalisation have also jeopardised population health via the erosion of social and environmental conditions, the global division of labour, the exacerbation of the rich-poor gap between and within countries, and the accelerating spread of consumerism.

Of these probably, one of the most significant impact of globalisation on health has been through direct trade in health-related goods, services and people (patients and professionals). India implemented its economic reform policies in the 1990s. Since then the country has enjoyed considerable economic growth. The most dynamic sector within the Indian economy has been the service sector, which itself has accounted for nearly 60% of India's overall economic growth.

The most visible and well-known services within this sector have been software and information technology-enabled services (ITES). However, there are plans to expand this sector and provide services in other domains as well. Most lucrative amongst these is the health service sector, which has been predicted to become a billion dollar industry in India. A major component of this health service sector that has a global appeal is medical tourism. The prospects and potential of medical tourism has attracted huge investments from the central government as well from private investors. However, there is inadequate documentation of the scope of these services in the country and its possible consequences on the public health system.

Here we examine the opportunities and challenges for medical tourism in India and attempts to assess its potential impact on the health workforce and health system. We draw upon published literature on medical tourism in India, however it does not address issues related to cross-border supply of services (telemedicine and processing of health information).

Health services are a heterogeneous group of activities, ranging from allopathic services (modern, facility-based health care services) to alternative health and wellness services provided in a hotel or spa setting or in a private practice. Globally, there has been tremendous growth in this sector. This growth has been assisted by inadequate national public health services, spiraling cost of health services in the developed world and the availability of cheaper alternative in developing economies. This has resulted in globalisation of health care worldwide and can be evidenced by growing cross-border delivery of health services that is estimated to be in excess of $140 billion.

In India, healthcare is one of the largest sectors, in terms of revenue and employment, and this sector is expanding rapidly. During the 1990s, Indian healthcare grew at a compound annual rate of 16%. Today the total value of the sector is more than $34 billion. This translates to $34 per capita, or roughly 6% of GDP. By 2012, India's healthcare sector is projected to grow to nearly $40 billion. A major proportion of this growth is predicted to be attributable to the growth in the business of medical tourism.

Medical tourism in India has gained momentum over the past few years. According to the Confederation of India Industries (CII), approximately 1,50,000 patients arrived in India in 2005 from across the globe for medical treatment and this is expected to increase by 15% each year. The medical tourism market in India was estimated at US$ 333 million in 2004 and has grown by about 25 per cent and is predicted to become a US$ 2 billion-a-year business opportunity by 2012.

Expansion of Medical Tourism in India

There are several characteristics that make India an appealing destination for visitors seeking health services. These include its well-trained health practitioners; a large populace of good English speaking doctors, guides and medical staff; availability of super-specialty centers that excel in cardiology and cardio-thoracic surgery, joint replacements, transplants, cosmetic treatments, dental care, orthopedic surgery and more; hospitals that provide the full gamut of health services which include full body pathology, comprehensive physical and gynecological examinations, echo Doppler, high strength MRI *etc.* using latest, technologically advanced diagnostic equipments; and finally, and more importantly the availability of these premium services at prices that are extremely reasonable for the foreign tourist.

In fact, the competitive cost of medical treatment in India has been the main catalyst for the growth of medical tourism in the country. The costs of comparable treatment in India are on average one eighth to one fifth of those in the West. For instance, a cardiac procedure costs anywhere between US$ 40,000-60,000 in the United States, US$ 30,000 in Singapore, US$ 12,000-15,000 in Thailand and only US$ 3,000 -6,000 in India. Likewise, the associated costs of surgery are also low.

India also has the potential to emerge as a hub for preventive health screening in view of the availability of low-cost diagnostic tests. At a private clinic in London a health check-up for men that includes blood tests, electro-cardiogram tests, chest X-Rays, lung tests and abdominal ultrasound costs around £350. In comparison, a comparable check-up at a clinic operated by Delhi-based healthcare company Max Healthcare costs US$ 84. A Magnetic Resonance Imaging (MRI) scan costs US$ 60 at Escorts Hospital in Delhi, compared with roughly US$ 700 in New York.

A study done by the India Brand Equity Foundation (IBEF) in 2004 showed that India is more cost-competitive as compared to other leading medical tourism destination like Thailand. Thailand has a cost advantage over India in only two categories: plastic surgery and breast augmentation. India is cheaper than Thailand across a whole range of other—and more serious surgery categories as the following chart indicates.

Surgery	Thailand	India
Bone Marrow Transplant	US$ 62500	US$ 30000
Liver Transplant	US$ 75000	US$ 40000
Open Heart Surgery (CABG)	US$ 14250	US$ 4400
Hip Replacement	US$ 6900	US$ 4500
Knee Surgery	US$ 7000	US$ 4500
Hysterectomy	US$ 2012	US$ 511
Gall Bladder removal	US$ 1755	US$ 555
Cost in US$		

Source: IBEF Research

The health services in India have the additional advantage of providing a good mix of allopathic and alternative systems of medicine. For instance, while New Delhi has emerged as a prime destination for cardiac care; Chennai has established a niche for quality eye care; Kerala and Karnataka have emerged as hubs for state-of-the-art ayurvedic healing.

The scope for profit in this sector has encouraged several large corporations, such as pharmaceuticals and industrial companies, and several non-resident Indians (NRIs) to invest money in setting up super-specialty hospitals such as Apollo, Medinova, CDR, Mediciti in Hyderabad; Hindujas and Wockhardt in Mumbai; Max, Escorts, Apollo in Delhi *etc.* These facilities now dominate the upper end of the private sector and cater predominantly to medical tourists and affluent sections of the society. These establishments have created a niche job market for health professionals predominantly trained in public sector institutes.

Even the Government of India has responded promptly to tap the potential of this sector. In its effort to capitalize on this opportunity the Government has untaken measures to promote India as a "global health destination". The National Health Policy 2002 strongly encourages medical facilities to provide services to users from overseas. It states that "providers of such services to patients from overseas will be encouraged by extending to their foreign exchange, all fiscal incentives, including the status of "deemed exports", which are available to other exporters of goods and services".

The Indian Ministry of Tourism has started a new category of visas for the medical tourists. These visas called the "M" or medical-visas are valid for one year but can be extended up to three years and are issued for a patient along with a companion. Efforts have also been undertaken to improve the airport infrastructure to ensure smooth arrival and departure of the health tourists. A brochure of the ministry predicts a "phenomenal expansion" of the Indian health-care industry in the coming years.

These factors have favoured the recent spurt of growth of medical tourism in India. Official figures indicate that medical tourists from 55 different countries come to India for treatment. While most of these patients are from developed countries, India is also seeing a surge of patients from countries in Africa and South and West Asia that lack adequate healthcare infrastructure. Among others, foreign health travelers to India comprise of a large number of non-resident Indians (NRIs). If the present trend continues trade in health and health-services will become one of the biggest sectors in India. However, there are several challenges that could impede the growth of medical tourism in India, more importantly the growth of this sector poses a threat to the already crippled public health system in India.

Challenges and Threats of the Expansion of Medical Tourism in India

The present growth in medical tourism in India has been encouraging but to sustain this growth and to achieve it full potential certain challenges have to be addressed. It is also important to understand the impact of the growth in this sector on the public healthcare delivery so that necessary corrective measures can be undertaken.

Create Inequitable Health Systems

Three decades after the Alma-Ata Declaration, "health for all" remains an unattainable goal in India. In sync with the fundamental principle of primary health care, the government has developed an extensive network of health facilities but regrettably the system has failed to deliver.

The nemesis of the public healthcare in India has been compounded by low government expenditure on health as well as by factors such as poor management of resources, acute shortage of skilled workforce, large-scaled absenteeism, corruption and conflicting job roles. These factors along with several policies of the government (such as release of prime building land at low rates, exemptions from taxes and duties for importing drugs and high tech medical equipment and concessions to doctors setting up private practices and nursing homes) have helped in the unabated growth of the private sector.

The private sector has gained a dominant presence and today it accounts for 82% of outpatient visits, 58% of inpatient expenditure, and 40% of births in institutions. A study conducted by global accounting and consulting firm Ernst and Young and the Federation of Indian Chamber of Commerce (FICCI), shows that the private hospitals in India earned Rs. 62,000 crore in fiscal year 2006 and revenues from the sector are expected to rise up to Rs. 130,000 crore in 2012, which represents an annual revenue growth rate of about 19% a year. In comparison to this public health care system in India has been seriously underperforming.

As per NSSO estimates between 1995–96 and 2004, the utilisation of government sources of treatment (including public hospitals, PHC/CHC, public dispensaries, ESI doctors, *etc.*) increased from 19% to 22% in rural India and declined from 20% to 19% in urban India. For hospitalised treatment, the decline in utilisation of government sources was from 43.8% to 41.7% in rural areas and from 43% to 38.2% in urban areas. The inadequacies in the public health sector has also stunted its growth and tarnished its potential of being a product that could be offered on an international market.

The underutilisation of the public health system coupled with the growth in the private sector will increase the disparities and poses as a major threat of medical tourism in the Indian context. The real challenge to expanding medical tourism as a strategy for economic growth and development will be to identify and implement mechanisms that prevent the development of a dual and inequitable health system with enclaves of high quality health facilities catering to foreign visitors; and foster mutually beneficial linkages between the private and public health sectors, and between state-of the art health services and community health.

Intensify Shortages of Skilled Health Professionals

An important reason for poor service delivery in the public sector is the shortage of trained and skilled health personnel. According to the recently released Planning Commission report, India is short of a phenomenal 600,000 doctors, 1 million nurses and 200,000 dental surgeons. With positions of 300,000 dental surgeons, only 73,000 are currently full. Meanwhile 1.1 million nurses are filling up vacancies for 2.1 million, a shortfall of nearly 50%. To aggravate matters, there is also a huge paucity of paramedical staff including radiographers, X-Ray technicians, physiotherapists, labouratory technicians, orthopedists and opticians. The report also highlights the highly skewed distribution of the available manpower towards the urban areas. The availability of medical specialist in local Community Health Centers, compared to the sanctioned posts, is also disquieting. The existing CHCs have a high shortfall of specialist manpower, such as obstetricians and gynecologists (56%), pediatricians (67%), surgeons (56%) and medical specialists (59%), with no provision of anesthetists. Such acute shortages of medical professionals in India is ironic as the country has approximately 229 medical colleges with an annual admission capacity of over 25, 600 students.

There are several factors that could explain the shortage of doctors in the public system. These include bottlenecks in the recruitment process, poor financial incentives, absence of a conducive work environment and the prevalence of corruption in the public health sector.

While the public sector is encumbered with staff and resource shortages, it has been estimated that over 75% of the human resources and advanced medical technology, 68% of the estimated 15,097 hospitals and 37% of 623,819 total beds in the country are in the private sector. These figures suggest that the private sector is the prime employer of health personnel predominantly trained in public health institutes. This also sounds an alarm that further growth of the private sector could aggravate the manpower crunch in the public sector.

An important expectation of increased trade in health services is that through the increased opportunities locally and regionally, it would encourage and facilitate a greater retention of skills in the region. However, considering that at present the growth is restricted to the private, it may not be a viable solution to the manpower crunch in the public sector.

Raise Quality of Care and Accreditation Issues

Variation in the quality of care provided and the asymmetry of information between providers and consumers regarding quality is a concern in the health service sector. A major reason for the underutilisation of the public health services in India is the lack of prescribed standards of quality. Still it remains a neglected area within the realms of government policies.

The quality of services is also one of the main arguments against medical tourism. In response to this, the Government and CII have taken the lead in the process of national accreditation and licensing for the private sector. The WHO supported Joint Commission International (JCI) has accredited 10 institutions in India, all of them being in the private sector. The process is underway to encourage other private health care facilities, including labouratories, diagnostic centers, outpatient clinics, and day surgery centers in the country, to attain JCI to accreditation.

Thus initiatives are being undertaken to standardize the quality of services in the private sector but they have completely bypassed the public sector facilities. This is disconcerting and is suggestive of the lack of government initiative to improve services in the public sector.

Promote Unregulated Growth of the Private Sector

There are several concerns that arise from the growth of the private sector and the government is supposed to play an important role in regulating this sector. However, in India, State interventions have been minimal, leaving the sector to grow *laissez-faire*.

In India, there is no policy framework to have a common set of regulations for the private health care sector. The implementation and enforcement of the existing regulation has been weak and many of these regulations have not been updated and hence have lost their relevance. The State does not consider concerns related to private sector growth as a high priority on the policy agenda. There are no institutional mechanisms within the government to address the private sector issues. Moreover, there has been considerable resistance from various constituents of the private health care sector to accept in principle the applicability of certain regulations to their profession.

This lack of regulation has allowed the private sector in India to grow unabated and has resulted in mounting dissatisfaction with the services offered by this sector along with an increase in cases of medical negligence. A major challenge in the promotion of the medical tourism in India will be to institutionalize and harmonize regulations within the private sector in the country. This is essential as if the present conditions persist there will be no quality control over the services provided. Besides, the present circumstances will promote mushrooming of super-specialty institutes providing health services to medical tourist and wealthy Indians, and monopolize the available human and material resource in health.

Increase Cost of Medical Treatment

As per NSSO 60th Round, during 2004, 24% of the episodes of ailments among the poor were untreated in rural areas and 22% in urban areas. Lack of finances was cited as a reason by 28% of persons with untreated episodes in rural areas and 20% in urban areas.

The health insurance market in India is very limited covering about 10% of the total population. Out-of-pocket payment by individual household is the main source of health care financing and accounts for 72% of all health expenditures. Around 24% of all people hospitalised in India in a single year fall below the poverty line due to hospitalisation.

Lack of insurance cover has also worked as a major disincentive for the growth of medical tourism. However, there have been recent developments that could help address this constraint. Insurance providers are currently expanding their network to include physician around the globe, and it is anticipated that within a decade a majority of large employers' health plan will include offshore medical centers. Already in India, US-based private health insurers Blue Cross and Blue Shield and British health insurer Bupa, now insure clients treated at a number of private hospitals in India. The option of health insurance is set to boost the growth of medical tourism in countries like India.

A trade-off of the increase in medical tourists will be the rise in the overall cost of health care in the country. Several studies have indicated the rising nature of the medical costs in recent years. According to their estimates, between 1995–96 to 2004, there was an increase of 55.67 and 77.28%, respectively, for government and private sources in rural India. In urban India, the corresponding increase has been, respectively, 76.6 and 116.2%. Such increases in cost will make medical treatment unaffordable and will further increase the percentage of untreated individuals.

Raise Medical Liability Issues

The provision of medical services is fraught with uncertainty of health outcomes and informational asymmetries. Difficulties by patients to ascertain provider qualifications, and to know the appropriate level, type, and cost of care required will be a challenge to expansion of health tourism. It would be necessary to establish a system that could deal with any legal liabilities associated with treating international patients. The issue of medical liability is equally pertinent for the public sector. An important challenge will be to develop a system to address medical liabilities, which also includes the services provided in the public health sector.

The current demand for health and wellness services has generated a global market in the health services. In India, the private sector has responded promptly to this demand, which is evident from the recent increase in the number of super-specialty centers offering services to medical tourists. Even the government has initiated measures to encourage growth of medical tourism but these have mainly benefitted the private sector, leaving the public sector unaddressed.

There are several factors that favour India as a hub for health related services, which include world-class medical expertise, competitive costs, well-equipped health facilities, no waiting period *etc.* Trade in health and health related services, has been predicted to evolve into a billion dollar industry in India. However, as outlined above there are challenges and the growth of medical tourism could pose as a threat to the public health system in India.

The threats could arise from intensified manpower shortage in the public sector, creation of inequitable health systems in the private and public sectors, increased cost of treatment and unregulated growth of private health facilities. To counteract these threats and to ensure that medical tourism has a favourable impact on the public health system, it will be necessary to undertake certain measures. The following are some recommendations that could help minimize the threats and maximize the benefits of the expansion of trade in the health sector:

1. **Harmonisation of regulations within the country:** It will be necessary to develop specific regulations for the health sector, improve transparency and ensure complete implementation. The regulations should restrict the uncontrolled growth of private sector institutes, maintain standardised quality of services and maximize the utilisation of the available resources.
2. **Addressing the availability of skilled health professionals:** The mal-distribution of human resources between private and public sectors is a concern and has been elabourated above. As a consequence of medical tourism, it is expected that job opportunities within the private sector will increase, leading to further migration of trained professionals to this sector. In order to confront the challenge, the public sector should readdress issues related to employee dissatisfaction and provide better incentives to retain its staff. There is also a need to increase the number of trained health professionals. Efforts have already began in this direction and the 11th five-year plan envisages setting up of six AIIMS like institutions, upgrading 13 existing medical institutions, establishing 60 new medical colleges and 225 new nursing colleges. It is also expected that increased trade may induce repatriation and retention of health professionals to work in private or public sector ventures.

3. **Reduce variation or gaps in quality of care provided in both the public and private sectors:** An important reason for the underutilisation of the public sector institutions is the poor quality of services. Instituting a common minimum standard of care could improve the uptake of services in the public sector and reduce the dependence on the private sector. Hence, a system to undertake national accreditation and licensing should be planned and implemented. The Indian Medical Association and Medical Council of India could play a pivotal role in this regard working through the Joint Commission International (JCI).
4. **Increase the coverage of health insurance:** As few health insurance plans offer clients insurance coverage for non-emergency medical treatments obtained overseas, the need to pay out-of-pocket for services provided abroad could limit the market to those who can afford to pay. While efforts have already begun to increase medical insurance options for overseas clients, similar efforts should also be undertaken to popularize alternative systems of health financing such as community-based health insurance, capitation, vouchers and social health insurance *etc.*, for the treatment of poor patients.
5. Identifying and implementing mechanisms that will prevent the development of a dual and inequitable health system with enclaves of high quality health facilities catering to foreign visitors. The government is responsible for providing good quality care to their citizens, and policies and strategies to expand and foster greater trade in this area should support, and be complementary to national health care efforts. In addition, strategies should foster mutually beneficial linkages between the private and public health sectors, and between state-of the art health services and community health. An effort should be made to

encourage the utilisation of the services provided in the public sector for the purpose of medical tourism.

6. Establish a system that can address legal liabilities associated with medical treatment. This is important as consumers will have less of an incentive to come to India for treatments if legal recourse is difficult. If such a system is instituted, it will be important to ensure that it is also sensitive to the grievances of the indigenous patients.
7. Establish, reactivate or strengthen mechanisms that can facilitate public-private sector partnerships. There is a need to provide support to local entrepreneurs in development of viable business plans for expansion of spa/wellness services, and in development public-private partnerships, including careful market analysis.
8. Because of the dearth of information regarding the number, origin, expenditures, and characteristics of tourists who may be coming to India for health and health-related services, it is highly encouraged that a tracking system be developed, implemented and maintained. As part of this effort, it may be useful to establish a health tourism desk at national level to collect and evaluate data.
9. Explore strategic options to train and retain health personnel in both the public and private sectors.

Thus, India has the potential to become a "global health destination", however this status will only be meaningful if the opportunities provided by medical tourism can also be utilised to improve the quality of services in the public health system in India.

Competitive Advantage

Competitive advantage refers to economic advantages realised in a competitive market. Traditionally it has been associated with the enterprise as the unit of analysis, but recent applications in regional economics, strategic management and international business have extended the concept to include its applications to industries, regions and nations. While comparative advantage is strongly associated with the initial endowment and availability of resources and their prices in different establishments, it is more connected to the evolutionary changes in the mix of resources employed to emphasise the dynamics of economic advantages in different market settings. Competitive advantages are either based on superior cost or the quality position of establishments. Having a superior market position in terms of costs or being a cost leader implies the capability to produce and market goods and/or services at average market quality but below market costs and prices. Competitive advantages in terms of costs can result from economies of scale, from business integration across related industries, or from superior location or from lower resource costs. Advantages in terms of quality are associated with the existence of distinctive capabilities and their maintenance or improvement over time relative to competing firms, industries or regions.

The sources of qualitative competitive advantages for tourism destinations are foremost, natural and environmental features, followed by built attractions. Included are general infrastructure ranging from retail services to personal and business services, and the tourism superstructure consisting of hotels, restaurants, travel and tourism organisations, special events organisations, and recreation and sports facilities.

Competitive advantages in terms of cost (cost leadership) in tourism signify value for money for tourists in major tourism businesses such as lodging, transportation, recreation, animation and sports facilities, as well as all other related activities which make up the chain of tourism services. Cost competitiveness in turn is determined by general price levels, inflation and exchange rates for all related services, and the efficiency with which inputs (human resources, technology, capital, infrastructure and superstructure) are converted into tourism products.

2

Territorial Economic Integration and Globalisation

In the present configuration of economic systems, moulded by the deepening of globalisation, productivity earns new dimensions to cover, besides the traditional efficiency dimension, new dimensions linked to value creation, where the design and development of solutions for customers, supported by immaterial components such as life style, patrimony, aesthetics, ethics or environment relations, are crucial.

Business efficiency, also gains new configurations with the growing importance of collective efficiency aspects associated to the entrepreneurial cooperation and to the competitive environment, with the growing relevance of support activities and specialised services , with the availability of qualitative strategic resources (people, capital, organisation, technology, information, markets) and with the worldwide spreading of business networks that configure procurement, distribution and value chains, each time more complex, diversified and global.

Social and economic progress is more and more associated to the "value" (*i.e.*, the value that can be attributed by the consumers, besides the simple reproduction of the production conditions) that can be obtained by the resources mobilised in a specific territory, in particular, the qualified labour, the scientific and technical knowledge, the information about social and individual needs revealed by the consumption markets and the experience and business capacity.

"Competitiveness", as a strong reference to public policies and entrepreneurial practices, emerges from the acceleration of world economic integration, *i.e.*, "globalisation". The globalisation process as generated a business environment where the competitiveness restriction tends to impose itself progressively, in hard or softer ways, in more or less depth, to all enterprises and to all regions, creating new challenges, namely, to policies and public actions aimed to promote territorial development and to dispute investments and strategic resources for specific regions.

The European Commission has been emphasising1 the importance of competitiveness as key indicator to public policies, noting, however, that analysis and action tend to be harder, when one changes from the enterprise dimension of competitiveness to the regional or national dimension, *i.e.*, to territorial competitiveness.

The vision, developed by the OECD Secretariat, namely through the project on "Framework Conditions for Industrial Competitiveness" has helped to support the emergence of competitiveness as a relevant concept for public policies' challenges and motivations, by an understanding of competitiveness as "the ability to produce goods and services that satisfy the needs of international market, keeping, at the same time, revenues at high and sustainable levels" or, in broader terms, "the ability that enterprises, industries, regions, nations and supranational regions have in generating, when exposed to international competition, relatively high levels of revenue and employment".

The new territorial dimension of economies and regions, moulded by a more demanding, complex and global competitive model, can be translated into two key aspects:

- The growing relevance in the approach of the specialisation of economies, the articulation between "how" and "what" for the construction of long term, dynamic, competitive advantages.

- The transformation of the nature of economic policy, namely, through the rising role of new horizontal and structural policies (centred in the search of collective efficiency in markets of open and fair competition) over the loss of effectiveness of traditional vertical and macroeconomic policies.

The importance of the quality and nature of the economic activities that configure the process of creating and sustaining wealth, in a territorial development basis, can be illustrated by the comparative framework presented below, related to the positioning of different European regions where the conditions and results of that process are considered simultaneously. The fully awareness of the nature of such distances between regions, namely with respect to the quality of human resources, is decisive to the promotion of competitiveness.

The evolution of the European economies has shown the possibility of real convergence between countries and real divergence between regions, *i.e.*, in simple terms, while the countries average values become closer, the regions average values spread apart, clearly indicating the existence of several speeds in the process of economic growth and in the process of accessing to its results. This only confirms the increased importance of the value of territories (cities, regions, "districts" with logistics, universities, infrastructures and people excelling in their actions) for "collective efficiency" factors that are becoming more and more determinant to create and sustain dynamic competitive advantages for global competition.

The organisation and development of new forms of efficiency, supported by the diffusion of information, best practices, knowledge and solutions, capable of stimulating business cooperation and giving a positive sense to the competition, constitutes the most adequate strategic approach, in order to help regions and countries in facing its real problems and challenges of territorial development.

The awareness of the importance in decentralising the construction of the territorial competitiveness seems to us sufficiently expressive in order to advise and support the necessary changes both in public policies and private strategies. Building "on time", "virtuous circles" of initiative and investment, polarised by globalisation but valuing resources and capacities that are strategic to promote territorial development.

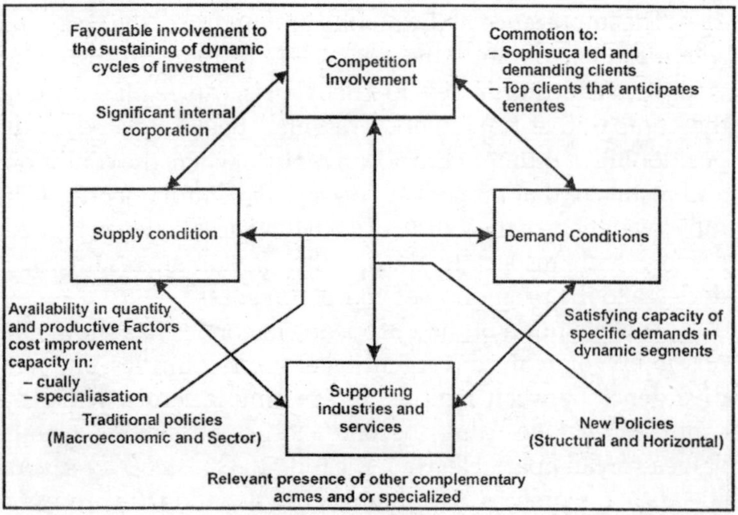

Fig. *The role of the new generation of public policies in the territorial development*

Aspects related to the agglomeration of dynamic economic activities (formation and consolidation of "clusters"), to the development of social and institutional capital (quick and strategic public decisions, cultural environments of human and patrimonial quality) and to entrepreneursh p translated in networks of specialised and innovative SME, are crucial in those strategic resources and factors.

Economic change transforms the combination of "flexibility" with "adaptability" in a key factor of competitiveness. A flexible and adaptable economy is able to accumulate and quickly develop existing or new resources in order to reach specific goals. It is in this context of structural change, where the territorial development strategies appear, that is important to locate the challenges that the public policies face, namely, the promotion of territory and region competitiveness.

The interaction of economic and institutional agent and the territory constitutes an innovating element in the modern notion of competitiveness. The structural factors located in the territory that help this interaction, only recently are being taken into account. The diversified factors that influence the articulation of "more" and "better" in successful growth dynamics in international competition produce, also, in each concrete process, a diversity of territorial competitiveness patterns. Competitiveness success will depend, nevertheless, decisively, in the way in which, in each territory, agents and organisations combine and use those factors to enhance the existing competitiveness conditions, generating positive externalities, developing active involvement channels in global markets and re-creating the quality and quantity of the strategic resources and infrastructures.

Territorial development implies the ability of valuating the potential specific advantages of each territory, consolidating them not only in sustainable conditions, but also with efficient processes. It becomes necessary, therefore, to develop a tight relation between vertical policies and regional policies, promoting complementarities and coherence. Consequently, the organisation and development of *collective efficiency* forms should be in the heart of the territorial development policies.

Globalisation, Reterritorialisation and the Political Economy of Tourism Development in the Middle East

A major limitation of most political economy studies of globalisation is that they view globalisation almost exclusively in terms of deterritorialisation. This essay, in contrast, emphasises how increases in the transnational mobility of people, capital and information can also result in reterritorialisation, which is the increased relevance of location and characteristics of place for global economic activity. In contrast to the erosion of the territorially based powers of nation-states often associated with deterritorialisation, the reterritorialisation of economic activity can increase the power and regulatory influence of state, societal and transnational agents who are able to exert control over territorial assets and the reterritorialisation process. The essay uses the concepts of deterritorialisation and reterritorialisation to develop a framework to analyse the changing political economy of one of the most understudied aspects of globalisation, the international tourism economy. With a focus on the development strategies of states in the Middle East and North Africa, the essay explores efforts to generate 'experiences of place' for tourists and territorial-based economic rewards for firms and their political consequences.

It would seem that there may be no better place from which to observe the process of globalisation than watching the rush of passengers through the transit terminal of an international airport. As travel writer Pico Iyer reports, airports are 'the new epicenters and paradigms of our dawning post-nationalist age'. Viewed from this perspective amidst the business lounges, foreign exchange booths, and duty free shops flows of people, currencies and commodities from around the world seem to glide effortlessly across the globe unconstrained by the geographies of distance or the territorial boundaries of national economies. At a glance, this perspective reflects a common trope in the popular and academic discourses about globalisation: increases in the transnational mobility of capital are eroding the territorially based capacities of nation-states to regulate economic activity, insulate their national economies and promote economic development. As Kiren Aziz Chaudhry explains, 'internationalisation exerts new pressures on institutions by opening up a rift between the political sphere, which is still nationally based, and the economic realm', which is increasingly organised by transnational firms operating in globalised markets.

On second thought, however, a visit to the airport, especially in the post-11 September era, might lead one to a different conclusion. Like Iyer, foreign policy scholar Walter Russell Mead observes that 'the international airport is both an agent and a symbol of the new global economy that is eclipsing the nation-state', but in contrast, he also suggests that 'from passport and customs control to air traffic control and international aviation agreements, the airport is one of the places in our society where the nation-state's power is most keenly felt'. This alternative reading of the airport is represented in the debate about globalisation by those sceptical of claims about the erosion of the regulatory power of nation-states. Many of these scholars suggest that the scale and scope of transnational economic flows have been overstated and misrepresented as most economic activity remains contained with statedefined national boundaries.

With a focus on the behaviour of firms and the regulatory institutions of governments, many political economists downplay the impact of globalisation, emphasising that 'governments...retain the authority to tax, regulate, and otherwise influence business activities'. Moreover, a growing school of statist-oriented political scientists argue that through interventionist industrial policy, domestic social policy and influence over the shape of international economic institutions, states are conditioning their firms and national economies to the globalisation of production while retaining or even increasing their powers to guide economic change and its social consequences within their territories.

Shaped by these rival perspectives, much of the debate about the impact of globalisation in the field of comparative and international political economy has been structured around assessing *to what degree* new patterns of global economic activity and economic policy regimes (such as neoliberalism and the so-called 'Washington Consensus') are eroding the capacities of nationstates – especially in developing countries – to regulate economic activity and insulate their populations from the impact of global markets. The frameworks employed by these studies, however, have generally failed to fully recognize the complexity of the transformations caused by globalisation and the full range of mechanisms states and local private firms have developed to respond to them.

A major limitation of this literature is that globalisation is almost exclusively measured in terms of deterritorialisation. Deterritorialisation, Gearóid Ó Tuathail notes, 'is the name given to the problematic of territory losing its significance and power in everyday life'. The concept of deterritorialisation, which remains the dominant measure of globalisation in popular and academic discourse, implies that as distances and national barriers become easier and cheaper to traverse, location comes to matter less to economic activity, resulting in the detachment of production systems and consumer markets from specific (national) territories.

To the degree that patterns of economic activity are becoming deterritorialised within particular economic sectors in particular countries (and this, of course, remains the focus of much debate) it is generally assumed that the nationally defined and territorially based powers of nationstates to regulate economic flows are being decreased. Regardless of the validity of various efforts to assess the scope of deterritorialisation affecting particular sectors of economic activity, these studies of globalisation fail to take into account how 'locations constitute both space and place'. As John Rennier Short observes, 'The popular view is that that globalisation leads to space. The particularities of place are overwhelmed by globalisation to create a bland space that covers most of the world.' But as Short explains, 'globalisation is a dialectic process that creates both space and place. The connection between location and globalisation is not simply the creation of space; it is the formation of new forms of a space-place nexus.'

This essay draws on recent work in the field of economic geography to show how increases in the transnational mobility of people, capital and information can also result in the *increased* relevance of location and characteristics of place for global economic activity. For example, as firms increase their ability to access resources and to distribute their products across greater distances, they will often seek to cluster themselves in specific localities in order to capture territorially defined economic benefits such as those generated by their proximity to other firms. I refer to this process as reterritorialisation.

In contrast to the erosion of the territorially based powers of nation-states often associated with deterritorialisation, I suggest that the reterritorialisation of economic activity can increase the political power and regulatory influence of state, societal and transnational agents who are able to exert control over territorial assets and the reterritorialisation process. In other words, viewing aspects of globalisation in terms of reterritorialisation gives us a tool to analyse alternative modes and scales of territorial regulation over global economic flows and better appreciate the role of state, local and global nonstate actors in supporting and challenging these modes. Globalisation should be analysed as a process entailing, often simultaneously, both deterritorialisation and reterritorialisation as each generates differing political dynamics in terms of the governance of territory and economic activity. The two processes often work in tandem where global transportation and communication networks (which are often themselves built upon highly territorialised infrastructures and nodes) promote the deterritorialisation of economic activity while enabling the formation of new spatial configurations characterised by reterritorialisation.

Using this lens, which views reterritorialisation as a critical aspect of globalisation, this essay explores the changing dynamics of post-war international tourism development across the Mediterranean and the Middle East. While international tourism remains an overlooked topic in the vast political economy literature on globalisation, the expansion and transformation of international tourism has long exhibited many of the core features of what has come to be characterised as globalisation. Tourism drives transnational flows of people, commodities and capital which circulate in globally coordinated production networks governed by large transnational firms such as airlines, tour operators and hotel management companies. International tourism also operates literally on the leading edge of globalisation by continually transferring consumer tastes, cultural practices, business people and capital across the globe.

The post-war global tourism economy has also exhibited distinct patterns of both deterritorialisation and reterritorialisation. The dominant form of international tourism in the early post-war period standardised mass beach tourism represented one of the earliest and most widespread examples of deterritorialisation in the post-war global economy. In contrast to the elitedominated pre-war international tourism market, in the 1950s and 1960s Fordist patterns of mass production and mass consumerism enabled a vast expansion of the international tourism market in the form of packaged holidays organised around highly place-substitutable low cost beach tourism along the shores of southern Europe.

This deterritorialisation of tourism allowed for the territorial expansion of tourism development across the Mediterranean and the integration of the Middle East and North Africa into the global tourism economy. By the 1980s, however, the market for beach tourism was becoming increasingly saturated while the ever-expanding international tourism market, incorporating new territories and practices into the global tourism economy, became segmented and increasingly dominated by many place-particular forms of tourism such as ecotourism, urban tourism and heritage tourism characterised by reterritorialisation.

Meanwhile, pressured by the decline of oil incomes and labour remittances in the mid 1980s, many states across the Middle East and North Africa sought to promote tourism development in an attempt to generate national wealth and state revenue. Tourism is a critically important sector to study because for many states in developing regions, such as in the Middle East, the promotion of tourism development has represented the most feasible means for them to foster reterritorialisation within their territories as they try to promote economic liberalisation and the incorporation of their economies into global markets. While tourism characterised by deterritorialisation forces tourism developers to compete with similar rival locations based on price, this essay explores how tourism characterised by reterritorialisation created new opportunities for states in developing countries to promote tourism development by means other than creating cheaper mass tourism products. While developing states have little power to reshape the global networks of transnational corporations dominating the international tourism economy, they have been able to exert territorial control over tourism spaces to generate 'experiences of place' for tourists and territorial-based economic rewards for firms.

This process, however, has also created new challenges for state building. States and local tourism developers must still negotiate relations with transnational tourism companies and mobile flows of capital, as they did in the context of the deterritorialisation of tourism development, but the reterritorialisation of tourism development has also forced them to engage in more intense struggles with local and transnational actors from private land owners and tourist firms to indigenous communities and archeologists – with rival objectives and interests in the development of territorial resources for tourism development and the symbolic representation of territorially based identities and cultures.

This study, while focused on the politics of tourism development in the Middle East, outlines a political economy framework for analysing the changing patterns of global tourism, alternative modes for the promotion of tourism development, and the political consequences of different patterns of development. International tourism is but one aspect of globalisation transforming patterns of economic development across the globe. Nevertheless, by using it as a case study through which to explore how globalisation generates deterritorialisation and reterritorialisation, this essay seeks to enrich the debate about globalisation and development in the field of comparative and international political economy. In particular, the essay suggests that the analysis of the political struggles over the governance of the local territorial economies generated by globalisation is critical to the formulation of an understanding of globalisation not as an inevitable, linear process leading towards increased deterritorialisation, but as an uneven, politically contingent process shaped by both global forces and local political struggles.

Reterritorialisation, Locational Economies, and the State

To analyse the dynamics of globalisation it is critical to understand how globalisation can result not only in deterritorialisation but also in the reterritorialisation of production where there is an intensification of the importance of location and territory for economic activity. The contemporary study of locational and regional economies has built upon Alfred Marshall's work on industrial districts that observed how economic activity becomes embedded in particular localities. Marshall and others since have studied the numerous ways in which spatially defined economic benefits are generated by labour market pooling, technology spillovers and increased ease of cooperation and learning between firms that are located in the same geographic cluster.

Building on these understandings, economic geographers have since studied how the spatial geography of production is being transformed by globalisation due to the increased ability of firms to access resources and technologies and cater to markets across greater distances as well as coordinate production networks with firms in other locations. This increased mobility caused by the reduction of spatially dependent transaction costs has led to the deterritorialisation of many aspects of production such as in the form of so-called 'footloose' factories and outsourcing which are driven by increased competition to constantly shift locations of production in search of lower labour costs, weaker regulatory frameworks and lighter tax burdens. The scope of this process, however, has often been exaggerated as not only do firms generally structure most of their operations from within the national regulatory context of their home base but each individual unit within an expanding global network operates within the context of local institutions and practices such that 'capital is more *territorially embedded* in places rather than having become "placeless".

Within the changing geography of global production, an alternative trend has been the formation of new patterns of agglomeration. In particular, many firms have sought to establish themselves in specific localities in order to exploit *locational economies* based on regional specialisation, concentrated pools of skilled labour and specialised service firms, well developed infrastructure networks, locational branding, and closer inter-firm relationships that require geographic proximity. This process is a recursive one where the locational benefits increase as more firms emerge in the urban or regional zone.

This form of reterritorialisation has characterised many aspects of production driving globalisation and economic growth in the last two decades such as the emergence of high-tech clusters and regional economies in Europe, North America and East Asia. Cities, in particular, have played a critical role as nodes of the global economy hosting the command centres of transnational firms operating within expanding networks of global markets and capital flows. Creative and design-intensive industries also often cluster in urban areas, attracted by their local facilities, services and quality of life features. Moreover, cities themselves have been transformed by tourism and entertainment-based downtown revitalisation efforts.

The process of reterritorialisation is even evident at the airport. As globalisation has led to increases in the transnational mobility of peoples, boosting the volume of international air travel, it has also led to the refashioning of the airport from a generic monofunctional space into a new sort of 'place' set within the geography of global flows. While in the wake of 11 September and the crisis of the international airline industry the future of airport operations remains unclear, by the early 1990s transportation planners and architects were seeking to reimagine the function of airports from efficient air travel gateways to commercial complexes anchoring intermodal transportation webs and regional business clusters. Supported by the demand for goods and services generated within a confined space by the flow of travellers, by the late 1990s airports were increasingly becoming 'shopping malls-with-planes' where the worlds of tourism, business and shopping fused together.

Reterritorialisation, as I use the term, can be analysed as entailing forms of production where firms are able to exploit spatially defined economic benefits called *rents* and *positive external economies*. Rents are incomes gained by holders of scarce property rights in excess of what would otherwise be earned (under perfect market conditions) without the addition or improvement of existing factors of production. As David Harvey explains, 'rent is the theoretical concept through which political economy (of whatever stripe) traditionally confronts the problem of spatial organisation and the value to users of naturally occurring or humanly created differentials in fertility'. In contrast, an economic externality 'is any occurrence or activity that lies outside the range of control of the individual firm, but that then has definite effects on the firm's internal production function'. Locational rents and locational external economies can be viewed as related aspects of the same phenomenon with locational rents referring to economic benefits which can be privatised and directly controlled by ownership, while locational external economies referring to the un-excludable aspects which are essentially public goods, or more often when they are exhaustible, common pool resources.

In contrast to the erosion of the territorially based powers of nation-states associated with deterritorialisation, the reterritorialisation of production can increase the political power and regulatory influence of state, societal, and transnational agents who are able to exert control over territorial assets and the reterritorialisation process. As Harvey explains, 'if capitalists become increasingly sensitive to the spatially differentiated qualities of which the world's geography is composed, then it is possible for the peoples and powers that command those spaces to alter them in such a way as to be more or less attractive to highly mobile capital'.

As a result, he concludes, 'the active production of places with special qualities becomes an important stake in spatial competition between localities, cities, regions, and nations'. To the degree that a territory is subject to aspects of production characterised by deterritorialisation, spatial competition is likely to create, for example, pressures for lower labour costs and more limited regulatory control which weaken local capabilities to promote social welfare objectives. In contrast, to the degree that these localities are able to encourage reterritorialisation, it is more likely that they will be able to expand their capacities to promote economic development and advance local social welfare objectives. While globalisation can lead to the reterritorialisation of capital flows and economic production based on where firms and investors perceive they can best capture rents and external economies, the territorial scope of these rents and external economies do not generally coincide with the territorial boundaries of national economies. National borders only came to sharply define the location and territorial scope of market contexts in the context of the era of national capitalism as states created national markets by enacting barriers to the flow of goods, capital, and labour at their borders.

However, with increased financial deregulation and economic liberalisation factors that have fostered globalisation the ability of nation-states to establish and protect these frontiers of their national economies have diminished somewhat. As advanced industrial economies, such as the United States, seek to guide the establishment of rules for the global governance of trade, finance, and intellectual property rights such that they conform to their own established neoliberal economic programs, the limitation these regimes put on state options to promote development is most strongly felt by developing economies. Chaudhry explains that 'economic liberalisation programs in many countries were initiated in response to fiscal crises prior to the construction of effective regulatory and extractive institutions that would undergird a market economy'. This leads her to argue that for developing states the relinquishing of control over their national economies in the context of increasing economic globalisation 'has resulted in the fragmentation of administrative, legal, political jurisdictions within already constituted "national" economies' while 'even in advanced industrial states fragmentation cuts at the administrative basis of the territorial national state, destroying the institutional infrastructure through which large national economies reduced transaction costs and enforced regulation at an earlier period'.

The process of 'fragmentation', however, has not necessarily eliminated the powers of government to promote development but has required a *rescaling* of governance regimes to arenas in which the interaction between the state, local actors, and transnational flows occurs. For example, in reference to the highly globalised information industries, Saskia Sassen writes, 'this would be a type of regulation focused not on the outputs of information industries which are indeed hypermobile and circulate in electronic spaces but on the material and socioeconomic infrastructure' which are territorially bound. Such a regulatory process does not require the integrative, extractive and boundary establishment activities which have long been seen as the foundation of centralised state formation, since it does not rely on states' ability to exert control over entire national territories, markets, populations or cross-border flows. In the context of globalised production networks characterised by reterritorialisation–which combine operations with low spatially dependent transaction costs (such as product distribution) and high spatially dependent transaction costs (such as frequent face-to-face meetings between the skilled workers of collabourating firms) the promotion of economic development requires that state agencies rescale some of their regulatory efforts from primarily integrated national regulatory systems towards fostering both global and regional systems of regulation.

This means, for example, on the one hand developing efficient global communication and transportation systems to keep marketing and distribution costs down, while, on the other hand, building locally the right social and technical institutions required to attract and train highly skilled professional workers into new industrial centres. While developing states have clearly very limited abilities to restructure global networks and governance regimes, they can nevertheless encourage decentralised, highly mobile global flows to become reterritorialised within their national boundaries through the establishment of conditions and infrastructures which generate spatially defined external economies and rents. Defining the specific policies and institutions required to do this is one of the current challenges facing the fields of economic development and industrial organisation. Much of this literature has highlighted worker education and training, technological development and diffusion, benchmarking and unifying quality standards, microfinance and rotating capital funds, regional marketing services, and institutions which foster more intense networking, collabouration and trust between firms. This work and the empirical findings from which it is derived show that public agencies *can* form alternative (sub-national) structures for reducing transaction costs and enforcing regulation over economic activity in order to promote economic development and advance social welfare goals.

Centralised state agencies, however, often cannot support the building of regional institutions and infrastructures without adequate cooperation from local firms and other societal actors which shape the nature of these regional economies and create the networks which sustain the generation of positive externalities or create opportunities for the creation of rents. Recognising this challenge has led some to conclude that the power of governments to regulate economic activity is being eclipsed. On closer inspection, though, the powers and capacities of nation-states are often not being eclipsed as much as being rescaled, decentralised or regionally subdivided. In many industrialised economies economic liberalisation and globalisation have often led to the enhancement of the responsibility and authority of local-level governments and to the decentralisation of the administrative techniques of central governments.

This process shifts the focus of the analysis of the dynamics of spatial competition from one between rival 'national systems' to one between subnational regions located within the same or different nation-states. One way to analyse the politics of 'spatial competition' at this level is to focus on the capacities of the state and other agents to shape processes of reterritorialisation through efforts to construct, define and direct the proceeds of rents and external economies. These powers, which I refer to as territorial control, can be viewed in the way that Joel Migdal understands the role of social control in the process of state formation. According to Migdal, 'increased capabilities of states include and rest upon increased state social control' which 'involves the successful subordination of people's own inclinations of social behavior or behavior sought by other social organisations in favour of the behavior prescribed by state rules'. Territorial control, by contrast, involves the ability to influence patterns of economic behaviour based on control over the territorial factors that shape patterns of economic activity.

In other words, I suggest that the political impact of reterritorialisation on state capacities and state–society relations is not only shaped by the nature of global forces but also by the configuration of control over the resources and institutions which promote reterritorialisation and the generation of territorial rents and externalities. These configurations include various social, legal and ideological regimes that shape, define and control access to territorial resources and the conversion of spaces into places valued by global markets and capital flows. In each case they are likely to be shaped by various historical state building patterns, contemporary political struggles, and state policy choices. Thus, to conclude this section, while deterritorialisation often erodes the power of nationally defined territorial-based regulatory capacities in relationship to global markets and transnational networks governed by private firms, viewing globalisation as composed of reterritorialisation as well allows us to analyse alternative modes for states to regulate global economic flows as well the political struggles between various state, local and transnational actors which both impede and assist the development of these capacities.

Tourism, the State and Reterritorialisation in the Middle East

The study of tourism exists as a specialised subfield within fields such as sociology, geography, anthropology and economics, but within the fields of political science and international political economy it remains highly under-theorised. A common question addressed by much of the existing political economy literature on tourism development is whether the economic and political impacts of international tourism are positive or negative for the host nation. On the one hand, many studies argue that tourism development brings in hard currency, creates jobs, draws investment capital, and can even promote industrial and agricultural development through fostering backward and forward linkages to other sectors of the economy.

On the other hand, tourism is also often portrayed as a neocolonial form of economic exploitation dominated by large transnational corporations that creates relations of dependency and distorts the local economies it comes into contact with. Most scholars, quite reasonably, see both sets of structural forces at work and treat the question as an empirical one to be addressed through a cost–benefit approach. This attitude, however, has helped contribute to the lack of theoretical development concerning the political economy of tourism. In the remainder of this essay, I seek to contribute to the formulation of a more sophisticated political economy approach to the study of tourism development by showing how the political and economic dynamics of international tourism development are shaped by local and global factors whose interaction varies depending on whether patterns of tourism development are characterised by deterritorialisation or reterritorialisation. Such an analysis is critical for understanding the role of the state in the process of tourism development, the possible future impact of shifts in the global tourism economy, and more generally, the impact of globalisation on economies and states in the Middle East (and elsewhere).

Tourism Development in the Middle East

I will elabourate this theoretical framework through an investigation into (though not a comprehensive survey of) the dynamics of international tourism development in the Middle East and North Africa. While international tourism flows to the region have never amounted to more than a 7 per cent share of world totals, over the past two-and-a-half decades the promotion of tourism development has become a central component of the economic development strategies of most states in the region. International tourism, moreover, represents one of the most prevalent aspects of globalisation affecting these economies and its impact and fate is likely to signal more general patterns towards the integration of these states into global economic flows.

By the mid 1980s most of the developing countries in the Middle East and North Africa were facing economic crises, due in part to the exhaustion of their state-dominated inward-oriented development strategies and the decline of oil incomes and labour remittances. These crises generated internal pressures for economic liberalisation and externally the International Monetary Fund and other donor agencies put pressure on these states to enact structural adjustment programmes in exchange for grant aid and loans. Such policies, however, threatened to erode these states' control over their national economies and their ability to insulate their populations from the social dislocation caused by the ongoing economic transformations. In this context, many states across the region sought to turn to tourism development as a new 'engine' of economic growth. While states in the Middle East and elsewhere had long viewed tourism development as a means to promote regime prestige and legitimacy and project an external image of stability and prosperity, the new wave of international tourism expansion beginning in the 1980s also seemed to offer an opportunity for these states to integrate their economies into global flows of capital and commerce while maintaining a significant degree of control over the process. In large part, I argue, this capacity was a product of states being able to promote forms of tourism development characterised as reterritorialisation. Over the last two decades Middle Eastern states have sought to exploit their capacities of territorial control in order to promote national economic development and gain revenues from tourism development but, as I will show, these capacities were sometimes limited or even challenged by societal actors seeking to shape the process of tourism development, drawing on their rival capacities of territorial control.

Tourism development is inherently a spatial activity which can be defined as the process of turning territorially defined experiences into commodities by the deployment of physical and human capital to create or enhance such experiences and provide visitors with associated goods, services and information. For this reason the concepts of deterritorialisation and reterritorialisation are particularly useful for studying the politics of tourism development because they help us both characterise and explain the changing dynamics of the industry across the post-war era. The dominant form of international tourism in the early post-war period–low cost, standardised mass beach tourism–represented one of the earliest and most widespread examples of deterritorialisation in the post-war global economy. As mass beach tourism became a highly standardised 'experience of place' it became cheaper and increasingly place-substitutable. As Burkart and Medlik note, 'To judge from the tour operators' brochures, the product being demanded by the consumer is a fortnight's holiday in a modern white concrete hotel with a swimming pool and a bar, the whole bathed in sunlight under a cloudless sky. Little or no concern is shown about the country in which the resort is situated, and it may be inferred that the international tourism passenger is quite indifferent to the nature or status of that country.'

This period of the deterritorialisation of tourism development, which involved the commodification of homogenous coastal space, encouraged the expansion of tourism flows to lower-cost underdeveloped regions along the Mediterranean coast. As the beaches of the northern shore of the Mediterranean became more crowed, tourists and tour operators began searching for lower cost and less crowded destinations.

These efforts led to the expansion of mass tourism development across the Mediterranean to destinations such as Morocco, Tunisia and Turkey on its southern and eastern shores. By 1975 Louis Turner and John Ash would note that 'what we are thus seeing is the rapid conversion of the whole of the Mediterranean coast into the Pleasure Periphery of Europe'. To some degree, these newer, more distant destinations could be marketed as adding a slightly 'exotic' element to beach vacations. In each location, however, the experience of otherness was not a product of territorial location, but rather, as Orvar Löfgren describes, was mass produced in virtually the same manner by tour operators and their local associates such that there was 'a constant standardisation of cultural difference'. For these mass tourists, their expectations of 'local culture' became so homogenised and alienated from territorial specificities that, for example, tourism 'entrepreneurs in Malta developed a new more flamboyant kind of folklore dance to meet the expectations of those tourists who had been to Spain or Greece' and handicrafts made in India could be sold as 'local crafts' on the beach in Morocco.

As mass beach tourism became the dominant model for tourism development, international tourism came to play a powerful role in erasing the specificity of cultures and locations across the non-industrialised world which became indistinct members of a larger homogenised geocultural grouping. As Löfgren notes, 'In many Northern European settings the Mediterranean simply became "the South" and this south stretched easily to include other sun destinations like Gambia and Thailand. "South" became the territorialisation of a certain kind of holiday, rather than a fixed geographical region.' The deterritorialisation of tourism experiences dramatically reshaped the organisation of the global tourism economy. As mass tourism became increasingly standardised, its production could reap greater economies of scale, further reducing its price, but this Fordist-like form of production also required firms to increase the volume of their operations. Increased affordability helped expand the potential market for mass tourism across the European middle and even working classes as well as encouraged the development of larger international tour operators which came to dominate the global tourism industry.

Transnational tourism firms, faced with increased competition and lower profit margins, were forced to grow larger through vertical and horizontal integration. As a result, the benefits to developing countries joining the international tourism economy became subject to an 'international division of leisure' in which the most profitable aspects of the tourism production process, such as transportation and hotel management, were dominated by transnational firms based in the developed countries of the originating markets. In other words, to a large degree the challenges faced by developing countries in the 1970s in their efforts to promote tourism as a means of economic development were a product of the extreme deterritorialisation which characterised the industry. While local states and developers were required to invest considerable capital in local hotel and infrastructure construction and had to produce a product that often required considerable import content (and thus an outflow of hard currency), the transnational firms which controlled the global tourism networks could easily redirect tourists to alternative locations if better prices or products could be found elsewhere.

By the late 1970s, however, a shift in the global tourism economy was underway. The rapid expansion of the market for low-cost standardised mass beach tourism across the Mediterranean began to wane. The cultural value of the homogenous beach vacation declined as the experience became routine and access to it widespread. And not only were beaches becoming more crowded and polluted, but an expanding environmental and health consciousness also dampened the demand for mass beach tourism which was increasingly viewed as having many negative environmental, social and cultural impacts on host communities.

For many individual beach resorts these changes posed a severe challenge requiring them to refashion and diversify the content of their products and services by, for example, adding more leisure activities (such as golfing and boating), shopping outlets and theme-park attractions as well as providing higher quality service and facilities. In the 1980s and 1990s lower transportation costs encouraged increased journey distances and tourist tastes became more sophisticated in search of more 'reflexive' and specialised cultural experiences. These transformations led to the diversification of the international tourism market, which included the rise of ecotourism and adventure travel and the expansion of cultural and heritage tourism markets.

In contrast to beach tourism, such forms of tourism development emphasised territorial location and particular experiences of place. This shift in the international tourism market also led to the growth of more organised tours and individual travellers exploring the rich cultural and natural heritage of regions such as the Middle East and North Africa.

The most lucrative links in the global tourism commodity chains remained dominated by large, transnational tour operators, airlines and hotel management firms. The trends towards the diversification and expansion of tourism markets also encouraged the cross-promotion of products between the movie, fast food and theme-park industries increasingly dominated by media corporations. While larger local firms in some states such as Mexico have been able to develop their own local brand-name hotel chains and capture one link in the tourism commodity chain, these overall trends in the global tourism economy have further narrowed the scope for states and firms in developing countries to participate in or bargain with the global networks of the international tourism industry. In contrast to the efforts of the 1970s and before, when states sought to start their own airlines and invest in hotel construction, by the 1980s most states were seeking to privatise their increasingly lossgenerating hotel and airline assets and promote tourism as a private sector-led, export-oriented engine of growth consistent with the constraints of neoliberal development strategies.

This shift in the global tourism economy and patterns of tourism development coincided with a period of acute economic crisis for most Middle Eastern and North African states. In the 1980s, pressured on the one side by declines in external incomes (such as oil revenues and labour remittances) and on the other side by structural adjustment policies, states across the region sought to promote tourism development as part of more export-oriented, private sector-based economic growth strategies. Tourism boosters in government and the private sector increasingly argued that the region's (territorially specific) natural landscapes, Biblically associated localities and historical monuments should be used to generate new sources of national wealth, encourage foreign investment and help their economies generate jobs and economic opportunities.

TABLE: INTERNATIONAL ARRIVALS (THOUSANDS)

Countries	1980	1990	2000
Egypt	1,253	2,112	5,116
Israel	1,116	1,063	2400
Jordan	393	437	1,427
Morocco	1,425	4,162	4,113
Syria		562	916
Tunisia	1,602	3,224	5,057
Turkey	920	4,799	9,587
Dubai	300	717	3,027

Above total	7,009	17,076	31,643
World	287,781	457,306	698,793
Subtotal share	2.4%	3.7%	4.5%

Source: World Tourism Organisation.
Note: 2000 data for Dubai and Syria is from 1999.

In the 1980s, as a consequence of increased tourism development and marketing efforts as well as the decline in oil prices, which gave a boost to the global tourism economy, tourism flows expanded across the region. International arrivals almost doubled in Egypt and Tunisia, nearly tripled in Morocco and increased more than fourfold in Turkey. In the late 1980s and 1990s, Middle Eastern destinations were also made more competitive by the devaluation of local currencies resulting from structural adjustment policies. The share of international arrivals across the region grew from 4.2 per cent of world totals in 1980 to 5.1 per cent by 1990 and climbed to 6.5 per cent by the year 2000. Meanwhile, the regional share of international tourism receipts, measured in US$, grew from 3.4 per cent of world totals in 1990 to 4.3 per cent in 2000. Across the region, international tourism revenues as a share of gross domestic product ranged from almost 3 per cent in Israel and Syria to around 8 per cent in Tunisia and Jordan. The tourism sector generally represented a leading source of hard currency earnings and accounted for up to one in ten jobs in the formal sector. The indirect impact of tourism spending is certainly even much greater.

TABLE: INTERNATIONAL ARRIVALS (MILLIONS)

Countries	1980	1990	2000
North Africa	4.0	8.4	10.1
Arab Middle East	6.0	9.0	23.2
Israel and Turkey	2.0	5.8	12.0
Regional total	12.0	23.2	45.3
World	287.7	457.3	698.7
Regional share	4.17%	5.07%	6.48%

Source: World Tourism Organisation.

TABLE: INTERNATIONAL TOURISM RECEIPTS
(CURRENT MILLION US$)

Countries	1980	2000
North Africa	2.3	3.5
Arab Middle East	4.4	10.7
Israel and Turkey	4.6	7.9
Regional total	11.3	22.1
World	263.4	475.8
Regional share	4.3%	4.6%

Source: World Tourism Organisation.

State-led policy changes encouraged local and foreign private investment in the tourism sector through regulatory changes and tax breaks as well as by making more territorial resources, from the land near archeological sites and beach resorts, available for tourism development. Along the Mediterranean coast most tourism development revolved around upscale and diverse beach resorts geared to European vacationers, but there were also increasing efforts to attract more sophisticated and higher income tourists to the natural and cultural heritage of states such as Morocco, Tunisia, Jordan, Israel and Turkey. While the 1990–1991 Gulf War brought a sharp decline to international tourism across the region, the market quickly rebounded. In the 1990s the tourism economy expanded as the end of the Cold War gave more people the freedom to travel and as peace negotiations seemed to be leading to Arab–Israeli peace and possibly the start of regional economic integration.

TABLE: INTERNATIONAL TOURISM RECEIPTS
(CURRENT MILLION US$)

Countries	1980	1990	2000
Egypt	808	1,100	4,345
Israel	903	1.396	3,100
Jordan	444	512	722
Morocco	397	1.259	2,040
Syria	156	320	474
Tunisia	601	948	1,496

Turkey	237	3.225	7,736
Dubai		169	713
Above total	3,636	8.929	20,526
World	105,313	263.357	475,526
Subtotal share	3.5%	3.4%	4.3%

Source: World Tourism Organisation.

TABLE: INTERNATIONAL TOURISM RECEIPTS AS % OF GDP (20000)

Countries	Percentage
Egypt	4.4
Israel	2.8
Jordan	8.5
Morocco	6.1
Syria	2.6
Tunisia	7.7
Turkey	3.8

Source: World Tourism Organisation and World Bank.

In a moment of great optimism, Jordan was able to greatly increase tourist flows by opening its borders with Israel after signing a peace treaty in 1994.60 Meanwhile, the decline in oil income led many oil-exporting states to expand their efforts to diversify their economies through the development of tourism industries. Leading the way in this regard were Dubai (in the United Arab Emirates) and Bahrain, which developed many high quality luxury hotels, night clubs and family-oriented leisure activities. Building on its access to capital and status as a trade and finance entrepôt, Dubai became the home to the world's tallest hotel, an annual 'Shopping Festival' and world class sporting events. While also seeking to build luxury resorts, Oman has put more emphasis on developing nature tourism and cultural attractions, such as remodelled forts. While Saudi Arabia has long hosted the annual Hajj religious pilgrimage to Mecca and Medina, the kingdom has been reluctant to support commercial tourism. Recognising the need for job creation and the potential to redirect its own tourist flows inwards, however, the kingdom commissioned a tourism master plan, allowed a very limited number of small, highly controlled group tours, and sought to expand religious-based tourism through granting *umra* or lesser pilgrimage visas seeking to attract off-season pilgrims who stay longer than the annual Hajj pilgrims.

Reterritorialisation and Tourism Development

States across the Middle East turned to or expanded their tourism development efforts, I suggest, in large part because tourism offered the most feasible means for them to promote reterritorialisation within their territories by exploiting the territorial rents and external economies generated through the production of tourism spaces. In contrast to the development of regional economies, high tech clusters and financial centres, or urban-based culture and design industries, tourism development generally does not require the same high level of technical knowledge, institutional capacities or investment capital to initially create positive externalities or rents. In fact, the spatial dynamics of reterritorialisation through tourism development turns on its head the economic geographers' understanding of the spatial construction of agglomeration economies.

According to the model of agglomeration economies developed by the California School of economic geography, as manufacturing systems become decomposed into their constituent parts with firms specialising in narrower aspects of the production process (as part of a trend often referred to as post-Fordism), firms tend to form locational clusters in order to minimise the costs of external transactions and to capture the positive external economies generated by the presence of other firms.

In this model consumers and consumer markets are viewed as territorial fixed while decreases in transportation and communication costs and the lowering of trade barriers make proximity to consumer markets less important. Meanwhile, highly standardised aspects of production, characterised by deterritorialisation, can be outsourced to locations with lower production costs. As a result, many firms, such as highly flexible high-tech and design-intensive manufacturing firms, are likely to emerge and develop in locations where they are best able to capture positive supply-side externalities, such as by locating in a cluster of other firms with which they can collabourate and learn from through close interaction often requiring face-to-face communications.

In contrast, tourism economies are constructed by mobile consumers visiting tourism sites which are territorially bound spaces developed by spatially fixed deployments of capital. The global mobility of international tourists and the spatially fixed nature of tourism development intersect to form a complex system for generating locational rents and external economies. At the centre of these systems are the globally known, high value tourism sites such as the Pyramids or the Luxor temples in Egypt; the city of rock-carved facades in Petra, Jordan; Roman ruins across Turkey and the Levant; and the Biblical holy sites in Israel, Palestine and Jordan.

While these exceptional sites have long attracted tourist flows, in the 1980s and 1990s the market for cultural tourism expanded as more tourists began looking for different, unexplored destinations as transnational tourism firms, meanwhile, sought to diversify their product offerings. As a result state tourism development policies and international marketing campaigns across the region focused on them to diversify and expand their tourism sectors. By themselves many of these sites generate considerable rents in the form of state revenues through entrance fees, but more critically they function as the central nodes of each states' tourism economy because they are often the main attraction drawing tourists to the region.

The challenge of local tourism development generally revolves around organising the movement of tourists through the nation's territory in order to create a network of territorial economies to extract rents and generate positive externalities for the state and private firms.

Even if public authorities divest themselves of assets in the tourism sector, they retain the ability to extract revenues from visitors through state-built tourist sites, such as national museums, and from their control of property rights near tourist attractions, such as archaeological sites. The expansion of tourism development around such sites allows the property rights holders of these spaces to extract rents from the developers of tourism facilities, and in turn, these tourism facilities are able to extract rents from the tourists. These tourist attractions also generate positive external economies in the spaces made available for tourism development in and around such sites and along the paths of the tourist flows to them. To enhance the generation and territorial expansion of the locational external economies, states can provide public goods such as marketing, infrastructure development, and tourism site development (such as improving the content and facilities of the sites to attract more tourists).

In contrast to the linear development model which characterised deterritorial forms of mass beach tourism (with long lines of hotels spread along the shore), an increasingly pronounced feature of tourism development in the Middle East and elsewhere over the past two decades has been the shift to a 'nuclear' enclave model of development. In this model, a large number of hotels and other tourism facilities (such as restaurants, bars, shopping arcades, golf courses, car rental agencies and gift shops) are built in a confined space, usually in a resort complex near a shoreline (called an integrated station) or within an urban 'tourist bubble', creating concentrated zones of tourist consumption.

This clustering process generates tourism spaces which are bounded territories or 'enclaves', limiting the economic or social interaction of tourists outside of them, while at the same time expanding the scope of available leisure tourist activities from golf and boating to high class dining and shopping. The spatial and cultural isolation of these complexes allows them to contain and capture (in other words, effectively privatises) the external economies generated by the tourists drawn to them. As Tim Mitchell explains, There is a larger reason for the creation of enclave tourism . . .Managers seek to increase their profit by channeling more and more tourist expenditure within their own establishments. The grand Egyptian hotels that used to provide little more than accommodation and a dining room have been replaced by complexes that offer three or four restaurants, several bars, shopping arcades, a swimming pool and fitness club, cruises and excursions, business facilities, and evening lectures and entertainment.

One of the first marina-focused integrated stations in the region, Port El Kantoui, was built along the Tunisian coast in the late 1970s under government direction as a means to diversify the Tunisian tourism product and compete against similar developments along the Spanish shore. Throughout the 1980s and 1990s the integrated tourism complex became the dominant model for the expansion of coastal tourism dotting the Mediterranean coast, the Red Sea and the Gulf of Aqaba. The reterritorialisation experienced in such tourism complexes is one confined to the space within the complex making it, like theme parks, re-locatable because the experience of place is one produced by the architecture of the tourism space more than the location itself. This transportability, for example, has allowed the Tunisian state to build several complexes across the country in an effort to spread the flow of tourists to a number of regions.

The spatial separation these tourism enclaves enforce between tourist and non-tourist zones and the organisational control it gives to the planning agencies which develop them has enabled tourism development to expand into regions where state authorities had previously shied away from low coast mass beach tourism. While more socially liberal than other Gulf States, Dubai and Bahrain have mostly limited tourism development to luxury hotels, resort complexes and shopping malls. Meanwhile, Oman and to a greater degree Saudi Arabia will only consider promoting tourism development if they are able to control who their tourists are and strictly limit the social impact they will have on their societies.

The other major trend in the reterritorialisation of tourism development has been the generation of external economies and rents by the construction of 'experiences of place' for the tourist. This process, in which territorial spaces are commodified and converted into tourism places, can also be characterised as an inversion of the geographers' model of reterritorialisation. Marshall explained how technology spillovers generated positive externalities within industrial districts by remarking that 'the mysteries of the trade become no mystery; they are as it were in the air'.

Contemporary geographers have expanded on his notion, suggesting that 'atmosphere in this sense represents an externality, a common set of resources facilitating the adaptation of workers to employment routines and providing a platform for creative and innovative activity'.69 In tourism development, by contrast, external economies and rents can be generated for tourism firms by the construction of an 'atmosphere', or experience of place, for tourists.

As noted above, integrated tourism resorts, while sometimes organised around various themes, generate experiences of place through their provision of a variety of leisure and commercial activities. Cultural, heritage and nature tourism attractions are also products of tourism development and promotion since even these sites are not simply discovered by tourists but are *created* by tourism promoters. As John Urry explains, the visual experience of place, what he terms 'the tourist gaze', has usually been 'self-consciously organised by (tourism) professionals' such as guide book writers, tour operators, regional tourism boards and local dwellers turned tourism promoters.

From the beginning of organised travel and tourism, first developed in the mid nineteenth century by Thomas Cook, tourism has required 'the development of a number of romanticised "place-myths" to attract potential travelers', usually 'constructed around literary and natural phenomena'. Across the Middle East and North Africa, place-myths have generally been constructed around romanticised images of ancient Egypt, the Biblical Holy Land, and essentialised Orientalist stereotypes of Arab and Islamic culture.

While cultural tourism to the Middle East has long been organised around popularly recognisable references to ancient Egyptian temples, Roman ruins and the Holy Land sites, over the past two decades states in the region have made concerted efforts to develop and promote these sites. Archaeologists, heritage preservation specialists and architects have been hired to restore antiquities and provide increased access and signage for them. International exhibitions of cultural artifacts from around the region have been sent on tours of Europe and North America with the hope of promoting interest in tourism to the region.

The Egyptian antiquities authority has even allowed the Fox television channel in the United States to broadcast the opening of an ancient tomb 'live'. Another major trend consists of rehabilitating and making more physically and visually accessible for foreign tourists the older urban areas and buildings in such cites as Fez, Tunis and Istanbul. Within these spaces craftspeople have been supported by state and international organisations to produce 'traditional' arts and crafts for tourist consumption. Moreover, states have even sought to discover new sites to attract tourists as when the Jordanian Ministry of Tourism and Antiquities put considerable resources into finding a collection of archaeological remains which it could use to promote as an alternative 'John the Baptist' site along the eastern bank of the Jordan river in order to compete with Israel's own site.

For some destinations, the construction of place-myths based on cultural, heritage and natural referents has been part of an effort to reshape their tourist image in order to attract tourists from different market segments. For example, Tunisia had for decades emphasised beach tourism and tourism development efforts focused on expanding its low cost beach tourism capacity. Then, beginning in the 1980s, as the mass beach tourism market began to wane, Tunisia sought to diversify its tourism product by, among other things, promoting its urban and Islamic heritage. And in the late 1980s the Tunisian government sought to create a new major tourism market segment by promoting tourism to its less developed, southern deserts region. The development of the desert tourism product was an attempt to fashion a more territorial specific place-image for the Tunisian tourist product and to augment Tunisia's reputation as a somewhat generic, low cost Mediterranean beach destination. This effort consisted of investment incentives, infrastructure projects, the hosting of cultural festivals, and new promotional efforts including international marketing campaigns promoting this more 'exotic' image of Tunisia's urban markets and desert landscapes with reference to the movies such as *Star Wars* and *The English Patient*, which were filmed in Tunisia.

The promotion of heritage tourism development involves a wide array of forms of symbolic representation – from international advertising campaigns to the plaques narrating tourism sites which are read by international tourists as well as domestic visitors. States have been able to use their influence over these texts to promote political interests such as state legitimacy, for example, by projecting images of domestic tranquillity for foreign investors or promoting national mythologies. In Jordan, the development of cultural heritage sites which emphasise Transjordanian (or East Bank) cultural and territorial identities have come to displace the country's previous reliance on West Bank Biblical sites (controlled by Jordan from 1948 to 1967) and Palestinian produced crafts. The development of Petra as an international tourist site also contributed to efforts to construct a territorially rooted national identity in Jordan.

Government-sponsored archaeological research, history displays and tourist literature often promote a connection between the ancient Nabateans, who built the city of Petra, and the current inhabitants of Jordan. In addition, the increased demand for cultural and heritage tourism in Jordan, combined with the desire of tourism developers to use design elements to 'brand' Jordanian tourism with a unique sense of place, has led to the rehabilitation and remodeling of unused nineteenth-century rural structures and early twentieth-century urban mansions, built in vernacular styles with local stones, into tourist hotels, restaurants and resort complexes. This has led to the creation (some would say fabrication) of a recognisable 'traditional Jordanian style' designed by contemporary architects inspired by elements of vernacular architecture.

This style has become the basis of hotel designs, handicrafts production, art work and even dining experiences. By infusing commercial experiences and commodities with a style which gives a sense of place, the rise of domestic middle-class consumerism and international tourism has help foster the emergence of a stronger, more coherent sense of a historically and territorially rooted sense of Jordanian national identity.

The Politics of Territorial Control

By asserting control over tourism spaces and the processes which convert places, cultures and experiences into territorial defined tourism commodities, social actors and organisations such as states, local communities or transnational corporations are able to drive the reterritorialisation process and control the generation of rents and external economies which draw both tourists and capital investment. As described above, different forms of tourismdevelopment are subject to different modes of territorial control. For example, in the development of tourism complexes territorial control is generally powerfully wielded by state authorities that own or can expropriate the land for the complex and can also tightly regulate or control the development process.

While the Tunisian government has chosen to maintain direct control over the development of its tourism complexes, in Egypt the state has often wielded its power indirectly by granting development licenses over government 'protected' coastal land to regime allies in the business sector. Other states, such as more democratically governed Turkey, have sought to decentralise the governance of tourism development. Turkish efforts to diversity its tourism product and forge a more sustainable pattern of tourism development have led to the emergence of new societal actors with needed skills and capabilities acting as partners and stakeholders in the process. This trend, however, 'has been hampered and sometimes diverted' by the 'prevailing centralist tradition and omnipotent bureaucracy'.

The reterritorialisation of tourism development generates the most severe challenges for state governance when states have limited capacities but still seek to maintain control over the tourism development process. The development of tourism sites often requires the technical and financial assistance of experts and international organisations–such as archaeologists, environmental activists, heritage preservation organisations and international development agencies to help convert cultural and natural features into tourism spaces able to generate rents and externalities and sustainable economic development.

These agents, however, often have rival interests to those of the state or the private firms in the tourism industry. For example, they might value historical 'authenticity', the preservation of biodiversity, or the rights of indigenous communities over the interests of tourism development. They also might have rival conceptions for the construction and representation of territorially based identities, which promote alternative nationalist, regional or religious ideologies or rival interpretation of histories. Furthermore, tourists themselves may present challenges and burdens for local states through their disruptive interaction with local populations, practices of conspicuous consumption or high use of scarce resources.

More critically, societal actors, such as indigenous populations and private land owners near tourist sites, may seek to assert their local territorial control to obstruct or exploit the plans of state authorities and private firms to development tourism sites. For example, while the Jordanian state controls the entrance gate at Petra, the land outside of the gate in the town of Wadi Musa is owned by members of the Lyathneh tribe who have long claimed the right to extract rents from the tourist trade. As a result, private tourism development in Wadi Musa proceeded at an uncontrollable speed and without planning or regulation, thus jeopardising the quality of the tourism experience offered to visitors.

In the wake of the 1994 peace with Israel dozens of hotels were built with inappropriate designs, no integration into the built environment, and lacking adequate infrastructure. Meanwhile land prices skyrocketed. Much of the ability of tourism spaces to generate territorial rents and externalities is built upon the construction of valued tourist experiences within an attractive environment, for it is the secondary spending in the tourism space which generates the external economies which drive reterritorialisation and sustainable tourism development. In contrast, reterritorialisation in the context of fragmented territorial control in Wadi Musa generated a pattern of tourism development characterised by haphazard and ill-designed construction. By 1998 Wadi Musa, while located in a stunningly beautiful and unique natural location, was burdened with a commercial and built environment replete with 'visual horrors'.

As travel writer Matthew Teller poignantly notes, 'Plagued by disastrously bad management of resources and town planning of the most tragically shortsighted kind, Wadi Musa is filled with a tawdry and rather sad air of powerlessness, a small agricultural community resigned to a collective free-for-all scrabbling at the whirlwinds of cash drifting through its fingers.'

The Limits of Reterritorialisation

The fragmentation of territorial control is only one potential challenge posed by the reterritorialisation process. In tracing tourism development patterns characterised by reterritorialisation I explained that these forms of tourism required the construction of a sense of 'place' and the diffusion of placemyths to attract potential travellers. These modes of place construction, however, can eventually be replicated by alternative, rival tourist destinations. A familiar example of this process can be drawn from the experience of urban redevelopment in the United States. One of the most celebrated efforts in the promotion of reterritorialisation has been the development of urban 'festival' shopping marketplaces developed in the late 1970s by James Rouse in such places as Quincy Market in Boston and Harbor Place in Baltimore. As Bernard Frieden and Lynne Sagalun write, Quincy Market's 'curious blend of historic setting and modern retailing was part of a deliberate strategy to merchandise history in the form of a unique shopping environment'. The 'plan was for small, independent merchants peddling their wares aggressively to create a lively, colourful atmosphere that would draw customers away from the chain store blandness of suburb malls'.

But by the 1990s this 'festival' style of commercial design was replicated across the country, not only in urban areas but also in suburban 'strip malls'. As the production of these 'festival'-style malls became more standardised they became more predictable and now include a recognisable set of national chain stores. In other words, the 'festival' style now represents a process of deterritorialisation making the commercial landscape of different territorial locations more similar. As Harvey notes in reference to the production of cultural commodities in an increasingly globalised economy, 'If monopoly rents are to be realised, then some way has to be found to keep commodities or places unique and particular enough to maintain a monopolistic edge in an otherwise commodified and often fiercely competitive economy.'

This example points to the limits of reterritorialisation as a tourism development strategy. Just as reterritorialisation can convert the homogenous space of a location into a place with special characteristics, the uniform replication of such a strategy for spatial competition across a landscape can reconvert these places back into nearly homogenous space. The fear of such are-deterritorialisation' represents one possible trend in the future evolution of patterns of global tourism development. This course, however, is not one that immediately threatens most tourist destinations in the Middle East. Rather, the most serious threats to the tourism economy in the Middle East are clearly those causes by the airplane hijackings and terrorist attacks of 11 September 2001, the subsequent wave of terrorist attacks on foreigners and tourist sites, and the continuing regional conflicts in Israel/Palestine and Iraq.

Tourism development characterised by reterritorialisation is particularly vulnerable to such events because they can over-write carefully crafted place-myths with images of insecurity, creating a geography of territorial fear made worse by increasing political tensions between regimes in the region and between the region and tourist-sending countries. Even without these transformative geopolitical events, cross-border tourism can generate its own domestic political cultural tensions. Discussing the case of regional tourism in and out of Israel in the mid 1990s, Rebecca L. Stein suggests that 'flows across state lines produced the need to defend and remake Israel's spatial and ideological divides, to shore up the borders around normative Jewish Israeli identity, culture, and territory'.

While the Israeli case has many unique aspects, similar challenges face other states in the region as they open their territories to transnational tourism flows but wish to maintain control over the boundaries of nationally defined spheres of religious, cultural and social practices. A growing concern, for example, is the reaction of Islamists to international tourism flows from non-Muslim states. At the same time, there is a growing fear on the part of American tourists in particular of travelling to Arab and Muslim countries regardless of how politically stable they are. The future of international tourism in the Middle East will likely be determined by how the territorialised politico-cultural gaps between guest and host societies are defended, remade or obscured.

At stake is not just the future of tourism industries in the region, but the future of the place of the Middle East within the expanding networks of global economic and cultural flows, as the Middle Eastern economies are not likely to be further integrated into the global economy if their tourism economies are not integrated first. Some have suggested that 'regime change' in Iraq will lead to an era of increased regional peace and openness. Plans for tourism development in Iraq were even being formulated before the US invasion. It is more likely, however, that increased regional instability will dampen international tourism flows and that tourism economies, to the degree that they survive, will shift their focus to domestic and regional tourism flows. The option of obscuration is likely only possible in the case of beach-side resort enclaves. Not only can these be built in remote locations in which tourist spaces are removed from the everyday life of the host country, their location can even be re-branded through international marketing efforts as some hotels in Sharm al-Shayhk, Egypt did as a response to a wave of terrorist attacks against tourists in the early 1990s. One hotel manager commented that 'most of the tourists who come here are under the impression that they are coming to some separate entity called Sinai, which has nothing to do with the rest of Egypt'.

But, at the same time, images of place can also become disembedded from the territorial location of the places they refer to, leading to new forms of spatial competition more akin to deterritorialisation. One example is represented by the development of the 'Luxor' casino hotel in Las Vegas, which consists of a massive hotel in the shape of a glass pyramid. Inside the hotel contains tacky recreations of Egyptian temples and artifacts and multimedia displays that bring to life images of the country as imagined by Hollywood films. Some have even called it a 'sanitised version of Egypt' real enough that a tourist from Kansas could conclude that she 'does not need to travel to Egypt anymore now that she has seen the Luxor, USA'. It is not likely that the place-myth of Egypt within the international tourism economy will ever be displaced by the place-myth of Las Vegas's version of Egypt. To consider such a suggestion would require viewing the globalisation of tourism as leading inevitably towards ever-increasing deterritorialisation where distinct notions of territory and location would some day collapse. Not only is deterritorialisation never so complete and unchallenged, but to view aspects of globalisation only in terms of deterritorialisation is to fail to fully appreciate the depth and complexities of the transformations caused by globalisation since, as I have argued, globalisation generates both deterritorialisation and reterritorialisation. More specifically, this essay developed a political economy framework to show how the political and economic dynamics of international tourism development are shaped by local and global factors whose interaction varies depending on whether patterns of tourism development are characterised by deterritorialisation or reterritorialisation. Using this framework, I situated the expansion of tourism development across the Middle East since the 1980s within the larger context of the changing nature of the post-war global tourism economy which has been increasingly characterised by reterritorialisation.

This expansion, I argued, was generally a product of state-led policy changes driven by the notion that tourism seemed the most feasible means for these states to promote reterritorialisation. As reterritorialisation can increase the power and regulatory influence of state, societal, and transnational agents who are able to exert control over territorial assets and the reterritorialisation process, it opened the development process up to new modes of political control and contention. As a result, this analysis shows, the physical and cultural space tourists now inhabit in the Middle East is not the product of an unchanging natural or historical landscape, but instead an ever changing political construction, the product of struggles between state, societal and transnational actors over the control of transnational flows, the use of space and the nature of cultural representations.

While international tourism is only one aspect of globalisation transforming patterns of development across the globe, using it as a case study through which to explore how globalisation generates both deterritorialisation and reterritorialisation this essay has sought to enrich the analysis of globalisation in comparative and international political economy by outlining a framework for analysing alternative modes for the promotion of economic development and the local political struggles over territorial control which help shape the impact of globalisation by reshaping the economic and political landscape of localities across the globe. This framework, I hope, can help contribute to an understanding of globalisation not as a linear process leading inevitably towards increased deterritorialisation, but as a dialectical and politically contingent process shaped by both global forces and local political struggles.

3

Tourism and Sustainable Development

Introduction

Tourism is a rapidly growing phenomenon and has become one of the largest industries in the world. The impact of tourism is extremely varied. On one hand, it plays an important and certainly positive role in the socio-economic and political development in destination countries by, for instance, offering new employment opportunities. Also, in certain instances, it may contribute to a broader cultural understanding by creating awareness, respecting the diversity of cultures and ways of life. On the other hand, as a tool to create jobs, it has not fulfilled its expectations. At the same time, complaints from tourist destinations concerning massive negative impacts upon environment, culture and residents' ways of life have given rise to a demand for a more sustainable development in tourism. Different parties will have to be involved in the process of developing sustainable tourism. This section focuses on what the tourism industry itself can do in order to increase its sustainability, defines three major problems, and suggests possible tourism initiatives to help solve these problems. Other problems should also be included in the discussion for it to become exhaustive.

Industry Initiatives for Sustainable Tourism Problems

Decreased Access to Natural Resources for the Local Communities and Environmental Degradation

Tourism is not, as many people assert, a clean and non-polluting industry. A major problem is the lack of a common understanding of what sustainable tourism or "ecotourism" means. This ambiguity leads to violations of environmental regulations and standards. Hence, the environmental problems evolving from tourism are manifold. First of all, the tourism industry is very resource and land intensive. Consequently, the interest of the tourism sector will often be in conflict with local resource and land use practices. The introduction of tourism will imply an increased stress on resources available. An influx of tourists into the area will lead to a competition for resources. Employees working at the tourist sites compound this competition. Almost as a rule, tourists are supplied at the expense of the local population. Tourist activities imply an intensified utilisation of vulnerable habitats. Investors and tourists do not necessarily possess awareness on how to use natural resources sustainably, and subsequently this utilisation often leads to a degradation of resources. Tourism is also a major generator of wastes. In most tourist regions of developing countries, sewage, wastewater and solid waste disposal are not properly managed or planned. Lastly, tourism is also responsible for a considerable proportion of increased volumes and mileage in global transport and hence the associated environmentally damaging pollutant emissions. The tourism industry has not shown sufficient willingness to (internalise or) compensate the cost of conservation of bio-diversity in, for instance, protected areas, even though they can profit from it.

Increasing Cultural Erosion and Disrespect for Human Rights

Tourism is a powerful agent of change. International tourism acts as a catalyst for the transition from traditional ways of life to so-called modern, Western forms of society. Accordingly, tourism often brings with it the introduction of new behaviour trends and norms. Very often, these are contrary to traditional norms existing in the host community, and can come into conflict with its cultural identity and threaten the traditional value systems there. The problem is that the investors seem to have a lack of cultural understanding of the invested society. There is a need for an increased awareness that establishment of new hotels *etc.* will have its consequences on the society and the people who live in it.

Tourism has become associated with violation of human rights. Many destination countries have experienced an increase in criminality, prostitution, alcohol and drug abuse as a consequence of tourism. Furthermore, child labour is commonplace in the tourism industry (particularly in the informal sector). According to estimates made by ILO (International Labour Organisation), between 3 and 19 million children and teenagers work in the tourism sector. A particularly abominable form of violation of human rights is child slavery and despicable abuse of children taking place in the booming sex industry in many countries. In these countries, tourism has led to an incredible increase in prostitution and also in the exploitation of children. The tourism industry has not yet come up with a general condemnation of these violations of human rights.

Unqualified Jobs and Foreign Exchange Leakage

The tourism industry is characterised by a high degree of monopoly, which implies a concentration of services and profits into very few big transnational corporations. In many countries, tourism facilities mostly belong to foreigners. Furthermore, in local host communities in many countries a relatively small number of people are involved in the tourism industry in host communities in many developing countries. Very often, there is a lack of qualified manpower in the locality. Hence, most employees are recruited form the big cities, neighbouring countries or even from the country of origin of the investors.

Multiplier effects from tourism are less significant than is often assumed. One reason is that tourism industries purchase most of their inputs (materials, products or services) in their country of origin. As a result, a considerable amount of foreign exchange revenues leaks from the destination countries. The more goods, services, physical capital and human capital a country must import for its tourism services, the higher the leakage. Very often the investors are not approaching the local community to see what it actually can provide. In addition to this, the General Agreement on Trade in Services (GATS), with its liberalisation of global trade and services, is increasingly undermining the possibilities of individual countries and regions to control their tourism industries and the possible economic gains from tourism.

Solutions

Decreased Access to Natural Resources for the Local Communities and Environmental Degradation

In general, the tourism industry should engage in promoting sustainability as a hallmark for investors. More specifically, investors in tourism should strive to adopt environmentally sound technologies or other measures to minimise the consumption of local ground water. In the case of water utilisation, such measures might be water saving equipment, desalination systems and collecting and utilising rainwater. Using other types of resources in a sustainable manner is, of course, also crucial. There is a need to use ecological materials and installation of renewable sources of energy systems (solar energy) in all new buildings and new construction. Furthermore there should be an acceleration of installation or solar/wind power in all public work projects of communities where tourism will be introduced. To prevent or minimise the impact of chemical inputs in soil, water and health, one should start utilising sound ecological methods, including IPM (Integrated Pest Management). Ecological methods need to be applied in all areas utilised for tourism, including in the maintenance of golf courts, gardens and recreational facilities. Pollution of ground and coastal waters must be prevented, and recommendations must be made (perhaps even legislation) for tourism investors to invest in proper sewage treatment facilities. Appropriate waste disposal systems and ways to separate garbage into organic and non-organic waste should be developed. Organic waste can be composted and possibly reused on hotel gardens or even for local farming. This could be done through collabouration with local residents. Residents could organise themselves and manage the allocated dumping sites, and hence benefit from the system in receiving payment from the hotel for services rendered. A system to separate the different materials, and recycle some should be in place at the landfill site, thus reducing the waste even further.

To avoid degradation of the natural environment, tourism projects can help finance protected areas and safeguard ecologically sensitive regions against further environmental deterioration. By empowering local populations and have them participating in the entire process, sustainability will be ensured as it becomes accepted by and adjusted to the local communities. Also, a protected area might certainly be a suitable tourist-attraction, where tourists can experience amasing nature and learn about conservation and traditional uses of natural resources in the area.

Investors in tourism should always respect the traditional land tenure system in the area and the traditional user-right systems of resources. In regard to this, the communication and consultation with the local communities about resource-use is important. Tourism investors should not exclude local people from using local resources, and thus take away what they depend on for maintaining their well being.

The tourism industry can and must take initiatives to implement that polluters pay a principle (or other forms of internalisation of externalities) for pollution related to tourism operations. This may be organised and carried out through local tax systems or through funds established by the tourism industry for local community development. However, the paid principle should be applied for minor pollution only and should not be developed into a possibility for investors to pay a symbolic fine for imposed irreversible negative impacts on the local environment. Inaccurate and mild environmental legislation in destination countries may possibly attract more foreign investors contributing to fast economic growth and development, but with environmental damage as a consequence. To avoid the dilemma, destination countries will have to choose between economic development and environmental protection international. Multinational enterprises must be committed to follow the environmental standards of their home country should these be stricter than those at the destinations.

Increasing Cultural Erosion and Disrespect for Human Rights

The tourism industry should promote projects, which are compatible with the cultural identity of the local population's way of life. Furthermore, the tourism sector should always make sure it acts in accordance with the cultural heritage, and respect the cultural integrity of tourism destinations. This might be accomplished by defining codes of conduct for the industry and hence providing investors with a checklist for sustainable tourism projects.

Establishing and developing tourist training programmes could be one way of managing codes of conducts for the tourists. Here, tourists can be informed and educated about the destination for their travel both before and after their arrival at the site.

At the site, tourist information centres can be established through funding from the investor. The information given to tourists should include codes of conduct regarding appropriate behaviour and clothing. It is reasonable to assume that people's offending behaviour is largely a consequence of ignorance rather than intention. Consequently, information and facts about the destination, ways of life, history, cultural heritage is crucial to help tourists get along.

It is an absolute must that tourism investors do not engage in or promote child labour and prostitution. Moreover, it is appropriate that the industry commit themselves to a global campaign against such and any other violation of human rights. Evaluating the sustainability of the tourism development, in regards to cultural and human rights aspects, is highly recommended for those responsible for the tourism projects. As with the case mentioned earlier of preventing environmental degradation, this must be carried out through communication and consultation with the local communities.

Unqualified Jobs and Foreign Exchange Leakage

By devising local training programmes and establishing educational projects, the tourism industry can ensure that qualified local people are employed in their projects. One should train the local people instead of foreigners to become guides due to their knowledge of the area and resources. The investors should be responsive to the kind of knowledge, abilities and skills found in the local communities. Very often such knowledge and skills are well fitted to be used in tourist activities be it fishing trips, nature trails, souvenir sales or dancing courses for tourists *etc.*

To constrain foreign exchange leakage, those responsible for the tourism projects should ensure that local inputs are purchased for their projects. A proper examination of local resources available will be beneficial for both the industry and the local residents. Usually, there is considerable local willingness to start producing new products if a market for these products exists. The tourism sector should also adopt measures to prevent foreign exchange leakage by a commitment to re-investment of a fair share of the locally accrued profit. We have already mentioned protected areas, training programmes on codes of conduct for tourists, or possible training of local employees, as projects in need of funds. Initiatives towards more local community development projects should also be appropriate. The tourism industry should promote the establishment of small and medium-sized tourism enterprises which, compared to large-scale hotels *etc.*, have far more moderate impacts on the environment. It is the industry's responsibility to act as a model for communities to show that it is possible to do business whilst protecting natural resources. The industry should also promote and support local communities to start tourism-related businesses and grant access to low interest loans. It is the responsibility of the tourism sector to ensure total transparency in all transactions, and to prevent tourism projects from being used as projects for laundering illicit money, as well as to refuse using bribes as a means to obfuscate or avoid government rules and regulations. There should be a global boycott against those investors involved in such or other types of illegal activities.

General Recommendations and Possible Solutions which Concern All Three Problem Areas

Empowerment of residents at tourist destinations, through local participation, may be facilitated by providing written and legally binding contracts between local people and tourism investors. The contracts will help to avoid broken promises, which too many examples and previous experience prove to be a huge problem. In addition to the mentioned examples (providing proper information for tourists and establishing training programmes for residents), the tourism industry, through for instance the WTTC or the WTO with NGOs in the selection panels, could issue awards especially for sustainable tourism projects as an encouragement for investors.

Agents and Partnerships for Change

In this section, the focus has been on what the tourism industry itself can do in order to augment and improve its environmental, cultural, social and economic profile and make sure this is sustainable. However, the industry's effort cannot be successful without a profound collabouration with all stakeholders.

Within the industry, it is important that both small and large-scale tourism operators are included in the collabouration and that they participate in solving problems related to tourism development. As mentioned, a sustainable development of the tourism industry can only be ensured through participation of all local residents in the destination countries. There is a need for a willingness and ability for the partners to work with this kind of bottom-up approach. In this context, both environment and social NGOs have an important role to play, putting pressure on the industry and facilitating contracts and local participation for community development. Governments in both destination and countries of origin of tourists and investors are responsible for providing appropriate legislation for sustainable tourism development, and to follow up the tourism projects with sufficient monitoring and appropriate sanctioning. Exchange of successful experiences of sustainable tourism projects is an important factor in this connection. Lastly, an interdisciplinary approach to the problem is necessary: using local, regional and/or international consultative forums.

Influencing Consumer Behaviour to Promote Sustainable Tourism Problems

International tourism plays an ambivalent role in contributing to cultural exchange and sustainable development. On the one hand, it involves a highly buffered, short-term consumer experience of other locales. Tourists can pay and leave, remaining isolated from negative impacts at the local level. On the other hand, tourism may increase recognition of the importance of respecting cultural diversity and developing an identity as a world citizen. It offers opportunities to educate consumers regarding responsible tourism and sustainable development. Consumers can play a major role in the transformation of societies towards sustainability. While mass tourism in the past was rather producer-driven, the industry today is becoming increasingly consumer-driven. In highly competitive tourism markets, well informed, responsible consumers can put increasing pressure on the industry to behave more responsibly.

A number of official proclamations have affirmed every individual's right to rest and leisure including tourism. However, tourism remains an unobtainable luxury for the majority of the world's population. Tourists primarily originate from affluent industrialised societies where tourism has become a mass phenomenon. Tourists' values, attitudes and behaviour are determined by their social environment, cultural identity and way of life which may be in conflict with local customs. Tourism is heterogeneous in nature, made up of many different types of traveller, seeking a wide range of tourism products. Demand is influenced by irrational factors, *e.g.*, fashion and trends. Demand depends on the availability of time and money, on images, perceptions and attitudes. Tourists have various needs, desires and motivations, both of a 'push' and 'pull' nature. While household incomes in major touristsending countries are declining, industry sales projections continue to grow, indicating increasing competition. The consumer mind is set on discount prices and "buy now/pay later" options. This poses serious threats, as prices already lag far behind any realistic accounting of tourism costs and impacts.

Many of the demand patterns in tourism reflect the unsustainable lifestyles of industrialised consumer societies. Tourism acts as an agent in exporting these life-styles and consumerist attitudes to less industrialised societies via demonstration effects and modelling. Tourism increases demand for imported consumer goods in the destinations, with detrimental effects on the environment, due to the ecological costs of transport and the high amount of waste generated. Increasing imports also reduce local/national economic gains, due to foreign exchange leakage.

The over-consumption of resources by tourists and tourism infrastructure (*e.g.*, the excessive use of water, firewood or food) is incompatible with sustainable development. The carrying capacity of natural environments is often exceeded with the addition of tourism demands. Tourist demand for resources (land, water, energy, food) may also compete with the needs of local people and may increase social inequality, gender inequality and injustice. Tourist transport, especially air travel, is highly energy intensive and causes pollutant emissions. Many tourism activities such as skiing, boating, mountain hiking, motorised water-sports (*e.g.*, jet skies), and trekking represent stress for fragile ecosystems. Tourists often lack information and awareness about their impact in a different culture and environment, about their impacts on socio-economic and socio-cultural development, and about the environmental costs of tourism. While tourists may be open to learning, they are often unaware of inappropriate behaviour and have little guidance on how to improve them. Others may refuse to adapt to local life-styles (even when informed) insisting on their freedom to behave as they want.

While the tourism industry may be willing to improve their products and services, there is a conflict between the industry's pursuit of economic gains and social and environmental responsibility. The industry lacks information on the requirements of sustainable tourism and on how to integrate economic forces with environmental and social requirements.

Tourists shopping for escapism generally abide by one fundamental consumer ethic: receipt upon payment. Consumer advocates may intervene where inferior customer service is delivered. However, the sustainability of corporate practices is self-regulated. This conflict of interest within the industry, and consumers' low awareness of tourism impacts, have led to a widespread abuse of 'green' labeling.

The mass media, especially television through films and reports about events, sights, *etc.* in other parts of the world, are increasingly influential on travel decisions and consumer behaviour in the destinations. However, these programmes often serve primarily as advertisements, painting images of destinations, rather than providing relevant information for potential travellers. There is a lack of reliable and appropriate (*e.g.*, age and gender segregated) research data on the determinants of tourist demand, motivation and behaviour. Few countries, whether tourist-sending or tourist-receiving, collect such data that are helpful under sustainable development criteria. Most studies of tourist behaviour focus on mainstream markets or market segments, rather than assessing or modelling sustainable alternatives.

Governments in many tourist destinations and local communities have little or no information on what to expect from tourism and the incoming tourists, and how to influence and control tourism and guide tourist behaviour; They are controlled by international/global institutions, the industry and the consumers. Governments of the affluent countries are only beginning to look at the issues of outgoing tourism. They are not yet sufficiently aware of their responsibility and methods to influence tourist behaviour by political and legal guidelines/criteria and appropriate planning and policies. Trade unions have fought successfully for shorter working hours and more vacation. However, they need to take more responsibility for helping to create a leisure industry that is more sustainable.

Solutions

Consumer behaviour can and must be influenced by:

- Fighting unsustainable forms and aspects of tourism, at the various levels, by sanctioning unacceptable behaviour and discouraging inappropriate consumer behaviour.
- Promoting responsible and sustainable patterns of behaviour, at the various levels, by promoting best practises and encouraging responsible consumer behaviour. There are different types of instruments and remedial measures available:
- Legal measures (rules, regulations, sanctions);
- Market based instruments, such as taxes to influence market prices;
- Promotion of and (financial) support for best practice;
- Industry self-monitoring/codes of conduct;
- Information, education and research.

Agents and Partnerships for Changes

Institutional Action and Possible Partnerships

Consumer behaviour in tourism is both a product and cause of policies by government and industry. Therefore, a comprehensive approach is required to solve the problems associated with market-driven tourism. Tourism should be viewed as a major development issue that all stakeholders need to be actively engaged with. To develop effective partnerships, the imbalance of power between the different stakeholders needs to be addressed.

UN Action

- Establish an NGO tourism advisory group for UN to provide technical support, analysis, and strategic advice;
- Create a 'best practices' information clearing-house, in order to collect consumer information useful to understanding and positively influencing consumer behaviour and to make documentation accessible on an equitable basis;
- Initiate a broad information and awareness campaign to highlight damaging forms of tourism and impacts, providing tools for informed decision-making. Initially, target participants in the CSD and CBD processes to clarify roles and responsibilities;
- Research and develop effective certification schemes, form a technical group under the
- CSD to assess how certification can be improved, *e.g.*, through the review of voluntary codes set up by CSD1998;
- Designate an 'ombuds' office jointly between the CSD, CBD, and UN-CHR to encourage diligent self-regulation and compliance with international standards for sustainable tourism;
- Develop guidance on tourism as an issue within Local Agenda 21 processes.

Governmental Action

- Introduce and enforce legislation to abolish child prostitution, implement effective control mechanisms, conclude judicial assistance agreements;
- Regulate tourist access to ecologically fragile or stressed natural areas;
- Tourist-sending countries: develop policies on outgoing tourism from a development perspective;
- Provide frameworks for ecologically appropriate pricing by strictly applying the polluterpays- principle to internalise external costs. This includes ecological tax reforms including the taxation of aviation gasoline and oil, removal of subsidies/other economic incentives with negative environmental impacts.
- Improve conditions for sustainable consumer behaviour by providing/promoting sustainable tourism facilities;
- Promote environmentally friendly modes of transport and transport concepts, reduce tourism-related traffic, shift demand to less environmentally damaging modes of transport;
- Promote renewable sources of energy (such as solar power), reduce the use of non-renewable energy and of limited local resources, through more sustainable practices/consumption patterns.
- Develop information and education programmes in co-operation with local stakeholders ensuring all stakeholders' involvement (*e.g.*, women's); provide information to tourists on appropriate behaviour (sensitivity, respect for/adaptation to local culture), *e.g.*, by establishing information centres in destinations, or by including briefing material for package tours;
- Take into account the specific information needs of various market segments, provide information to the local population on the opportunities and risks from tourism and on how to influence tourist behaviour;

- Adopt, observe, implement and promote codes of conduct, *e.g.*, the planned WTO-OMT
- 'Global Code of Ethics for Tourism';
- Integrate sustainable development education including tourism in the curricula of schools at all levels, universities and training institutions, involving all stakeholder groups, create and promote open networks for information and research on sustainable tourism, disseminate and implement results;

Tourism Industry Action

- Promote sustainable tourism products, using market related instruments and incentives, such as contests, awards, certification, model projects, culturally sensitive quality labels covering both environmental and social sustainability;
- Reduce inappropriate consumption, use local resources in preference to imports in a sustainable manner; reduce and recycle waste, ensure safe waste disposal, develop and implement sustainable transport policies and systems, *e.g.*, efficient public transport, walking, cycling in destinations;
- Provide tourists with authentic information, enabling them to understand all environmental and related aspects (*e.g.*, human rights situation) of tourism when selecting any destination or holiday package; educate visitors in advance of arrival and give guidance on 'dos' and 'don'ts'; make tourists aware of their potential impact on and their responsibilities towards host societies;
- Provide information on respecting the cultural and natural heritage of destination areas; employ tour guides who portray societies honestly and dispel stereotypes;
- Ensure that the marketing of 'green' tourism reflects sound environmental policy and practice; use non-

exploitative marketing strategies that respect people, communities and environments of destinations, dismantle stereotyping, integrate sustainable tourism principles when creating new marketing strategies;

- Train staff to foster tourist responsibility towards the destinations, encourage multi-cultural education and exchange;
- Actively discourage exploitative sex tourism, particularly sexual exploitation of children, and tourism which causes or contributes to social problems;
- Adopt, observe, implement and promote codes of conduct.

NGO Action

- Disseminate information to a wide public about the complexity of tourism and about the objectives and criteria of sustainable tourism;
- Educate tourists to change consumption patterns and promote appropriate, environmentally and socially acceptable behaviour in the destinations;
- Launch broad awareness campaigns on the worst impacts of tourism, to be funded by international governmental and non-governmental agencies;
- Promote relevant research on tourism impacts, criteria for sustainable tourism and possibilities for implementation;
- Monitor tourism development, policy, industry initiatives, and local people's reaction to tourism development and policy, and implementation of stakeholder action.

Promoting Broad-based Sustainable Development

Early tourism development has given little consideration to natural resource limitations, impacts on wildlife and indigenous cultures. The human environment and development has been largely ignored. Within the process of globalisation local communities' participation and nature conservation are threatened and often overlooked.

If tourism is to be sustainable, it must improve the lives of local people, protect their environment and health, and offer them a better future. In many instances, tourism can be seen as a vehicle to empower local communities and protect the environment through the development of new employment opportunities, the enhancement of local economies, preservation of indigenous knowledge and practices, public awareness and education. Sustainable tourism can create positive opportunities for community development in remote areas. The business sector can choose sustainable tourism over other more polluting ventures. Long and short-term development plans should be developed so that tourism and its benefits are spread within the area. To develop tourism in a sustainable manner, it is necessary to define optimal tourism destinations in local areas and regions, ensuring enjoyment for the tourist and minimum impact or disruption for the environment and local communities. Complex and broad-based local communities' involvement in tourism development requires targeted investment strategies implemented by local decision-makers. Those strategies do not exist in many areas and the development of tourism is not planned. Often, tourism investments are imposed from the outside, and the potential for sustainable forms of tourism is weakened. Alternatives to mass tourism (*e.g.*, cultural and "ecotourism") can be influential in changing the nature of tourism. Tourism can benefit both tourists and local communities and allow for two-way interaction and education.

Solutions

In order for tourism to become a sustainable industry, countries, states, regions, and individuals must work with new technology, natural resource management and marketing concepts. Ideally, participatory planning and implementation will be a part of Local Agenda 21 processes. To ensure community involvement and to safeguard local cultures, sustainable tourism development should therefore involve all stakeholders in tourism development at all appropriate levels, facilitate the development of tourism services that are planned, managed and reviewed by the host community in Local Agenda 21 processes. This will also ensure that tourism revenue stays in the host communities to enhance livelihoods and generate a profitable source of income, empower and motivate local groups to direct cross-cultural exchange in the way they wish and adopt practices which conserve, protect and preserve the environment.

Local and regional Tourism Boards should be created, involving all stakeholders. These Boards should:

- Promote sustainable tourism concepts in co-operation with local governments and all stakeholders, in line with Local Agenda 21 priorities;
- Work systematically to attract investment in sustainable tourism;
- Help other institutions in developing marketing strategies and training programmes and developing educational materials;
- Work together with different public institutions to involve all stakeholder groups in tourism activities, and bring greater benefits to the entire community; and
- Co-operate with grass-roots organisations to develop employment strategies through sustainable tourism.

Agents and Partnerships for Change

Institutional Action

The UN-CSD should:

- Invite countries to integrate tourism into their sustainable development strategies for the 2002 review;
- Ask the review progress in local communities involvement in tourism development in their country

profiles to the preparatory meetings for Earth Summit III in 2002 as part of the review process;

- Instruct DESA in co-operation with relevant UN agencies and convention secretariats, major groups and all stakeholders to develop indicators of sustainable tourism;
- Invite convention secretariats and the Committee on the Environment of the WTO-OMC to report annually to the CSD;
- Establish an international "ombuds" office to deal with human rights abuses and environmental destruction in tourism;
- Ask UNEP, through their Technology Industry and Economics Division, to work with industry associations at all levels, trade unions, local authorities and NGOs to develop a framework for 'good practice' and to develop a database on good practice, criteria, examples and analysis which should be accessible to governments and stakeholders alike; ask UNEP together with UNCHS, the Sustainable Cities Programme and relevant stakeholders to develop guidance notes on tourism within Local Agenda 21.
- Ask the UN Regional Commissions to prepare a report for the preparatory meetings for Earth Summit III in 2002 on sustainable and community-based tourism activities within their region and to work with UNEP/ WTO to develop regional agreements to address sustainable tourism.
- Invite UNDP to share its work on guidelines for "good practice" and to involve indigenous peoples and local communities this work;
- Ask the UNDP country offices to bring together UN agencies, bilateral donors and other stakeholders to work together on sustainable tourism, as well as involve the gender development programme in this process;

- Ask UNDP to include sustainable tourism into its poverty alleviation strategies and programmes.
- Ask the United Nations Conference on Trade and Development to integrate tourism into their development strategies and include a progress review on the role of indigenous and local communities' involvement in tourism for the Earth Summit III (year 2002) review, and to support community-owned and controlled initiatives in tourism and bio-diversity through its BIOTRADE initiative.
- Invite environmental conventions and treaties secretariats to include community-based tourism in their action plans and programmes, and to promote it as an incentive for the conservation and sustainable use of bio-diversity.

Multilateral financing and assistance agencies should:

- Provide funds for applied research through pilot projects to determine optimal mechanisms for tourism development in a range of differing circumstances;
- Create small-scale credit lines to assist small enterprises to invest in tourism without excessive risk on personal property;
- Support community controlled tourism initiatives that are directed to poverty alleviation, bio-diversity conservation and promotion of human rights;
- Assess their projects' effectiveness on local, sub-national and national levels involving all stakeholders, and publish the results by the Earth Summit III in 2002;
- Take part in a discussion forum on minimising leakage, with findings to be brought back to the finance discussion at CSD-8 in 2000. Possible outcomes include the development of a purchasing/procurement strategy for the tourism industry, local/ national investment strategies, improved mechanisms for informed choice

by consumers, and a linking of aid with capacity building in tourism-dependent areas.

Governments should, at national level:

- Establish/clarify institutional and departmental responsibility for developing outgoing tourism and harmonise institutional interventions;
- Initiate the use of tourism for local economic development by involving all sectors alongside the tourist ministry; to build the capacity to work at the destination level,
- Including product development and effective management of existing destinations;
- Facilitate research grants on sustainable tourism, methodologies, impacts and analysis of good practice; finance pilot schemes to develop 'good practice' and establish systems for ongoing evaluation and monitoring;
- Establish sustainable tourism policies and regulations, ensuring responsibly zoned development; natural and cultural heritage and resource conservation and protection;
- Rreview land ownership in potential tourism areas and where possible transfer ownership to local communities and provide the necessary training for them;
- Include the perspective of local and indigenous communities into local and national sustainable development strategies;
- Increase funding for local NGOs to enable them to engage in a dialogue on tourism;
- Support public education programmes which encourage responsible consumption, natural resource use, environmental protection and local culture conservation;

- Give priority to the following investment suggestions: create funds to help tour operators improve their technical capacity for sustainable tourism development; create funds to develop recreational facilities for the public;
- Encourage local banks and other lending institutions to set up regional investment funding programmes, including micro-credit programmes;
- Create Regional Tourism Boards, fully staffed, to help in planning, promoting, regulating, and expanding sustainable tourism;
- Initiate special marketing programmes by local governments and Tourism Boards, in which local tourism programmes will be advertised in the media;
- Initiate programmes to improve the management of eco-tourism in protected areas;
- Set up training programmes for guides, tour operators, marketers, *etc.*

Governments should, at local level:

- Harmonise laws on tourism including regulations, fee standards, licensing, *etc.* so that they will be more favourable to sustainable tourism in the region;
- Ensure that tourism development is in line with Local Agenda 21 priorities and land-use plans and that the public can participate in local and regional decision making;
- Regulate tourism to ensure that profits benefit local people and conservation efforts;
- Develop and support programmes to revitalise the diverse aspects of local cultures.

The tourism industry should:

- Reduce financial leakage and support local economies by buying food and resources locally, develop long-term partnerships with local operators, businesses and suppliers;

- Train and hire local staff and contract with local businesses, promote management opportunities for women;
- Prefer accommodations owned, built and staffed by local people, promote locally made handicrafts and traditional products;
- Encourage clients to study and understand their destinations, respect local cultures and co-ordinate visits with local communities, authorities and women's organisations, being aware of and being sensitive to local customary laws, regulations and traditions, whilst respecting historical heritage and scientific sites;
- Educate staff to avoid negative environmental and cultural impacts and create incentive schemes to promote sustainable behaviour.

NGOs should:

- Initiate stakeholder dialogue on community involvement in tourism development, recognising social and gender divisions in communities;
- Promote consultation processes in tourism planning, involving local communities;
- Launch educational and awareness programmes on tourism for local communities, support and promote history research and museums;
- Promote the respect for indigenous peoples and local communities' self-determination, autonomy and social and cultural integrity;
- Strengthen their efforts to empower disenfranchised groups (in particular women) to become involved in local tourism planning and management;
- Develop participatory programmes to support the integrity of local cultures and economies;
- Support the sustainable resource use and initiate environmental actions on different levels to conserve the environment while the tourism is developing;

- Analyse the experience with sustainable tourism in different parts of the world, in order to disseminate methodology/positive examples of community involvement in tourism;
- Support the use of traditional knowledge, practices and innovation systems relevant for the conservation and sustainable use of biological resources and promote actions on different levels to eradicate poverty, protect human rights and conserve the environment while working in tourism.

Possible Partnerships

There is an urgency to constructively shape tourism in order to support local development and conservation goals. UN bodies and institutions, governments, industry and civil society should co-operate to launch a dialogue process on sustainable tourism. This must be planned within the framework provided by the various UN treaties and declarations. All the stakeholders involved in and affected by tourism should be involved in the development of action plans for sustainable tourism. Identifying mechanisms to achieve sustainable development goals in tourism must be a priority for co-operation. 'Good practices' in conserving culture and nature while developing sustainable tourism should be collected worldwide, involving all stakeholders. This process should lead to a multi-stakeholder round-table on strategic planning of local community involvement in tourism to be organised by UNEP as a side event at the Preparatory meetings for Earth Summit III in 2002.

There is an urgent need to assess the impacts of globalisation and the role of multilateral and bilateral development organisations in unsustainable tourism practices. An independent international assessment commission should be created under the CSD. NGOs, indigenous peoples, women's organisations and local communities should be involved in this assessment process together with all other stakeholders. The UN Working Group on Indigenous Peoples should be invited to monitor impacts of tourism on indigenous peoples and local communities. The assessment is to be completed and published by the year 2002.

Coastal Impact of Tourism Problems

The United Nations Commission on Sustainable Development in 1999 will address both Oceans and Seas and the review of SIDS. Therefore, it is recognising that: "The survival of small island developing States is firmly rooted in their human resources and cultural heritage, which are their most significant assets; those assets are under severe stress and all efforts must be taken to ensure the central position of people in the process of sustainable development." With these words, the Report of the Global Conference on the Sustainable Development of Small Island Developing States identifies the single most important issue to be borne in mind as we address the challenge of survival and development for our islands.

Article 25 of the Programme of Action from the United Nations Conference on the Sustainable Development of Small Island Developing States (SIDS) focuses our attention on another significant consideration: "Sustainable development in small island developing States depends largely on coastal and marine resources, because their small land area means that those States are effectively COASTAL ENTITIES".

Tourism is one of many anthropogenic activities with a special focus on coastal areas. The two most popular locations for holidaymakers are the mountains and the coast. The coastal area or zone (as it is often called) is hard to define as the area where fresh and salt waters mix, containing many complex, diverse and productive ecosystems on and offshore interacting with each other. New concepts including the whole watershed area seem to be the best approach, especially when aquatic pollution problems are considered. Most problems are related to conflicts between different uses and access restrictions. Tourism leads to increased traffic flow and overcrowding in already densely populated areas. Up to 130 tourists has been calculated per inhabitant in the most popular coastal regions.

Therefore, tourism adds substantially to the following pressures:

- Pollution by waste water, garbage, heating, noise and traffic emissions;
- Encroachment of buildings, facilities and roads close to the coastline;
- Beach erosion due to building, dune removal and dredging;
- Excessive use of natural areas;
- Destruction of natural areas to accommodate tourism or other needs;
- Inter-sectorial competition and conflict over (marine and terrestrial) space;
- Exclusion of local communities from any role of significance in decision-making;
- The loss of natural and architectural heritage in the face of rapid expansion;
- Strain on public utilities and facilities;
- Displacement of local population;
- Creation of restricted exclusive zones that are off-limits to the local people;
- Loss of business by local enterprises as all-inclusive resorts supplies all the needs of their guests.

Additional typical tourism impacts are socio-economic conflicts as property and general costs of living increases, and social structure can be changed significantly, when summer guests overrun small communities. Foreign customs and expectations can create conflicts and a deterioration of cultural and regional values.

Solutions

A major focus should be on the integration of tourism planning and operation of tourist facilities into local planning instruments. Local agenda 21 can play a key role here in ensuring the involvement of all stakeholders. Ideally, this would be done in the context of integrated coastal area management (ICAM). This instrument bridges sectorial approaches in order to avoid or mitigate user conflicts, and it ideally takes into account ecosystem features and physical, not man-made borders.

New tourism developments should be planned together with municipal, industrial, agri-/aqua-cultural and nature protection activities, to allow for multiple complementary uses and to segregate conflicting activities. Area development plans should inform sector plans which should then be incorporated into a coordinated national development plan. All planning should be accompanied by widespread public information dissemination and provide opportunity for discussion leading to integrated coastal zone management. The tourism development strategy should protect local culture, respect local traditions and promote local ownership and management of programs and projects, so as to foster community stewardship of the natural resource base. Environmental Impact Assessment (EIA) on a strategic level as well as for projects is an invaluable tool for this stage. Criteria for planning and EIA should be:

- Strict environmental standards for solid, liquid and gaseous waste emissions;
- Taking the integrity of coastal values and resources into account;
- Enhancement of public transport infrastructure (train, boat, bike, bus);
- Locally adapted styles and maximum height/size limit for facilities;
- Setting of local/regional carrying capacities on a case-by-case basis;
- Limits to sale of property to foreigners;
- Maintenance of public access to the coastal strip;
- Safeguarding cultural values and customary uses.

During the operation of tourism facilities, several instruments can be applied to enable sustainable development.

The details have to be developed according to the use, and together with the local community, the facility operator and local NGOs. Local Agenda 21 could play an important role here (They will be different for a diving site than for a big hotel complex). Modern instruments, which should be, and partly are, already applied in the tourism industry are:

- Introducing environmental management, (according to ISO 14.000 or the European EMAS Initiative);
- Increasing cultural and nature awareness of guests through interactions with local initiatives, guided nature walks, museums, *etc.*;
- Integrating the local economy by giving priority to local produce (*e.g.*, fish, fruit, vegetables, furniture, and building materials).

However, all these efforts will be in vain, unless carrying capacity limits can be agreed upon in a dialogue and on a case-by-case basis. These limits have to follow sustainability criteria and have to come out of discussions on the development objectives and the natural and cultural values to be protected. They can be tiered in respect to nature used, number of beds and other facilities for guests, and amount of property to be sold to foreigners. (But management efforts for sustainable development cannot allow an ever increasing growth, which will destroy and, in fact already has, the resources the guests have come to see and experience.) To diminish conflicts a better use of facilities over the year, instead of only in a short season of two to three months should be aimed at. These limits probably have to be stricter for "nature use". Here the introduction and implementation of ranger and guide systems together with limits, regarding the number of visitors, can lead to increased awareness and control at the same time. A simple example is the different approaches to beach litter: Instead of excessive beach cleaning of all organic matter, a plastic litter clean-up by volunteers plus hands-on teaching on the biota originally inhabiting the beach and its natural detritus (like algae and wood) could reinstate an appreciation of natuie.

We also believe that the recommendations for action at the national, regional and international levels have been detailed in the SIDS Program of Action (1994), at the CTO Conference on Ecotourism in Dominica (1997) and more recently in the CEP Technical Report No. 38(1997) need to be implemented.

Agents and Partnership for Change

Institutional Actions

Actions on several levels are necessary. First and foremost, the historically grown sectorial approach to managing coastal issues, relating to tourism and other uses, has to be changed substantially. Under the lead of one coastal agency, all stakeholders, especially local people and NGOs, and also sectorial agencies, small and medium enterprises and industry representatives should meet regularly to promote sustainable development of their coastal area. The planning process and the operation of tourism developments should reflect the country's commitment to the guidelines set out in international accords such as Agenda and the SIDS Program of Action. Depending on the region, this could mean enhancing human resource development including public awareness building and training; institutional strengthening and networking. Lessons learned in one community should be accessible to others. This will start the ICAM process, which is a goal-directed planning and decision- making process. ICAM leads to inter-agency and inter-sectorial collabouration, resulting in operational decision-making with strong public participation and feedback mechanisms. ICAM could mean in practice:

- To start an environmental management initiative through an award scheme;
- To raise an environmental tax from visitors for small projects, *e.g.*, for funding ranger;
- Training or environmental training for tourism staff;
- To start joint actions with local fishermen, farmers, hotels, or other local initiatives;

- To develop a tourism master plan for the region.

In the long term, a development plan should be devised and discussed thoroughly in order to achieve a common understanding on the objectives and necessary restrictions. As all coastal areas contain particularly sensitive sites, environmental protection has to feature strongly in this planning process, with representatives from government nature protection agencies and NGOs having an equal standing with all other participants. Depending on the nature of the coastline, regional and intergovernmental collabouration may be necessary in addition to local initiatives. For some issues, such as the reduction of pollution and especially "eutrophication", co-operation on a larger regional scale is necessary. Maybe the Baltic Sea States, consisting of very poor and rich states (can serve as example) are co-ordinating their fight against pollution under the Helsinki Convention, funding projects in neighbouring countries according to a list of hot spots. They have just finished the development of a joint Agenda 21 for the development of the Baltic region, including tourism. Generally, national plans should be converted into area development plans, which would provide the local context within which enterprise-level proposals can be evaluated. All these plans should inform and be incorporated into wider regional plans.

As integrated processes take time, tourism umbrella organisations should start with voluntary selfrestraint, until locally adapted objectives have been reached. In the north, which bears the brunt of world-wide tourism, a development of quality tourism should be the focus for the future instead of an increase in quantity.

The term quality should include ecological and social carrying capacities at the same time as being economically sustainable. In the south, tourism development objectives should be developed according to the local needs. A specially developed Code of Conduct, taking into account inter-area, the Coastal Code of Conduct by EUCC and the Berlin Declaration on Biological Diversity and Sustainable Tourism, could lead the way. Environmental management should become a standard of operation as well as social accountability thus leading to sustainable development.

Possible Partnerships

Additional to those partners mentioned above, there is a major role for environmental and social NGOs to play. The involvement of local initiatives, heritage and nature protection organisations and agencies can lead to a balanced ICAM process in the spirit of the Agenda.

Umbrella organisations, such as scuba diving, boating, and yachting associations should develop and promote the application of codes of conduct focussing on environmental and sustainability issues in their respective fields.

The Convention on Biological Diversity contains an ecosystem approach, which is consistent with the ICAM logic. Its experts could sensibly focus on questions of nature use and ecological carrying capacities for sensitive sites in order to obtain harmonised world-wide standards with legal standing. The instruments and strategies are all already developed, now is the time to utilise and combine them in local dialogue processes.

4

The Tourism Phenomenon—The New Tourist and Consumer

Times are changing and so are the demands and expectations of the 'new' traveller, the search for different experiences, different adventures, different lifestyles has paved the way for this concept called the 'new tourism' Attention is being turned to exploring new frontiers or daring to go where traditional thought did not allow. "New" tourists however, are increasingly being seen to be environmentally sensitive, displaying respect for the culture of host nations and looking to experience and learn rather than merely stand back and gaze. "New" tourists are participators not spectators. Things that would never appear on the list of the "mass" tourist such as adventure, getting of the beaten track and mingling with the locals are now the foundations of the new tourist experiences.

Typically these tourists are turning away from travel and prefer to have a high level of involvement in the organisation of their trip. Responding to the shift in market dynamics towards a "New" style of tourist, a number of initiatives have or are likely to fuel the growth of experiential tourism, these include:

- Network tourism initiatives;
- The development of interpretive highways;

- The explosion of interpretive centers;
- The latest trend towards regional base camps.

A new era has arrived, and a new kind of tourism is emerging, sustainable, environmentally and socially responsible, and characterised by flexibility and choice. A new type of tourist is driving it: more educated, experienced, independent, conservation-minded, respectful of cultures, and insistent on value for money. Attempt is made in this paper to study the expectations and desires of this new tourist in this new age of tourism.

Until 19th century, travel for recreation was only undertaken by the elite. With the advent of rail, mass travel was available for the first time and destinations such as Brighton, UK and Coney Island, NY developed. Status was then defined by the mode of travel. In 20th century status was revealed by the nature of the destinations. Travel and tourism has been going on since time immemorial, and for the 'twentieth century tourist, the world has become one large department store of countrysides and cities' (Schivelbusch, 1986). By 21st century, travel became a new economy tourism available to all with enough money.

The focus of the tourism industry has shifted from air travel, overnights, meals and so on to total experiences or fantasy worlds associated with specific destinations (Keller and Koch, 1995). This new tourism phenomenon is not only influenced by economic factors but also by new cultures and a new generation of tourists. In tourism, the different destinations compete worldwide through globalisation (Saayman, 1998).

The paradigm shift from mass tourism (also known as *Fordian Tourism*), which was the norm for more than three decades, no longer suffices to achieve competitiveness in tourism enterprises and regions. A new paradigm, or new tourism, is gathering momentum owing to its ability to face prevailing circumstances (Fayos-Sola, 1996).

Modern information and communication technology development in symbiosis with the transformation of tourism demand gave rise to a new tourism. This paradigm shift is not easy to define but is indicative of a new type of tourist who wants a new or different product. The new tourists are more experienced, more educated, more "green", more flexible, more independent, more quality-conscious and "harder to please" than ever before (Cater and Goodall, 1992; De Villiers, 1996). Furthermore, they are well read and know what they want and where they want to go.

The different approach of the new tourist's creates a demand for new products. The small, medium and micro entrepreneurs within the tourism industry are dependent on major tourism developments. It is essential role of these small entrepreneurs be increased to deal with the changing demands of the new tourists. In Canada, 20% of the population is truly entrepreneurial while in South Africa the role of entrepreneurs is still extremely small. Only about 4% of the South African population is truly entrepreneurial. (Van Gijsen, 1998)

What is New Tourism?

New Tourism is characterised mainly by super segmentation of demand, the need for flexibility of supply and distribution, and achieving profitability through diagonal integration and subsequent system economies and integrated values, instead of economies of scale (Fayos-Sola, 1996). This paradigm permits the tourism industry to offer products adapted to the increasingly complex and diverse needs of demand, while being competitive with the old standardised products. These markets of experience have become global, affecting the demand as well as the supply side of the tourism industry. The tourism industry has undergone profound changes, which have been categorised by Poon (1993) in the following groups: (a) new consumers, (b) new technologies, (c) new forms of production, (d) new management styles, and (e) new prevailing circumstances.

As a result of the super segmentation of demand there is a very strong need for in-depth knowledge of the market in order to identify the clusters of consumer traits and needs. This knowledge will enable the tourism enterprises to develop those products that will give a greater competitive edge, and to place them on the market using efficient methods of communication and distribution. Flexibility is also a very relevant factor since it can assist the enterprise in adapting to the new demand requirements. This factor is relevant in several areas: flexibility in the organisation and in the production and distribution of tourism products; flexibility in reservation, purchasing and payment systems; and flexibility in ways in which the tourism product is consumed. New technologies are fundamental in this respect and, in particular, in the expansion and development of new systems of tourism information (Fayos-Sola, 1996).

Diagonal integration is the final basic element. Compared with vertical and horizontal integration, which characterise the mass-standardised production paradigm, this is a process by which the tourism enterprise can develop and compete not only in one activity, but also within a wider framework, seeking profitability on the basis of system economies, obtaining synergies between different products and offering services well integrated in the value systems of consumers (Fayos-Sola, 1996).

Key shifts in global tourism market trends are as follows:

- In the long term, the average standard of living in western developed countries will increase, as will the amount of discretionary money available for travel;
- Rising affluence will bring with it increases in the amount of free time available. Longer weekends and increased paid holidays have helped to stimulate expansion in attraction visitation;
- There is a shift in emphasis from passive fun to active learning;
- Activity or special interest holidays are likely to gain at the expense of conventional sightseeing, visiting and other passive experiences;
- There is growing concern about the impact of modern industry, including tourism, on the physical and social environment;

- There is growing awareness of risks to personal health and safety;
- Leisure time will be used more actively, for mental development as well as physical exercise;
- People aged 45 to 64 years of age will be growing significantly in number to the year 2010. In the United States alone, this age group is forecasted to grow by 31% by the year 2000;
- The potential visitor of the future will be: older, more affluent; more demanding; more thoughtful and discriminating; and more active physically and mentally;
- Timeframes for decision-making windows will be smaller. Hence, one-stop-shopping for all-inclusive packages will continue to be appealing; and
- Consumers will increasingly seek low impact tourism facilities, consistent with environmental values and the desire not to contribute to negative impacts.

The New Tourist

The travelling consumer of today (let alone in the future) is very different from any other time in history. The most successful businesses in the travel industry are those that respond to the challenge through the use of technology, innovative marketing programs, better training of staff and by developing a closeness and understanding of its customers/ guests. The differences in travel patterns in the next century will be more related to what consumers are seeking in a travel experience than in how they travel.

Today's traveller, the well-heeled or footloose back-packer, is usually informed, educated, and more often than not, fully aware of what he or she wants from their travels. For them the optimisation of time and money is the key and they prepare for their trip by researching their destination through the Web and the experiences of friends and fellow travellers. Mass media has responded to this shift and further fuelled the search for experiences through the promotion of a vast range of lifestyle/adventure programs which have evolved more recently into experiential voyeuristic docu-dramas referred to as reality programmes. Attention is being turned to exploring new frontiers or daring to go where traditional thought did not allow. In *Tourism, Technology and Competitive Strategies,* author Auliana Poon speaks about the changes in consumer behaviour and values which are the critical driving forces for the new tourism. The new tourist is experienced, more flexible, independent, quality conscious and harder to please.

"New" tourists however, are increasingly being seen to be environmentally sensitive, displaying respect for the culture of host nations and looking to experience and learn rather than merely stand back and gaze. "New" tourists are participators not spectators. Things that would never appear on the list of the "mass" tourist such as adventure, getting of the beaten track and mingling with the locals are now the foundations of the new tourist experiences. Typically these tourists are turning away from travel and prefer to have a high level of involvement in the organisation of their trip.

TABLE: COMPARISON OF OLD AND NEW TOURISTS:

		New Tourists
Search for the sun	=>	Experience something different
Follow the masses	=>	Want to be in charge
Here today, gone tomorrow	=>	See and enjoy but not destroy
Just to show that you had been	=>	Just for the fun of it
Having	=>	Being
Superiority	=>	Understanding
Like attractions	=>	Like sports
Precautions	=>	Adventurous
Eat in hotel	=>	Try local fare
Homogeneous	=>	Hybrid

Source: Tourism, Technology and Competitive Strategies, Auliana Poon.

Travel is no longer a novelty to the new tourist. Studies support what industry executives have been noticing for the last few years. People expect more out of their vacations than they used to and they are more adventuresome. Surveys done by the Canadian Tourism Research Institute indicate a high degree of interest in getaway vacations, ecotourism, cultural tourism and combining a business trip with a pleasure trip.

Over the next ten years, tourism products and attractions will have to cater to visitors who are more demanding and discriminating, as well as more active and more purposeful in their choice of destination. There will be a shift in emphasis from passive fun to active learning, and the quality and genuineness of visitor experiences will be crucial to future success in a competitive market. An Acronym that is relevant to describe the 'new' tourist is REAL, which stands for:

- Rewarding
- Enriching
- Adventuresome
- Learning Experience

A key underpinning concept for REAL tourism is authenticity of experience, which is often related to the environment and culture and seen to be unaffected by "mass" tourism. The New Tourists prefer to be regarded as travellers and not tourists. Some specific points which need to be kept in mind while dealing with the New Tourist are:

- This type of traveller requires a completely different marketing approach. They avoid conventional glossy marketing mechanisms and prefer to use reliable sources such as word of mouth referrals, their own independent research and trusted publications;
- They desire experiences as opposed to products and services;
- They can be called experiential traveller s, they extend across all age groups and traditional market segments;

New Tourism for the New Tourist

To enable new tourism attractions to stand the test of time and satisfy the demanding requirements of the evolving 'new' tourist, the following criteria should be applied to existing and proposed attractions:

That the attraction offers a distinct, unique experience that cannot easily be replicated by competitors;

- That the attraction is value added through 'best practice' interpretation, which preferably utilises a 'human element' such as interpretive guides, seasoned veterans and/or local characters;
- That, where possible, the experience is externalised within the natural/actual setting rather than internalised within a false/reproduced
- The development of interpretive highways;
- The explosion of interpretive centers;
- The latest trend towards regional base camps.

Network Tourism Initiative: Tourism experience consists of a large number of factors, which have different levels of importance dependant on the perspective of the visitor. For experiential travellers, the experience may be strongly influenced by the experiences between attractions such as the expert commentary provided by a trained guide or the friendliness of locals along the way.

The aim of Network tourism is to package a diverse range of products and services throughout a broad region to create a quality experience that capitalises on a region's strengths and comparative advantages. This principle recognises that the combination of discreet experiences within the network creates a greater attraction than its individual components and serves to increase economic benefits and market profile for the entire region. To satisfy the diverse experiential requirements of the "new" tourist, it is imperative that a strong referral system is developed between attractions contained within the network. This therefore goes beyond current promotional attempts by the tourism agencies to promote the entire network, and rests with the individual attractions within the network themselves and the need to actively cross promote between attractions.

Interpretive Highways: Travel is seen to be a part of a network of experiences as opposed to the mere mechanism for going from point A to B. Interpretive highways have been a successful device to link a number of disparate experiences to provide a more comprehensive visitor experience. Whilst principally a tool for satisfying the travel desires of self-guided travellers, a framework should be developed that has also serves to assist experiential requirements of commercial guided tour operators. This is primarily attributed to improved interpretation offered along the travel path to break the monotony of long haul travel between attractions.

The Explosion of Interpretive Centers: The purpose of the center is to educate the general public and children in particular on the importance of a particular tourist site, historical monuments, natural resources, wetland ecosystems *etc.* These centers can contain permanent and evolving exhibit galleries, meeting space, a classroom and teaching labouratory, an auditorium, and a gift shop, along with offices and other support facilities. Indoor exhibits on natural history and other objects of tourist interest can be complemented by regular showings of multi image presentations.

The Wildlife Institute of India, United States Fish and Wildlife Services and Madhya Pradesh Forest Department collabourative programme aims to achieve long term conservation of the park by increasing awareness and appreciation towards Panna National park among visitors as well as local people through the use of interpretive centers. The main components of the programme are:

- *Outreach Programme:* It is aimed at sensitising the local community about the benefits of the programme to the park and eventually to them.
- *Resource Material:* In the form of books, brochures and CD-ROMs would be developed to highlight the conservation needs. An exclusive website on Panna National Park is also planned for attracting international attention.

- *Interpretation Center and Visitor Center:* They are an important component of the project and would comprise of exhibits on Panna National Park and its conservation needs. This is a means of education mainly targeted to the tourists, School children and local community.
- *Capacity Building:* Training of local youths as guides, Park staff and tour operators on Interpretation and communication skills to enable them to run the programme.

The Latest Trend towards Regional Base Camps: While the traditional centralised awareness centre can be thought of as a strategic hub located at a major strategic travel point, it is proposed that a 'hub and spokes' approach be the next evolutionary step. The hub can be thought of as the 'base camp' for regional exploration and provides advice, essential services, orientates the visitor, provides all the necessary supplies and equipment to enable the visitor to safely and sensitively explore the region. In delivering these services, the hub can also become an important community asset by encouraging mixed use. The spokes visit important remote sites and recognise that where possible, interpretation should be undertaken in the authentic setting. The 'hub' attempts to put the heart back into a township and revitalise the local economy.

A new tourism is emerging, sustainable, environmentally and socially responsible, and characterised by flexibility and choice. A new type of tourist is driving it: more educated, experienced, independent, conservation-minded, respectful of cultures, and insistent on value for money.

Starting in the eighties and mid-eighties (depending on the tourism receiving region in question) a number of dramatic environmental changes occurred which moved the "tourism industry" much closer to the characteristics of the new economy. Used to more convenience, faster service and more options from his/her every-day-life the new tourist also insisted on more options, more entertainment and fun, more diversified sports facilities and cultural variety in his/her vacation (see *e.g.*, Weiermair and Fuchs, 2000). This new consumer (tourist) thereby has exercised pressure upon the tourism industry and tourism enterprises to develop new products, services and experiences. Information technology is opening up an astonishing array of travel and vacation options for this new tourist. To remain competitive, tourism destinations and industry players alike must adapt. For many, the challenge is to "reinvent" tourism. Market intelligence, innovation, and closeness to customers have become the new imperatives. Thus, on the horizon of the postmodern landscape, a New Age of tourism is dawning: New Age tourism for New Age people.

New Demand Factors in Tourism

The Consumer in a World of Change

Tourism has to face a challenging change in its framework conditions: The geopolitical as well as the economic situation require new strategies. Technological innovations, demographic change and a powerful costumer have to be met in politics, marketing and planning. New destinations, new products with prices on a level, which would have been incredible some years ago, compete with the established tourism offer. This paper tries to structure the impacts of a world in change on the consumer's behaviour in tourism and to identify some of the aspects being the most important for the foreseeable future.

Focusing on the consumer the paper does not ignore the importance of the tourism offer, the industry, the destinations *etc.* They constitute some of the factors leading to a change in consumer behaviour, and they are together with others the field where the behaviour of the consumers shows up and where the knowledge of the consumer can be applied.

Two Perspectives

We may look at the "New Demand Factors" from two perspectives. On the one hand we have those factors influencing the demand, *i.e.*, the motivation to travel and the ability to travel, directly or indirectly. They cover a wide range from the general economic situation, over politics to technological innovations, just to name some examples.

On the other hand we have emerging factors, *i.e.*, the changing face of consumer behaviour in tourism like destinations preferences, quality expectations, booking behaviour *etc.* But what the tourist does can not only be explained by external factors alone. The experienced and educated traveller will change his behaviour even in a constant framework.

Thus, there is an endogenous dynamic within the tourist behaviour. The emerging (from external and endogenous factors) patterns characterize the tourism consumers and their behaviour within the next years.

The Situation

Before we start looking at the factors influencing future tourism demand we shall have a quick glance at the actual situation: Statistics record a high volume of tourism demand for Europe (WTO: close to 450 mn. intern. arrivals p.a.) and from Europe (338 mn. international trips of Europeans in 2003, with 2/3 being holiday trips; IPK, 2004). But with national holiday travel propensities ranging from 31 to 77% (Eurostat, 2002) source markets are different: from *close to saturated* (like in Germany) to *offering growth potentials* (*e.g.*, Portugal or Poland). Holiday travel does not generally mean international travel. In most European countries domestic travel exceeds the international holiday trips. Of course, there are some exceptions like Germany or the Netherlands or quite naturally small countries like Luxembourg.

The total volume of European tourism demand has been quite stable, but the structure underneath showed quite a dynamic *e.g.*, with growth rates in Eastern Europe and a stagnation in the West, with new destinations preferences *etc.* Vacations are not only for the fun of the travellers: Holiday tourism has become an important economic sector (for both destinations and the travel industry), a social achievement, a political Instrument, and an educational tool.

Influencing Factors

As we all experience the change around us the questions arises how these developments will have an impact on tourism demand. To name just a few categories:

- Economy: (*e.g.*, from BIP over exchange rates to perceived risk of loosing the job)
- Politics: (*e.g.*, the enlargement of the EU, taxation, environment)
- Crisis and threats: (*e.g.*, terrorism, epidemic diseases, earth quakes)
- Demographic Change: (*e.g.*, age structure, migration, educational level)
- Technology: (*e.g.*, transport, communication, information)

In addition we have to take into account the influences coming from general changes in consumer attitudes and, finally, the tourism industry itself, of course influencing the demand side of tourism (*e.g.*, standardisation of products, information channels, (over) capacities and price strategies). All these factors are linked to each other.

How Can These Factors have an Impact?

Holiday demand is driven by needs, motives, and expectations, its realisation depends on the individual economic situation and the freedom to travel.

Thus:

- External factors may have an impact on tourism demand by affecting the ability to travel (freedom, time, money, fitness) and the motivation to do so.
- Consumer Behaviour is not a reaction on a single factor but on the whole set of influencing external factors. In addition it is driven by internal factors (*e.g.*, motives, abilities *etc.*). Thus, the impact of a change in a single external factor is limited. Most of the external factors seem to be in favour for a sound development

of tourism demand in Europe in the years to come. However, there are no signs for a general boom.

Emerging Factors

As we can't limit our attention to a single external factor and its impacts, we look at several of the emerging factors, new trends in tourism emerging from the whole set of influences and the endogenous dynamics of tourism. These emerging trends will not change tourism over night. Trend research has shown that the future developments will most probably come as a step-by-step development, not as a revolution.

Giving the global and nearly unlimited offer in tourism with capacities still on the rise at least in Europe the power in the market is clearly with the consumer. He will only choose products which fit into his motivation and expectations. Taking the efforts to reduce seasonality in tourism as an example, we clearly see that the limitations to these efforts are only partly due to *e.g.*, school holiday regulations but predominantly due to the motivation of spending a holiday under nice weather conditions.

New Source Markets

The enlargement of the European Union in 2004 and 2007 sure is important for the whole continent. Poland, Hungary, the Czech Republic, Estonia, Latvia, Lithuania, Slovenia, Slovakia, Malta and Cyprus have joined the European Union on May 1, 2004. The EU since then embraces 25 countries. The size of the EU has grown by 25%, the population by 20%, the GDP by 5% (European Commission, 2003). However, its short time effects on tourism are limited. But the general political process, under way since some 20 years, which the EU enlargement is a "natural" part of, contribute a lot to a changing tourism demand in Europe.

As destinations, the new EU-members benefit from a bonus this year: The extensive coverage in the media will influence the growing interest in these countries and the felt distances will decrease. However, for most holiday makers, almost the whole world is accessible for a vacation. For holiday destinations this means a continuously growing competition a competition in which the new EU-member countries will have to participate as well: No guarantee for success for anybody, but chances for everybody.

There is a growing interest for holiday trips to Eastern Europe in the old EU-member countries, but the volume is still very small. This is remarkable as there were no more real barriers to travel for example to Poland in the past couple of years. The old populations continues to prefer their old holiday destinations in the near future: Domestic trips, holiday in Spain and Italy will remain the most popular holiday countries. The dynamic in holiday tourism is based on continuous, long-term developments, not in sudden changes. Naturally there are not only potentials and chances, but also barriers preventing a fast development in tourism. Experts mention the following reasons for Eastern Europe: Low investment rates, undeveloped traffic system, undeveloped infrastructure in the countryside, unsatisfactory quality of hotels and gastronomy, weaknesses in tourism marketing. Of course this does not go for every single destination.

There are also limits on the demand side. Images are playing an important role when deciding upon a holiday destination. In case of the new EU-member countries in Eastern Europe they can limit demand. Most holiday makers from the old EU-member states probably know very little about their new neighbours, or they have incorrect assumptions about them. Not automatically they combine these countries with holiday. Closely connected to images are holiday motives. People choose holiday destinations mainly based on their suitability of fulfilling their holiday motives.

Political settings or changes, like the EU-enlargement, are comparatively unimportant. To raise the demand for the new EU-member countries, (potential) holiday makers must be convinced that their holiday motives can very well (or better) be fulfilled in these countries. Now is the time for a powerful marketing. In medium terms the new EU members will contribute to a considerable change in Europe's tourism as *source markets*. People are going to make use of their new freedom and the opportunities connected to rising welfare (at least those, who participate in the economic upswing).

What we already can see in the statistical data is a growing importance of these countries as source markets for international travel, while some of the classic source markets like Germany experience a *ceiling effect*: There is a very limited room for a general growth in the "old" source markets. Thus, the quantitative impulses in Europe have to come from the East and the South.

Demographic Change

Demographic change is a constant process but has got a lot of public attention in recent years. It is said to be one of the important drivers for new trends in consumer behaviour in most European countries (*e.g.*, Lind 2001, Smeral 2003, Wallace 1999). Two important demographic trends, often being in focus at conferences as well as in publications are:

- An older growing society due to rising life expectancy (developed countries taking the lead) (*e.g.*, Lind 2001, OECD 1998; Ruskin 2002; Wallace 1999; Horx 2002),
- A declining number of children due to sinking fertility in many industrial countries combined with the dissolution of traditional family patterns (*e.g.*, Lind 2001, Wallace 1999, Schafers 1995, Horx 2002).

These are major demographic changes that are already influencing society today and that are worth a closer look on how they may have an impact on holiday travel behaviour. Examples for other important demographic trends are: Rising educational level, a more colourful society due to migration, a changing role of women in society. Research has shown (Lohmann and Danielsson 2004) that people do not change their travel behaviour just because they turn 60 or 65, or because they retire. In most cases they stick to the holiday patterns acquired till the middle of their life. This fact allows for predictions of the tourist behaviour of future senior generations: The 'new' *senior citizens* in five or fifteen years time will be different from the present senior citizens when it comes to travel behaviour. While senior travellers today are already relatively active, the new senior generations to come are more than likely to surpass them. The effects of demographic change (more and bigger share of older people) and consumer behaviour patterns (stick to once learned travel patterns) will show up as: *more senior trips with different preferences. e.g.,* in Germany we expect within 15 years the number of holiday tourists in the age group 70 to 80 years to rise by more than 50% (from 4,2 mn. in 2003 to 6,6 mn. in 2018) with more than 2/3 choosing a destination abroad (today: 50%; 2003 figures from RA 2004).

Less dramatic are the changes in the segment of *family holidays*: Taking again Germany as an example: The number and share of Holiday trips with children (up to 13 years) has proved to be stable in Germany for more than a decade with some 22% of all holiday trips. In 2003 this share resulted in 14.4 mn holiday trips. With an 8% decline in 10 years in the number of children would lead to a number of 13.2 mn trips, still an important segment. One can expect even a higher number when considering the fact that the decrease of the number of families will be slower as the one of the number of children. Thus, there is no need for a complete re-orientation of the tourism industry towards new target groups replacing the family holiday. But of course given not only the demographic change but also the strong competition between destinations a strong focus on the needs and expectations of this segment (cf. Danielsson, Lohmann and Sonntag 2003) is recommended.

Old with young: The share of people aged 50 years or older within all German family trips has been 11.5% in 2003 (RA 2004, F.U.R 2004). This is already today a significant segment which could be considered more closely by the tourism industry, especially as a further increase can be expected. In addition, this segment shows a specific behaviour as tourists, *e.g.*, compared to all family holiday trips a lower seasonality, higher spending, longer stays, and other destinations choices. Against expectations they are not very fond of culture trips and prefer holiday homes or apartments to hotels.

Finally, the one-kid-trip: It seems to be the standard of family holidays (58.5% in 2002). So, this is not a development to come but today's reality. Again, this segment has specific travel behaviour patterns as *e.g.*, more flight trips and more use of tour operators and as it offers further increase. In addition one-kid travellers have special needs (*e.g.*, other kids being around in the destination) which the tourism industry has to take into consideration. What we can see from these examples is that demographic change will sure has its impacts which are reflected in the structure of tourism demand.

Information Search and Travel Decisions: Skilled Consumers with Low Involvement

Along with this structural developments the consumer behaviour changes as well. One of the important fields is in the pre-trip phase the search for information and the way a decision for a certain tourist product is made.

The immense tourism offer available able to fulfil the individual needs leads the way to *interchangeable products*. For the consumer it doesn't make much of a difference whether travelling to destination A or B, with the tour operator X or Y *etc.* Actually, with all the communication channels and the more and more detailed information available the consumer is in a state of *information overload*. Impossible to consider everything.

Thus, the holiday decision is not the final result of a comprehensive search-evaluatechoice process but a *good-enough solution* considering a few aspects of a few products (those being in the relevant set) from a few information sources. Rational arguments are not very important. This is the state consumer researcher call "*low involvement*". With basic needs fulfilled and low involvement conditions *convenience* (taking the easy way) and *experience* orientation together with *variety seeking* are getting more important. Naturally, there is nothing new about experience orientation in tourism.

The point is, that these experiences and the accompanying emotions are now part of the product, promised by the producer. In addition to these consumer attitudes we observe a growing *price orientation* which is expected to get more important as well. In this case this attitude is induced by industry strategies. Low prize is a strategy of the industry selling high quality trips for a tremendous low price. In a saturated market that may lead to higher market shares, perhaps to a slightly higher turn over and probably a lower profit.

Even experiences from the retail sale show that convenience and product quality comes first for the consumer. But having learned that the same products and services are on the market for a cheap price, this industry induced price orientation grows more and more.

The tourist consumer is much *more flexible* than the tourism industry. This is one lesson we have learned from the geopolitical changes in the last five years. If I don't have the feeling of being welcomed in a destination, I don't stop travelling, I simply chose another destination. If I'm afraid of travelling in an airplane, I just look for an alternative means of transportation.

The key-concept is "*contingency*" (For everything what exists, there is a possible alternative; well not in every way, and not necessarily better, but it is there) as opposed to the old TINA concept ("there is no alternative") (Bolz, 2004). The tourist does not consume because he has to, but because it's fun. His decisions are not related to a feeling of lack or shortcoming, everything is on the market, more than the tourist needs. This leads to a lack of predictability of the *individual* behaviour. At the same time it is more important than ever before to have reliable figures and information on the actual and the potential customers. General market conditions, skilled consumer and vast capacities in tourism are a challenge for tourism marketing, especially in the big close to saturated markets.

Consumers' Paradox: Meet the Standards and be different

With globalisation of the tourism industry, a computer based distribution, and the strive to offer high quality, *standardisation* of tourism products is a must. That constitutes a risk for tourism because "standard" is nothing offering new experiences or meeting the trend for variety seeking. At the same time the tourism demand and the products get more and more *differentiated* and fragmentised, *e.g.*, with winter sports, study trips or family holidays. The consumer expects both: *quality* and *difference. Standardisation* and *differentiation* are main trends of both the consumers' and the industry's side. Again, this is an additional challenge for the industry, because this means more efforts necessary without a growing demand or even a growing turn-over.

Looking at the mayor trends we can summarize:

- High volume of tourism demand around Europe with a few growth potentials in some source markets.
- Source markets are different: from *close to saturated* to *offering growth potentials* and need specific treatment in marketing.
- General market conditions, skilled consumer and vast capacities in tourism are a challenge for tourism marketing, especially in the big close to saturated markets.

But holiday tourism has manifold functions. It is an economic sector (for both destinations and the travel industry), a social achievement, a political Instrument, and an educational tool. Different sectors see tourism as a tool for different objectives. The evaluation of the situation and the future perspectives may vary with the sector. But with all the sectors is a need to focus on the customer: Holiday travel is a behaviour of individual consumers, their perception of the reality is important. Now is the time for real marketing: Consumer behaviour in tourism is less determined by the general framework conditions than at the end of the last century. The tourists have in their decisions many degrees of freedom. Consumer research is a necessary base, not only for projections into the future, but to determine the starting point, to have an orientation to formulate own objectives and plans to reach them. Without the consumer, in tourism as in every service industry, you will go nowhere. That does not go not only for the industry and their marketing activities, but as well for politics/tourism related policies.

What do the new demand factors in tourism mean for the different sectors or functions? For *destinations* it is of utmost importance to recognize the international competition they are in. Master plans and marketing activities need realistic objectives considering not only what one wants to reach but as well what others do, then the own resources (financial and human which will be limited *e.g.*, with demographic change), and of course the consumers' motivation and the trends in consumer behaviour in tourism. Giving the situation of the demand and its expected future trends, it's not sufficient to have a good product. It's not sufficient either, that the consumer perceives a product as a good one. The product or the destination has to be in the consumer's *relevant set,* and to be judged a *very good choice* within this set.

The same goes for the *industry, i.e.,* tour operators and travel agencies, transport companies *etc.* Tour operators and travel agencies may *e.g.,* take advantage from the fact of the information overload. They can take the role of a guide in the information jungle and thus offer convenience.

Politics have not only to watch carefully the market conditions and how the consumers behave under these conditions. The time to just formulate and express good objectives like sustainability, strengthening specific regions, support third world countries, stressing the importance of the environment, supporting the European integration through more international travel, where everybody agrees. They have to identify the contradictions and inconsistencies arising from the whole set of objectives and to find solutions or priorities. It does not seem very useful to provide funding and financial support for everybody just because he intends to follow one of these objectives. Another challenge for politics is to keep the *social balance* within the source markets: Some experts claim that the economic development tends to widen the distance between the poor and the rich within European societies. But tourism needs a broad base of more or less middle class people with time and money to travel. Coming back to the tourism demand we can state that the future in a quantitative perspective seems to be quite stable:

> There is no boom ahead, but no bust either. Of course, the future is predictable only within close limits, and unexpected events (*e.g.*, crisis, terror attacks, war, epidemic diseases) will always cause confusion. Still it is important (and possible) to prepare oneself for the trends that can be identified with some reliability today. Demand potentials for good products are there, but you will not be able to sell just anything to the skilled consumer.

In this way the future is open: Room to move for everybody who has a sound marketing plan or political perspective, and respects the consumer. There is a strong need for *orientation* and decision for every organisation involved in tourism: Where do you want to go from now and here? What is your objective? Different paths of development are possible, so you have to decide which road to take. You may call that a vision.

While elabourating your vision, you need to have a strong focus on the customer, on what other market actors are doing, and what resources are at hand. Visions will be and have to be different on different levels (pan-European, national, regional, local), and different with different destinations or other segments of the industry, but linked to some extent. Success shall be based on safeguarding the core values (the distinctive qualities and related experiences) while constantly adapting to new market trends. A deep understanding of the consumer and his perpetual learning processes as well as the changing structure of tourism demand is a prerequisite for successful planning. A bright future for both, tourists and the tourism industry is within easy reach. Just take your responsibilities to make it real.

THE TRANSFORMATION OF CONSUMER BEHAVIOUR IN TOURISM INDUSTRY

The emergence of new information and communication technologies (ICTs), higher levels of wealth, more leisure time, and changes in values and lifestyles due to a new consciousness regarding one's own needs as well as regarding social responsibilities, have led to a new breed of tourism consumers. The new consumers of tourism products and services are more informed, more independent, more individualistic and more involved (Poon, 1993). In addition, the new travellers are used to having many choices, expect speed, and use technologies to overcome the physical constraints of bodies and borders. However, consumer behaviour has also become increasingly contradictory (Marobella, 2004).

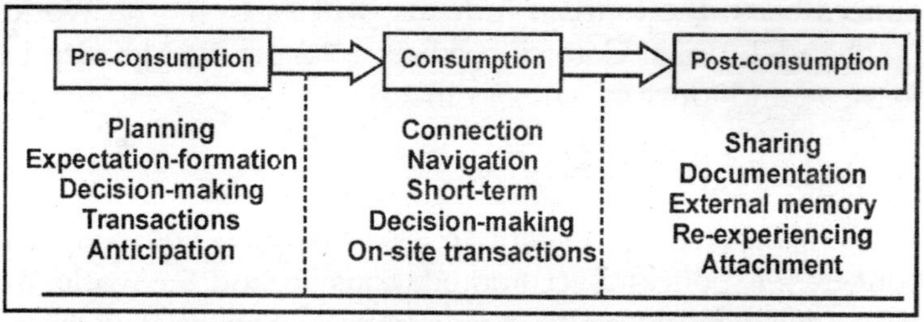

Fig. Communication and information needs in the three stages or tourism consumption

Many travellers are 'trading up' (Silverstein and Fiske, 2003), and are more willing than ever to pay for luxury travel experiences. At the same time, they will fiercely search the Web for 'the best deal' on hotel rooms and flights.Travel behaviour has also become more unpredictable: a traveller who bought an organised city sightseeing tour the previous year might engage in a month-long trekking adventure the year after.

Factors Influencing Travel and Tourism Consumer Behaviour

As of 2010, the global travel industry contributed 9.2 per cent of the world's total gross domestic product, according to the World Travel and Tourism Council. People travel for work, to visit family and friends and for pleasure. When it comes to making choices about where and how to travel, multiple factors influence travel and tourism consumer behavior.

Global Economy

Travel is often seen as a luxury, and when people are earning less or worried about earning less, they may eliminate travel from their budgets. As the world economy struggled in 2009 and into 2010, the travel industry suffered along with other businesses.

According to the World Travel and Tourism Council, global travel and tourism was down nearly 5 per cent in 2009, specifically due to a struggling economy. Still, as the economy bounces back, the tourism industry will as well. The World Travel and Tourism Council predicts a 3.2 per cent growth in the travel and tourism industry in 2011.

Internet and Social Media

Consumers have instant access to reviews and opinions about travel spots and accommodations around the world, as well as airlines, car rental agencies and other related travel companies. More and more, people turn to the Internet to research potential trips and seek out bargains. Thus, the Internet and social media can influence consumers' travel choices.

According to The Digital Letter, reviews on sites like TripAdvisor "can make or break a destination." Prospective travelers can read reviews and find out if others found the hotel to be clean and the staff courteous, or if the "service (they will) receive is worthy of (their) time and money."

The Digital Letter points out that travelers can learn everything they want to know about a destination in a matter of minutes on sites such as Facebook, Twitter and Google. While a business's website can also play a factor in consumer choice, if independent online reviews aren't consistent with the company's claims, travelers are likely to make a different selection.

Personal Budgets

Even with a bad economy, some people still need or want to travel. In 2010, savvy travelers have many ways to find deals online and cut their costs before heading out the door. Airlines offer online specials for discount flights and last-minute trips, and companies such as Kayak exist solely to gather the best travel deals on the Internet into one place, so shoppers can compare prices. Travelers no longer need to rely on the standard price for transportation or accommodations. They may now make their travel choices based solely on price.

Influencing Consumer Behaviour to Promote Sustainable Tourism Development

Problems

International tourism plays an ambivalent role in contributing to cultural exchange and sustainable development. On the one hand, it involves a highly buffered, short-term consumer experience of other locales. Tourists can pay and leave, remaining isolated from negative impacts at the local level. On the other hand, tourism may increase recognition of the importance of respecting cultural diversity and developing an identity as a world citizen. It offers opportunities to educate consumers regarding responsible tourism and sustainable development. Consumers can play a major role in the transformation of societies towards sustainability. While mass tourism in the past was rather producer-driven, the industry today is becoming increasingly consumer-driven. In highly competitive tourism markets, well informed, responsible consumers can put increasing pressure on the industry to behave more responsibly. A number of official proclamations have affirmed every individual's right to rest and leisure including tourism. However, tourism remains an unobtainable luxury for the majority of the world's population. Tourists primarily originate from affluent industrialised societies where tourism has become a mass phenomenon. The values, attitudes and behaviour of tourists are determined by their social environment, cultural identity and way of life which may be in conflict with local customs.

Tourism is heterogeneous in nature, made up of many different types of traveller, seeking a wide range of tourism products. Demand is influenced by irrational factors, eg fashion and trends. It depends on the availability of time and money, on images, perceptions and attitudes. Tourists have various needs, desires and motivations, both of a 'push' and 'pull' nature. While household incomes in major tourist sending countries are declining, industry sales projections continue to grow, indicating increasing competition. The consumer mind is set on discount prices and "buy now/pay later" options. This poses serious threats, as prices already lag far behind any realistic accounting of tourism costs and impacts.

Many of the demand patterns in tourism reflect the unsustainable lifestyles of industrialised consumer societies. Tourism acts as an agent in exporting these life-styles and consumerist attitudes to less industrialised societies via demonstration effects and modelling. Tourism increases demand for imported consumer goods in the destinations, with detrimental effects on the environment, due to the ecological costs of transport and the high amount of waste generated. Increasing imports also reduce local/national economic gains, due to foreign exchange leakages.

The over-consumption of resources by tourists and tourism infrastructure, eg the excessive use of water, fire wood or food, is incompatible with sustainable development. The carrying capacity of natural environments is often exceeded with the addition of tourism demands. Tourist demand for resources (land, water, energy, food) may also compete with the needs of local people and may increase social inequality, gender inequality and injustice. Tourist transport, especially air travel, is highly energy intensive and causes pollutant emissions. Many tourism activities such as skiing, boating, mountain hiking, motorised watersports (eg jet skies), and trekking represent a stress to fragile ecosystems.

Tourists often lack information and awareness about their impact in a different culture and environment, about the impacts of tourism on socio-economic and socio-cultural development, and about the environmental costs of tourism. While tourists may be open to learning, they are often unaware of inappropriate behaviour and have little guidance on how to improve. Others may refuse to adapt to local life-styles, even if informed, insisting on their freedom to behave as they want.

While the tourism industry may be willing to improve their products and services, there is a conflict between the industry's pursuit of economic gains and social and environmental responsibility. The industry lacks information on the requirements of sustainable tourism and on how to integrate economic forces with environmental and social requirements. Tourists shopping for escapism generally abide by one fundamental consumer ethic: receipt upon payment. Consumer advocates may intervene where inferior customer service is delivered. However, the sustainability of corporate practices is self-regulated. This conflict of interest within industry, and consumers' low awareness of tourism impacts, have led to a widespread abuse of 'green' labelling.

The mass media, especially television through films and reports about events, sights, *etc.* in other parts of the world, are increasingly influential on travel decisions and consumer behaviour in the destinations. These programmes, however, often serve primarily as advertisements, painting images of destinations, rather than providing relevant information for potential travellers.

There is a lack of reliable and appropriate (*e.g.*, age and gender dis-aggregated) research data on the determinants of tourist demand, motivation and behaviour. Few countries, whether tourist sending or tourist receiving countries, collect such data that are helpful under sustainable development criteria. Most studies of tourist behaviour focus on mainstream markets or market segments, rather than assessing or modelling sustainable alternatives. Governments in many tourist destinations and local communities have little or no information on what to expect from tourism and the incoming tourists and how to influence and control tourism and guide tourist behaviour.

They are controlled by international/global institutions, the industry and the consumers. Governments of the affluent countries are only beginning to look at the issues of outgoing tourism. Governments are not yet sufficiently aware of their responsibility and methods to influence tourist behaviour by political and legal guidelines/criteria and appropriate planning and policies. Trade unions have fought successfully for shorter working hours and more vacation. However, they need to take more responsibility for helping to create a leisure industry that is more sustainable.

Solutions

Consumer behaviour can and must be influenced by:

a. Fighting unsustainable forms and aspects of tourism, at the various levels, by sanctioning unacceptable behaviour and discouraging inappropriate consumer behaviour.

b. Promoting responsible and sustainable patterns of behaviour, at the various levels, by promoting best practises and encouraging responsible consumer behaviour. There are different types of instruments and remedial measures available:

   - Legal measures (rules, regulations, sanctions);
   - Market based instruments, such as taxes to influence market prices;
   - Promotion of and (financial) support for best practice;
   - Industry self-monitoring/codes of conduct;

- Information, education and research.

Institutional Action/Possible Partnerships

Consumer behaviour in tourism is both a product and cause of policies by government and industry. A comprehensive approach is therefore required to solve the problems associated with market-driven tourism. Tourism should be viewed as a major development issue that all stakeholders need to be actively engaged with. To develop effective partnerships, the imbalance of power between the different stakeholders needs to be addressed.

UN Action

- Establish an NGO tourism advisory group for UN fora to provide technical support, analysis, and strategic advice;
- Create a 'best practices' information clearing-house in order to collect consumer information useful to understanding and positively influencing consumer behaviour and to make documentation accessible on an equitable basis;
- Initiate a broad information and awareness campaign to highlight damaging forms of tourism and impacts, providing tools for informed decision-making. Initially, target participants in the CSD and CBD processes to clarify roles and responsibilities;
- Research and develop effective certification schemes, form a technical group under the CSD to assess how certification can be improved, *e.g.*, through the review of voluntary codes set up by CSD1998;
- Designate an 'ombuds' office jointly between the CSD, CBD, and UN-CHR to encourage diligent self-regulation and compliance with international standards for sustainable tourism;
- Develop guidance on tourism as an issue within Local Agenda 21 processes.

Governmental Action

- Introduce and enforce legislation to abolish child prostitution, implement effective control mechanisms, conclude judicial assistance agreements;
- Regulate tourist access to ecologically fragile or stressed natural areas;
- Tourist sending countries: develop policies on outgoing tourism from a development perspective;
- Provide frameworks for ecologically appropriate pricing by strictly applying the polluter pays principle to internalise external costs. This includes ecological tax reforms including the taxation of aviation gasoline and oil, removal of subsidies/other economic incentives with negative environmental impacts.
- Improve conditions for sustainable consumer behaviour by providing/promoting sustainable tourism facilities;
- Promote environmentally friendly modes of transport and transport concepts, reduce tourism-related traffic, shift demand to less environmentally damaging modes of transport;
- Promote renewable sources of energy such as solar power, reduce the use of non-renewable energy, reduce the use of limited local resources through more sustainable practices/consumption patterns.
- Develop information and education programmes in co-operation with local stakeholders ensuring all stakeholders' involvement (eg women's); provide information to tourists on appropriate behaviour (sensitivity, respect for/adaptation to local culture), eg by establishing information centres in destinations, or by including briefing material for package tours; taking into account specific information needs of various market segments, provide information to the local

population on the opportunities and risks from tourism and on how to influence tourist behaviour;

- Adopt, observe, implement and promote codes of conduct, *e.g.*, the planned WTO-OMT 'Global Code of Ethics for Tourism';
- Integrate sustainable development education including tourism in the curricula of schools at all levels, universities and training institutions, involving all stakeholder groups, create and promote open networks for information and research on sustainable tourism, disseminate and implement results;

Tourism Industry Action

- Promote sustainable tourism products, using market related instruments and incentives, such as contests, awards, certification, model projects, culturally sensitive quality labels covering both environmental and social sustainability;
- Reduce inappropriate consumption, use local resources in preference to imports in a sustainable manner; reduce and recycle waste, ensure safe waste disposal, develop and implement sustainable transport policies and systems, *e.g.*, efficient public transport, walking, cycling in destinations;
- Provide tourists with authentic information, enabling them to understand all environmental and related aspects (*e.g.*, human rights situation) of tourism when selecting any destination or holiday package; educate visitors in advance of arrival and give guidance on 'dos' and 'don'ts'; make tourists aware of their potential impact on and their responsibilities towards host societies;
- Provide information on respecting the cultural and natural heritage of destination areas; employ tour guides who portray societies honestly and dispel stereotypes;

- Ensure that the marketing of 'green' tourism reflects sound environmental policy and practice; use non-exploitative marketing strategies that respect people, communities and environments of destinations, dismantle stereotyping, integrate sustainable tourism principles when creating new marketing strategies;
- Train staff to foster tourist responsibility towards the destinations, encourage multi-cultural education and exchange;
- Actively discourage exploitative sex tourism, particularly sexual exploitation of children, and tourism which causes or contributes to social problems;
- Adopt, observe, implement and promote codes of conduct.

NGO Action

- Disseminate information to a wide public about the complexity of tourism and about the objectives and criteria of sustainable tourism;
- Educate tourists to change consumption patterns and promote appropriate, environmentally and socially acceptable behaviour in the destinations;
- Launch broad awareness campaigns on the worst impacts of tourism, to be funded by international governmental and non-governmental agencies;
- Promote relevant research on tourism impacts, criteria for sustainable tourism and possibilities for implementation;
- Monitor tourism development, policy, industry initiatives, local people's reaction to tourism development and policy, implementation of stakeholder action.

5

The Economic Globalisation of Tourism

Globalisation, as one of today's most controversial issues, can be defined as the increasing integration of economies, societies, and civilisations. It includes, and goes beyond, the more simple internationalisation defined as relations among and within nations. Globalisation is a restructuring process that works across units and affects all aspects of human life: from capital flows, through political collabouration, to the flow of ideas. It also includes environmental pollution, criminal behavior, disease, and, ultimately, terror. Travel and tourism are among the many causes and results of globalisation processes.

There is a huge body of literature on internationalisation from the point of view of the individual enterprise (Pugh and Plath 2003). Johanson and Vahlne (1977) carried out a pioneering study of incremental stages of internationalisation of the firm. In the first stage, a purely national firm sporadically enters export markets. This is often followed by more systematic marketing efforts through agents in neighboring countries. The next step is own sales representation in major markets, and, as knowledge accumulates, investments in production and/or distribution facilities abroad. The internationalisation process continues until increasing costs outweigh the growth potential. Following up on Johansson and Vahlne, later contributions emphasize the need to understand both the behavioral mechanisms of the single enterprise and the driving forces that make whole industries of the economy—for better or worse—undertake an increasingly intensified and multifaceted global orientation (Jones 2005; Wolf 2004).

Given the current climate of increasing international acquisitions and mergers, the assumption of a uniform and logically progressing internationalisation with a clear national face is thus coming under frequent attack (Luo 1999). According to Hedlund (1993), after a first ethnocentric (or missionary) phase, the internationalising firm will enter a process of polycentrism, with a looser and more pragmatic coupling of activities without a clear center; the national identity will fade and become less important. Starting a firm is usually a purely national activity, and international relations are established only when it has grown to a certain size. However, this assumption is also under revision.

Some new enterprises are simply "born global" (Chetty and Campbell-Hunt 2004; Knight 2000), seeing markets and supplies in a wider perspective, without national restrictions, from the very beginning. The emerging hyper-global enterprises challenge economic theories that assume the unchanged persistence of a nation state. This can be considered of major importance in connection with the globalisation of tourism (Cornelissen 2005).

Conceptualisations of the ongoing globalisation of firms are dominated by stage models (Hedlund 1993; Johanson and Vahlne 1977). However, in spite of their intuitive use as guidelines for strategy and practical action, these models have also been strongly criticised. Cannon and Willis (1983) found that, rather than moving from one stage to the next, firms chose to move in and out of markets, depending on specific conditions.

Others could ignore particular stages, and leap directly to more advanced formats, or back to an "inward" strategy (Bjo¨rkman and Kock 1997). Danmarks Erhvervsrad (2005) investigated a large number of Danish firms and found support both for the idea of "born globals" (enterprises that adopt such a concept from the very start) and for the idea of "reborn globals" (those that reengineer operations entirely over a short period of time to the conditions of a larger market). While the present article is also based on a stage model, the aim here is to apply this theoretical framework both to single enterprises and to national tourism systems, those comprising tourism and related industries and institutional and political structures. Thus, the article attempts to apply the stage paradigm in a broader context.

While globalisation in tourism has attracted some research interest, most studies have tended to focus on international hotel chains and airlines (Dunning and McQueen 1982a, 1982b; Johnson and Vanetti 2005; Rodriquez 2002; Williams, 1995). It is, however, remarkable how little the literature has discussed the broader manifestations of globalisation in tourism, and how limited interest has been in applying theory to the field (Bianchi 2002; Cornelissen 2005; Fayed and Fletcher 2002; Knowles, Diamantis, and El-Mourhabi 2001; Smeral 1998; Wahab and Cooper 2001).

Even though the positive and negative impacts of globalisation are on the agenda at all policy levels, there is a widespread assumption that tourism is an exception, an industry where global mechanisms and consequences do not come fully into play. This is what two agents in the Danish tourism industry have to say:

Tourism cannot be outsourced. Therefore, in an era with growing globalisation, tourism is a particularly interesting industry. It is really incomprehensible that politicians have not opened their eyes for the benefits in the form of income and employment, and acted accordingly with an effort to promote tourism to and in Denmark (Jørgen Hansen, manager of the regional tourism development agency for North Jutland, January 2005).

It is a matter of fact that jobs created by tourism are guaranteed to stay in the country. . . Tourism also creates opportunities for categories of people in the labour market who cannot easily get jobs in high-tech industries (Ulrik Bu¨low, managing director of VisitDenmark, January 2005).

Both statements appeared in the press after shock lay-offs in major manufacturing firms. At the time, there were calls for an increased emphasis on the service industries and for increased public financing of tourism marketing campaigns. The tourism industry and its associations thus simply wanted more of the conventional type of action on the international scene, assuming that it was somehow immune to the more complex influences of globalisation. The shortcomings in the literature demonstrate a clear need to conceptualize globalisation in tourism further and to carry out theoretical and empirical studies of its causes, direction, extent, and consequences.

Tourism is a "hyper-globaliser" (Held, McGrew, Goldblatt, and Perraton 2000), and there is a need to address this in research as well as in practice. Such efforts may eventually guide the development of appropriate policies and inspire the modernisation of business strategies. However, any further discussion in these fields is beyond the scope of this contribution.

In this article, a descriptive model of the globalisation of the tourism industry is constructed, the aim of which is to comprehend the increasing complexity of dynamic interactions across borders. The model is then adapted and developed further with inspiration from McKinsey's (2003) 5-step model. The level of analysis is the tourism community and its actors: enterprises, destinations, the state, and more. Accordingly, the globalisation process is seen as the result of both business decisions of single enterprises and political decisionmaking.

The model, Table, consists of four stages. Stage one embraces the attempts of the national tourism system to reach out to new markets. Stage two describes the integration and incorporation of its business across borders. Stage three addresses the fragmentation and flexible relocation in space of production processes.

TABLE: STAGES IN THE GLOBALISATION OF TOURISM

Features	Los Globalization Profile			High Globalization Profile
Stage title	1. Missionaries in the markets	2. Integrating across borders	3. Fragmentation of the value chain	4. Transcending into new value chains
Logic	Access to profitable new markers for existing products	Utilization of market access and brand profiles in foreign markers	Creating profitability in services and getting access to specified material and immaterial resources	Adding value by integrating economic logic in other sectors
Manifestations in the tourism sector	A. Tourism board representation and operations in the markets. B. International marketing collaboration by regional/national tourism enterprises C. Market expansion of larger tourism corporations	D. Transnational integration through business investments and mergers E. Import and export of business concepts through franchising and licensing	F. Splitting the value chain, outsourcing G. Flexible human resorting and enhancing of the international labor markets	H. Development, production and marketing of knowledge I. Sales of market positions and brand extension and spin-off J. Tourism in the global media production

Source: Developed from MCKinsey (2003)

Finally, in stage four, the industry identity will be challenged, and new market types and business concepts will appear that go beyond previous definitions of tourism. Although the model suggests a logical progression toward the last more complex phase, in practice they overlap.

The basic assumption of the model is that, by embracing globalisation in stages, individual firms, destinations, and countries may be able to control costs, gain market shares, and enjoy access to competencies and other important resources. By joining still more complex international networks, tourism agents can address institutional and investment pressures at home, also at several levels (Knowles et al., 2001). Globalisation is further enhanced by developments in information and communications technologies and transportation opportunities.

In principle, actors in the tourism system will experience a gradual, albeit inevitable, need to take account of the next phases and to adapt to the subsequent opportunities and competitive forces. Another assumption is that the evolutionary process takes time. Along the way, specific organisations may become obsolete, and established routines and modes of operation will lose effect. New patterns will emerge, possibly after painful transformations. However, this process will not evolve in parallel in all countries and all continents. On the national scene, some segments of the economy will be more advanced in the globalisation process than others, thus contributing to the complexity.

The pace of globalisation may be affected negatively by, for example, increased energy prices. Stage One: Missionaries in the Markets The main aim of tourism missionaries in external markets is to attract customers to the enterprise, destination, or country where the tourism product will be sold and consumed. This phase is similar to the "sales subsidiaries" step in Johanson and Vahlne (1977). Promotion in international markets is undertaken jointly by tourism associations and other collabourative bodies, or by these enterprises individually. Over the decades, tourism promotion has developed in comparable ways in most Northern European countries, and the organisation of sales efforts tends to be embodied in stable institutional structures (Statens Offentliga Utredringar 2004). Evidence from many countries shows that organisations such as tourism boards tend to resist radical changes for as long as possible and coexist for long periods of time with new types of organisations and businesses (Smeral 1998; Statens Offentliga Utredringar 2004). There are three traditional forms of positioning and promotion of regional/national tourism products in the international arena.

Tourism Board Representation in the Markets. Placing agents and offices in foreign markets is one of the most commonly used globalisation strategies, and has been employed by almost all business sectors as an engine for growth. In particular, it has been crucial to exporting large product volumes to markets with a need and willingness to pay. Those most frequently selected for expansion are closest in terms of geography and culture. Tucker and Hall (2004) mention that, to some extent, the choice of markets also reflects colonial relationships. The strategy is based on a number of assumptions. First, a presence in the markets helps bridge cultural and language barriers. There is a two-way need for "translation": the market has to be informed about the products through consistent marketing efforts, and producers in the home market have to be informed about the nature of demand; and in this sense, market offices function as qualified observation posts (Johanson and Vahlne 1977).

Over the past few decades, most countries have established publicly financed tourism promotion offices in the main or upcoming markets (Middleton 1988; Yusal and Fesenmaier 1993). The Danish Tourist Board, for example, is represented in nine countries. These offices are active in public relations, participation in fairs and exhibitions, and the distribution of brochures and other marketing material to wholesalers and directly to potential tourists. The industry is dominated by small and medium-sized enterprises, with limited ability to carry out systematic and simultaneous marketing in several countries.

Such efforts of tourism boards is thus one way to reduce the costs connected with spatial and cultural distance, and, in addition, also results in significant economies of scale. The rationale for tax-financed marketing is that country/region branding goes beyond the financial interests of the single enterprise. In more recent years, some business sectors outside tourism have dramatically revised their representation strategies (Freytag 2003; Lindholm and Stokholm 2003), leading to the almost daily closure of a number of market offices. Though this is partly due to the dismantling of cultural and language barriers, the main reason is a need to save costs. Customers' information search behavior has changed as result of the Internet and cheaper communication, which together have reduced the need for advanced representation in the market. In consequence, firms and organisations are building new types of alliances that ensure a more flexible and cost-effective collection and dissemination of information. The national boards are gradually adapting, as shown in Statens

Offentliga Utredringar (2004). In coming years, therefore, there are likely to be major reorganisations here too, including revisions of the presence of collabourative structures in the markets. Representation in foreign markets may become irrelevant in later stages of tourism globalisation. Marketing Collabouration. Marketing collabouration among many actors—including public subsidising agents—aims at creating advantages of scale in promotional activities. The tourism market is characterised by a large number of small firms, which typically only supply part of its complex product, characterised by a large number of individual purchasing decisions. Given such a structure, joint marketing is an advantage for both enterprises and customers, since it tends to reduce complexity for both. Over the years, joint marketing campaigns have been a very important part of promotion (Middleton 1988). Some campaigns are destination-based, and often organised by regional associations, whose marketing efforts are sometimes partly publicly financed. Tourism enterprises allocate some of their marketing budget to the coordinating agency and in return receive advertising space or other types of promotion according to their contribution. The scale of public co-financing is sufficiently large to ensure that the enterprises find it attractive.

Public subsidies to some categories of campaigns notwithstanding, there are numerous privately organised marketing collabourations. Research in the field indicates that joint marketing is growing (Morrison, Lynch, and Johns 2004). Hotel chains, such as the Best Western Hotels, which operate from a transborder base, are one example of high-powered cooperative efforts with a strong coordinating unit. The permanence of the structures allows the organisation to develop loyalty programs, quality systems, management training, and joint purchasing that further knit the units together and enhance the economic advantages of co-operation (Tepeci 1999).

Marketing groups have become popular because they appeal to identical customer needs and interests. Golf clubs, for example, group together in order to encourage golfers to take tours and experience other golf courses (within the controllable and mutually benefiting framework of the group). The European Union has launched efforts to unite and interconnect tourism supply across borders in special interest trails. Of course, this is supposed to have positive economic benefits for the enterprises, but it is also meant to develop European coherence and a feeling of common roots, culture, and history (European Commission 1999). The global nature of some categories of tourism is thus two-tiered, politically and economically. A precondition for the success of joint marketing initiatives is cost savings, as in connection with the printing and distribution of promotional material.

However, paper-based modes of communication are increasingly being challenged by the Internet, as growing numbers of consumers surf the net to book their holiday (Marcussen 2003; Wynne, Berthon, Pitt, Ewing, and Napoli 2001) rather than going to a travel agency or acquiring brochures. With good links and a strategic position vis-a-vis search machines, even very small suppliers can attract potential customers the world over at low cost. The expected development in mobile communication will boost marketing and sales to many young and experienced tourists, for whom purchase decisions are more spontaneous than the industry has been used to. The arguments for collabouration in marketing are thus becoming less compelling, and are likely to remain so until new forms of attractive information and communications technologies-based structures appear. The ease of advertising on the Internet also implies that private individuals can offer their small-scale facilities in a large spot market. It has now become much more common to see summerhouses, motorboats, horses, and more for rent from own homepages or on various platforms. As new categories of mediating services are added, the traditional industry will meet increased international competition from unconventional sources.

Market Expansion of Larger Tourism Enterprises. Larger businesses will naturally find it more advantageous to create and develop their own market positions rather than participating, and potentially drowning, in a collective effort. High volumes and market concentration are further arguments for going it alone. For example, the Danish firm Dansommer, which rents summerhouses, has been successfully represented in main towns and cities in northern Germany, giving it an impressive market share in this particular region. Over the years, airlines have also benefited from sales offices in the capitals of most countries, as tour operators have skimmed the market in neighboring regions (Cavlec 2000). For example, guests from southern Sweden are conveniently flown out of Copenhagen airport, with Danish as well as Swedish operators as intermediaries.

For the same reasons, the large tourism enterprises are busily revising both the servicing of their markets and their presence in them. Perceived conditions for the original international strategy are changing. Modern and well-informed customers feel less need for face-to-face service before making purchase decisions, and much can be handled by telephone and electronically. One consequence of this is that activities are withdrawn back to the country of origin, thereby potentially consolidating employment in the domestic tourism industry.

However, this is only part of the story. While the telephone services of most airlines appear to be national, without customers' knowledge calls are transferred to the first available employee, no matter where in the world he or she is located. Recently, Scandinavian Airlines moved its ticket handling to India, and other airlines are in the process of outsourcing flight maintenance. These examples show that operations in a value chain are subdivided. Airlines feel the need to keep only the most necessary jobs in high-wage countries. Common sense dictates that jobs requiring high qualifications remain in Western welfare states, but even this assumption is being contested (Davies, Moutinho, and Hutcheson 2005).

The subcontracting of selected marketing tasks to local business contractors is a classic approach to international market expansion, and is still much used, despite the growing trend of firms' own representation in foreign markets (Buckley and Casson 1998). In tourism, a continual development of contractual forms is taking place, and a new division of labour emerging. For example, the MICE (meetings, incentives, conferences, events) field is undergoing a professionalisation and specialisation, and new categories of agents are offering promotional services to enterprises—across borders (Swarbooke and Horner 2001). The nature of the competencies, capacities, and, not least, interlinkages of the culturally indigenous agents can become a major success parameter for a enterprise based in another country.

Stage Two: Integration Across the Borders Investing abroad is a topic treated extensively in the globalisation literature (Buckley and Casson 1998). In tourism, the reproduction and foreign expansion of successful business concepts recognised by many customers are a major driving force for globalisation. The transfer of capital and concepts is prominent in the industry, and the pros and cons of cultural and economic hegemony are much debated, particularly when exported to developing countries (Britton 1991). Here two methods of integrating across borders will be elabourated, first business integration through investments, mergers, and acquisitions abroad, and second, the global trade of business concepts through, for example, franchising and licensing arrangements.

Transnational Integration Through Business Ownership. Foreign investment has long occupied a prominent position in the economic literature (Hymer and Cohen 1979). Unsurprisingly, the development of ownership across borders is a significant driving force of globalisation processes. There are several motives for making foreign investments. First, if growth opportunities at home are scarce, expansion may continue elsewhere, where markets are still relatively undeveloped. Second, investing abroad can mean access to new markets for the products of the home country. Third, foreign investment has traditionally been used to gain control over raw materials or other physical assets.

Fourth, and most ambitiously, the investment can aim at achieving market dominance in specific fields, but including all steps of the value chain in a larger number of countries. Tourism businesses have invested abroad for decades (Johnson and Vanetti 2005). During the charter holiday boom period in the 60s and 70s, tour operators invested heavily in hotel capacity, thereby building up their own resources and freeing themselves from dependence on local (less capable) actors. While outward investments from northern Europe have sometimes been quite significant, foreign investment in tourism facilities there have not been particularly impressive and are concentrated in hotels in metropolitan areas, discouraged by low earnings and high costs, particularly in high-wage countries such as Denmark (PKF and Danmarks Turistra°d 1998). While this means that ownership is kept in local hands, it also implies that the enterprises concerned may miss out on market access and knowhow that is often a side effect of business integration.

Tour operators and travel agencies have intensive experience of mergers and acquisitions (Cavlec 2000). National pioneers in the field have been swallowed up by the bigger European actors, possibly with positive impacts on quality, variety, and price, but also with reduced employment in some countries and growth in others. As regards attractions, Euro Disney is an example of business expansion that has inspired others, such as Danish Legoland, which established a themepark outside London (Richards and Richards 1998). Legoland is an example of a genuine effort to enhance both the market for toys and the market for entertainment, just as Disney combines media products and amusement. One of the effects of ubiquitous integration in multinational corporations is a reduction in variety and local flavor of the tourism product worldwide.

However, small-scale micro-investment flows are also taking place. The free movement of capital, labour, and social benefits across European borders gives small-capital owners an increased incentive to set up business in other countries. For example, early retirees from the north have established small lifestyle-based bed-and-breakfasts in southern France. These investments will most likely be from north to south, and not in the opposite direction (Hall and Williams 2002). Import and Export of Business Concepts. Control of markets can be achieved by direct investments in and ownership of physical facilities, as already noted. However, resource-based theories emphasize knowledge as a key asset of globalisation, and increasingly so. Knowledge is not cost-free, and is a tradable commodity in its own right (Penrose 1958). Franchising and licensing are examples of specific manifestations.

Many tourism services are well suited to franchising and licensing arrangements (Quinn and Doherty 2000). The prevalence of trademarks is important for the image and general recognition of the products. Operation and delivery can be standardised and conceptualised, and the dependent units can often be operated in any local setting with a relative minimum of prior experience and education. Head office is responsible for the provision of raw materials and supports the local units with marketing, financial advice, personnel management systems, and more.

The concepts must be considered as transnational sales objects. Franchising and licensing thus have a potential for rapid expansion in larger markets (Hoffman and Preble 2004; Yakhlef and Maubourguet 2004). It is through these organisational constructs that the transfer of transnational payments and knowledge takes place. Sometimes, both immaterial substances and physical products are transferred, since purchasing is tightly controlled. This can give a boost to national economies. For example, Danish poultry slaughterhouses, chosen for their high sanitary and veterinary standards, supply McDonald's restaurants throughout most of Europe. Nonetheless, large and primarily North American concepts dominate Europe and the rest of the world. In spite of successes in some areas, the European food industry has failed to generate franchised or licensed catering spin-offs to any great degree. There is no doubt that many franchise concepts appeal to many categories of tourists and fit in well with their preferences, enabling them to travel away from home without having to change their purchasing behavior (Scarpato and Daniele 2003). But since the driving forces originate almost exclusively from North America (Altinay and Roper 2005), the main managerial and development functions are not localised in Europe. Franchising or licensing is usually an all-or-nothing concept, with no half solutions or scope for adaptation. Notwithstanding, some arrangements can involve the transfer of parts of business concepts with significant local adaptation. A beneficial side-effect of many franchise and licensing arrangements is a dissemination of technology that in these types of organisations may take place more rapidly than under other circumstances.

Stage Three: Fragmentation of the Value Chain Recent years have seen a greater emphasis on the creation of profitability through an expanded fragmentation and optimisation of the whole value chain (Arndt and Kierzkowski 2001). While much of the sourcing is purely local or national, the accessibility of world markets is increasingly affecting the composition of local tourism product and the production process. In this service with a high degree of labour input, the sourcing of human resources and immaterial inputs are of major importance. In northern Europe, one of the main driving forces for the fragmentation of the value chain is the substitution of costly labour inputs.

Outsourcing: Many of the raw materials or semimanufactured ingredients in tourism services have their origin in other countries. The wine in the restaurant is French; the towels in the hotel room have been manufactured in India. While some researchers have expressed concern over the leakages (Dwyer and Forsyth 1997), according to theories of foreign trade, the exchange of goods and services across borders contributes positively to product quality and diversity, and helps keep prices down and profits up.

From this point of view, outsourcing cannot simply be regarded as a threat to domestic tourism employment, since outsourcing firms are unlikely to be as competitive without this intensive import and product exchange (Lamminmaki 2005). However, current patterns of purchasing and outsourcing in tourism are developing rapidly, a process most often claimed to result from the high cost of human labour. For example, many restaurants increase their purchases of semimanufactured items, which only need to be heated before being served. Food manufacturers in France, Belgium, and the Netherlands have developed a high level of expertise in catering, and supply broad segments of the restaurant sector in Europe (Hjalager 1999). While tourism boards and agents would like to see the development of closely integrated regional food ways, the reality is that very few restaurants get their supplies directly from local stables, fields, barns, and fishing fleets.

Differences in labour costs are not the only motivation for sourcing from other countries. Variations in the tax and VAT systems across Europe create an extra dimension in the sourcing decision game. The Danish tax authorities frequently uncover illegal international sourcing related to tourism. This primarily concerns wine, beer, and other drinks imported into the country through unofficial channels. While this results in cheaper liquor prices, possibly with the savings being passed on to tourists, the traffic is of course problematic for other reasons (Hjalager 2006). Merchandising is becoming increasingly important for the survival and continual development of museums and attractions (Bryman 2004), although, while often claimed to be authentic, the Viking daggers and reproductions of van Goghs, and the like, are produced outside the countries where the originals first appeared. For many museums, books, postcards, posters, and such, make up the bulk of sales, but local authenticity is limited to the authorship or planning activity, while production is outsourced. One might think that publicly owned cultural institutions are "patriotic" in their sourcing, which is not the case. Managers of museums, theaters, *etc.*, constantly search the international market for "footloose" performances and exhibitions.

They also offer their own popular contributions on the global "wholesale" market (Wang 2003). Precious heritage is no longer maintained solely by local craftspeople and conservators; in recent years museums in Western Europe have increasingly drawn on the expertise of Eastern European conservators, who can also offer significant advantages in terms of price and quality.

The design of hotels and restaurants can be a task for specialised enterprises, some of which sell their designs as "turnkey" solutions. IT (information technology) solutions for administrative and booking purposes and entertainment are often also standardised, which the need for transnational data exchange intensifies (Buhalis 2003). An international division of labour and specialisation is taking place; for example, Danish manufacturers have had some success in developing and making equipment for discotheques and nightclubs. This continual division of labour between the tourism industry and its suppliers may represent considerable turbulence in economic composition, but the advantages or disadvantages for national economies are not necessarily observable in the tourism statistics.

Human Resourcing: There is a good deal of focus in the international business literature on expatriates and related issues about management, control, and knowledge transfers to subsidiaries in other countries (Bartlett and Ghoshal 1989). There is also a significant focus on international careers, the general impression being that working in other cultural settings will benefit employability and look impressive on one's curriculum vitae (Jayawardena 2000). In more recent years, expatriation for longer periods of time has become less common (Davies 2002). Not only is it costly and difficult, but improved transportation and communications make it less necessary. This does not imply that segments of the workforce are not increasingly operating internationally, however. As Sklair (2001) claims, the "transnational capitalist class" is emerging as a parallel process to globalisation—integrated, but also governed by the specific forces of careers, capital accumulation, and consumerism, albeit less predictably than previously. Large hotel chains, airlines, and tour operators have commonly offered ambitious and committed employees international career opportunities (European Institute of Education and Social Policy 1991). Some high-profile companies in tourism operate with successive management contracts, for example in connection with the opening and implementation of new resorts. Switzerland produces an internationally oriented management elite from its well-known private hotel schools.

Other countries do not have similar institutions and reputation in this field. Divisions of labour in the provision of human resources tend to emerge across countries. For example, seamanship traditions in Denmark have led to a demand for Danish officers from the international cruise fleet (Hjalager and Jeansson 2002). This industry is a major employer of a migrating labourforce, where a strict ethnic stratification is in operation (Wood 2000). With international personnel flows prevalent, most of the labour market does not have any high degree of formalisation. On average, tourism labour markets are dominated by short employment contracts (Hjalager 2006; Lucas 1995).

One important reason for this is seasonality, which causes variations in the need for the labour. However, the rapidly developing short-term labour market also has an intrinsic international dimension. Students on world tours represent a workforce that tends to accept nonstandard working conditions and contracting. Most countries have flows of youth labour in both directions, with some more popular than others. In Europe, the traffic is supported by the European Commission's labour exchange offices. Illegal work thrives in the industry, not least because many functions do not require any particular knowledge of languages and culture. Authorities find that the supply of labour, as in hotel and catering, increasingly takes place through a systematic clandestine exchange. In particular, through family and other networks, many proprietors with an ethnic background supply the labour market from countries with lower wage levels (Hjalager 2006; Razaei 2004).

It is worth noting in this context that the voluntary labour market, as for archaeological excavations or marine research, is fast becoming an international phenomenon. Participating in social projects or in rescue missions during a holiday mixes work and the tourism experience. In addition, courses for foreign students are turning into a booming business for universities and other educational institutions, which in some cases is of major regional importance. The melting together of travel experiences, education, and (voluntary) labour and humanitarian alliances across the world (Prahalad 2005) provides entirely new prospects for the industry, and the international dimensions are potentially very different from purely recreational tourism. New categories of tourists no longer respond to traditional marketing efforts, which means that the institutions and organisations that cater for emerging markets will have to reinterpret the notion of both tourism and work.

Stage Four: Transcending into New Value Chains Many organisations and researchers are involved in the attempt to define and distinguish tourism logically in traditional economic and statistical categories (OECD 1995). While difficult, the attempt is understandable, since there is significant political focus on the ability to document economic importance and growth rates. The ongoing globalisation processes tend to compromise the industry's courageous attempts to legitimate such claims. Tourism is increasingly transcending into other—and highly international—value chains, and vice versa. Various manifestations of this radical fragmentation and global reorganisation of activities are tourism-related. As will be shown, the division Tourism in the Knowledge Economy. The main aim of the industry is to provide services and facilities for tourists. But its operations and creative developments also create a spin-off of knowledge, which may be further cultivated, commodified, and offered for sale as consulting and expert services. The sophistication of a national, home-bred tourism may be important for the quality of consulting services offered abroad: Spanish consultants and experts seem to be strong in accommodation development, Germans are at the forefront of sustainable tourism, and the British in heritage management and development. One example of the intermingling of value chains is the Roskilde rock festival (Denmark), where an environmental management model was introduced which eventually became an export object to other festivals around the world. However, the actual exporter was not the festival organisation itself, but the consulting engineers who had helped in the development process. The transcending mode of development has continued, with the festival becoming involved in a major initiative called "Musicon Valley". The parallel with Silicon Valley is not a coincidence, the intention being to establish a cluster of music-related services, production facilities, and educational systems which can create real competitive advantages across a number of business sectors. Musicon Valley is planned to be a learning environment and a place for the expression of an intelligent demand (Caves 2000) that will benefit from international sales from both festival tourism and other businesses.

National and international foreign aid organisations, the UN system, and numerous nongovernmental organisations are facilitating the exploitation of knowledge resources in a global context (Wearing, McDonald, and Ponting 2005). Organisations such as the World Tourism Organisation and more trade-based and commercial transnational associations also contribute to the establishment of a knowledge pool that transcends national borders.

Sales of Market Positions and Brand Extension: Many trademarks and brands have a high credibility among customers. With these crucial to sales and profitability, owners put great effort and large investments into establishing and maintaining their brands. Once established, the intrinsic value of the brand name can be capitalised on (Aaker 1991), and other, less recognised products may benefit from being connected with the "parent brand". For instance, Disney lets its name and figures integrate in the marketing of hotels, restaurants, and more (Richards and Richards 1998). However, a brand's value can also be extended to less well-known products and firms outside the parent firm.

Capitalising on these and market positions is an increasing—and very international—activity. Of course, it is important that the parent firm and user of the brand market position are compatible in terms of quality, image, customer category, and the like, and that mutual trust can be established between the partners. For example, a spa resort has entered into an exclusive agreement with providers of beauty products and fashion items. McDonalds' and Disney have close alliances. Events of many kinds, such as sponsor contracts, create close relations with high-profile trademarks if there is a perceptual fit.

Since tourism flows are international, it is important that the brands are recognised at this level. Increasingly, efforts are focusing on the joint marketing of products and tourism, thereby attempting to reap the benefits in both areas (Mitchell and Orwig 2002). For example, Scottish whisky distilleries combine the tourism experience with their own marketing. Plant tours and visitor centers have a greater effect than commercials, since the tourists relate the product to a positive experience. Combining brand equity management with tourism is a mode of operation which has yet to be fully exploited. The way that its products have traditionally been marketed is likely to be modified and developed considerably in the future, with less emphasis on the hitherto implicit regional/destination connection. Tourism in the Global Media Melting Pot. It is common knowledge in the industry that a few minutes on prime-time television or features in newspapers can result in massive marketing savings. Contact (especially paid) with journalists is thus increasingly being used by many tourism enterprises, since the media are very suitable for the types of unbiased mental image promotion that the industry needs to influence customers' purchase (Goessons 2000).

However, the media business is undergoing rapid structural change, one of the main trends being an increasing globalisation in a diagonal process: Media are merging across borders, and media conglomerates diversifying into TV, films, publishing, the Internet, marketing, and so on. In this process, content becomes a shared international resource, and space concepts dissolve (Beeton 2005; Holmes 2002). In the near future, content linked up to the GPS (Global Positions Systems) will push developments further and put news and commercial information on tourists' mobile telephones. Tourism enterprises that need the media for exposure will find that access to it is harder, but they will get a far more widespread effect if they succeed. As discussed by Crouch, Jackson; and Thompson (2005), media and tourism represent converging cultures. Smaller enterprises will not have the resources to approach and manipulate global media providers (Smeral 1998). Government and regional marketing bodies will also find it a major challenge to move information beyond national borders.

There are significant ongoing counter-developments to the trend described above. Technological developments and the globalisation of the media are creating new modes of information-sharing among tourists on popular weblogs, thus empowering the tourists at the expense of the business (Hjalager 2001). This study has attempted to systematize the modes of internationalisation and globalisation in tourism, demonstrating that it is becoming more global in ways which tourism enterprises and organisations, as well as political actors, are not always likely to recognize. The article suggests a stage model for the evolution of globalisation in tourism. The underlying logic is the advance from simple forms to more complex ones. Globalisation is progressing in scale and scope, but the practical outcomes are unevenly distributed across enterprises, countries, and regions. Accordingly, a stage model such as the one discussed here should be seen more as a tool for reflection and development than a clear-cut forecast of future developments.

Globalisation has still not been discussed to any great extent in tourism research, and the literature tends to focus on selected manifestations only. Therefore, there is a real need for further investigation and improved empirical documentation. In particular, there is a lack of a genuine and more detailed insight into the changed composition of value chains, which are relocating economic assets, employment, and earnings in the industry across national and regional borders, as described in stage three of the model. There is also a need to look into the ways small enterprises and selected tourism subsectors grasp opportunities across all stages. Eventually, globalisation manifests itself in different ways in different parts of the world, an issue that has not been treated in this article, which has a predominantly northern European focus.

When analysing communities of enterprises or the industry as such, rather than single enterprises, a stage model is appropriate. At this level, and allowing for substantial overlaps and underlying leaps back and forth, there seems to be support for an incremental development from stage one to four. Potentially, the model can guide tourism policymaking by helping actors discard outdated modes of operation in time, and review and renew their policies according to the real global potential. If applied to the level of national and destination policies, there is in most countries in northern Europe a scope for far more advanced globalisation formats than simple market representation and promotion. A better understanding of globalisation potentials and a hedging of the threats require increased innovation and the structural development of commercial tourism industries, and also that government bodies enter into new types of alliances. Models of boundarycrossing systems in other industries, such as pharmaceuticals or music and entertainment, may also apply to tourism. Basically, globalisation in tourism is not a new issue, and the industry has been undergoing an internationalisation process for decades.

6

Economic Impact Analysis in Tourism

A knowledge of economic trends and conditions is fundamental to strategic planning and project development in any business. Yet, despite the fact that tourism has become the world's largest industry, until now, there were no textbooks devoted to the economics of tourism. A book whose time has finally come, Tourism Economics arms students and industry professionals with a solid working knowledge of economic concepts and analytical techniques as they apply to tourism.

Tourism can be viewed as an institution with millions of interactions taking place, an institution with a history, body of knowledge, and a constituency of millions of people who feel themselves a part of the institution. Tourism is an economic activity involving billions of dollars exchanged each month, a social science to be analysed, trends to be identified, and costs/benefits to be computed. The past two decades have been a time of fast and furious growth for world tourism, accounting for more than 6% of the world's gross national product ($3.2 trillion in 1993) and employing 127 million people worldwide, tourism is now, beyond a doubt, the world's largest industry. And with an average of 20,000 new jobs created per each additional $1 million spent on travel, tourism is also the most prolific generator of new jobs. As a consequence of tourism's growing preeminence, a new field has emerged over the past few years to help the tourism industry and public policymakers better understand the impact of tourism on other segments of the economy and to recognize and facilitate current and future economic trends in tourism—tourism economics.

Tourism Economics operates with a singular objective: combine a deep understanding of the tourism sector with proven economic tools to answer the most important questions facing destinations, strategic planners, and investors. Tourism Economics designs market strategy models, tourism policy recommendations, tourism forecasting models, and tourism economic impact studies. The core issues involved in economic impact analysis are the manner in which income is created and how this income flows through the local economy. It is hoped that this clearinghouse assists communities to better understand the impact of tourism on the local and regional economy. With that in mind, the organisation of the applied economic impact analysis literature is designed for two different types of users:

1. The practitioner wanting to learn more about the methodology of tourism economic impact analysis
2. The practitioner wanting to see examples of how economic impact analysis has been applied to different components of the tourism industry.

We have not applied a strict definition of economic impact analysis and this clearinghouse includes much research that falls outside of many definitions of economic impact analysis. Community development practitioners are less concerned with definitions and more interested in answering questions.

Tourism, Economic Development and the Global–local Nexus

We take the reader on a brief trip through the theoretical terrain of the past three decades and conclude with a discussion of the 'new' economic geography of tourism, in which cultural and economic boundaries are being transcended across a variety of scales.

Our discussion begins by underscoring the rise and increasing importance of tourism locally and globally. A brief overview of the industry's economic role at the international and national scale leads us into a discussion of local and regional involvement in the tourism industry. We argue that communities and individuals that depend on tourism are faced with an over-arching problem: how can the industry be developed while also ensuring that local quality of life is maintained. In particular we are interested in how local economies can thrive, and unique socio-cultural and environmental resources survive, in a globalised environment.

We emphasize the need to develop a more rigorous understanding of the evolving tourism industry and how it influence processes of local economic development. We present a brief review of theoretical frameworks developed during the 1970s and 1980s, focusing on dependency, life-cycle and community approaches. We then analyse the influence of the so-called 'new political economy' that began to permeate the tourism literature during the early 1990s.

We then highlight the ways in which current attempts to understand the links between tourism and economic development are embracing the complexity of the industry and its influence on everyday lives. We advocate 'new' ways of seeing and studying the economics of tourism geography, ways that reflect the cultural turn in the 'new' economic geography, and the increasing significance of networks and new information and communication technologies (ICTs). We argue that the cultural analysis of economic relations, and a willingness to embrace complexity, are essential if we are to unpack the 'global' nature of tourism development processes.

Tourism from the Global to the Local

There can be no denying that tourism is a major global economic force. Hardly a day goes by without a new pronouncement about the wider significance of what many call the world's largest industry. International tourism has grown substantially in recent decades, with technological improvements, rising living standards and broader processes of globalisation leading to rapid increases in visitor numbers. Receipts from international tourism rose from US$2.1 billion in 1950 to US$445 billion in 1998. During the same period international tourist arrivals rose from 25.3 million to 625 million. In 1999, tourism generated some US$3.5 trillion of GDP and almost 200 million jobs across the world economy.

World tourism GDP is forecast to increase in real terms by 3.0 per cent per annum in the decade to 2010. As a result, the industry's share of world GDP will rise from 10.5 per cent in 1990 to 11.4 per cent by the end of 2005. In the same period, employment is expected to grow at 2.6 per cent per annum. This equates to creation of over 5.5 million jobs per year over the first decade of the new century (WTO 2000; WTTC 2000). In its longterm growth forecast document, *Tourism: 2020 Vision*, the WTO (1999) predicts that the tourism sector will expand by an average of 4.1 per cent a year over the next two decades, surpassing a total of 1 billion international travellers by the year 2010, and reaching 1.6 billion by the year 2020.

The economic and societal significance of tourism varies dramatically across the global stage. Twenty rich nations (17 European, USA, Canada and Japan) accounted for 81.8 per cent of all tourist expenditure in 1995, with five nations (USA, Japan, Germany, the UK and France) accounting for almost half of all spending (WTO 1998). While the growth of international tourism from nations like China and Brazil is significant, there seems little likelihood that this uneven global division of expenditure will change dramatically in the near future.

Despite the relatively strong performance of the tourism industry in many western nations, most are characterised by travel account balances that are in deficit. With residents from developed economies generating the bulk of international tourist expenditure, it is not surprising that the travel account balance in developing economies has been persistently in surplus, widening from US$4.6 billion in 1980 to US$33.7 billion in 1989 and US$62.2 billion in 1997. Indeed, it is estimated that in 1997 the travel account surplus in the developing world offset more than two-thirds of its accumulated current budget deficit (WTTC 2000; WTO 1999).

A key issue is the way in which these processes of global tourism expansion, uneven development and, in some cases, retraction, play themselves out at the sub-national levels of regions and communities. Urban communities and rural settlements are all influenced by tourism to some degree and also play important roles in shaping the structure and nature of the industry. To help us conceptualize the links that exist between the global and the local we adopt the notion of the global–local nexus (Alger 1988). We argue that it is essential to look carefully at how interactions between the global and the local shape development outcomes for individuals, households, communities and regions. Tourism, in simple terms, must be viewed as a transaction process which is at once driven by the global priorities of multi-national corporations, geo-political forces and broader forces of economic change, and the complexities of the local where residents, visitors, workers, governments and entrepreneurs interact at the industry 'coal-face'. At the global scale tourism's development outcomes are influenced by broad-based economic change, evolving structures of corporate governance and the unrelenting evolutionary pressures of demographics and technological change. Global institutions, such as the IMF and World Bank, play a vital role in shaping the economic environment for tourism investment and development in much of the world.

Multi-national trade bloc formation drives increases in business and leisure travel as restrictions to trade and human movements are relaxed. At the same time it is the transnational corporation that stands astride the global economy as the dominant form of enterprise in both the tourism industry and other sectors. It is impossible to understand the global–local nexus unless we examine the prevailing discourse on internationalisation and globalisation is highly critical of what he calls the prevailing conception of globalisation in the business literature: 'In this hyper-globalised world, transnational corporations call the shots, labour has to learn to be "realistic" and (globally) competitive, and the nation state shrinks to insignificance, both as a unit of analysis and as a political agent'. He argues that this notion of globalisation is too simplistic and reduces the role of nations to one of de- and re-regulatory facilitation. At the same time regions and localities are discussed in terms of 'learning networks' and 'reflexive institution forms' and are simply, he argues, viewed as vital competitive assets on the supply side of the global economy.

At the national scale macro-economic policy frameworks, infrastructure provision and issues of socio-cultural cohesion play a vital role in influencing tourism's development outcomes. Some commentators argue that the role of the nation state has diminished as the 'stateless' multinational corporation has come to dominate global economic affairs and neo-liberal policies have led to a retreat of the welfare state. We argue, however, that the national scale remains significant to any understanding of tourism's development outcomes. What is seen by many as a wholesale retreat, is argued by others to be more of a qualitative reorganisation of structural capacities and strategic emphases. Indeed, from a tourism perspective national governments often appear to be playing a more active role in coordinating the tourism marketing campaigns and broad-based product development that play such an important role in shaping tourism demand and behaviour.

In recent decades the region has been seen to be an increasingly vital component in the global–local context of development. Notions of regions stimulating economic growth through a mixture of networks, and cultural/political attributes have dominated much of the social science discourse on economic development since the early 1980s. The Third Italy and Silicon Valley are known the world over as 'smart regions' that have managed to create the right mix of circumstances to enable economic growth. In tourism too the region has become seen as an important driving force in linking disparate segments of the industry and enabling destination networks to form. It is also, of course, true to say that many of the natural and cultural resources upon which the industry depends are regional in nature – ranging from complex ecosystems through to patterns of culture and economic identity. Since the early 1980s the community level has also been viewed more seriously as a key factor in influencing economic development outcomes.

Community is of vital importance as an intermediate level of social life between the personal (individual/family) and impersonal (global/institutional). Community structures built around modernist cultural identity, architectures and work practices are frequently depicted as being in decay. The 'breakdown' of community is often highlighted by the media as being at the forefront of growing problems of lawlessness and family dissolution. Indeed, during the 1990s many governments placed community at the centre of attempts to create economic regeneration and remedy social ills.

The theoretical underpinnings of such initiatives can be found in the work of the 'communitarian' movement, where scholars such as Amitai Etzioni have challenged the atomising nature of free market liberal economics and its detrimental consequences for socio-economic well-being. Tourism has not been immune to these trends. 'Community-based' approaches are central to many tourism development plans around the world and there is a growing realisation that localised cooperation, trust and networking are essential ingredients in providing the right mix for successful tourism development outcomes. Indeed, tourism is often seen as a key element that can enable communities devastated by economic restructuring to regain and enhance their economic foothold in regional and national economies. The complexity of the global–local nexus and how its economic, cultural and environmental elements interact to create local development outcomes is breathtaking. We cannot understand the context of local tourism development unless we grapple with this complexity and better understand how key stakeholders interact both within and between multiple 'nested' scales. We now turn to a review of how tourism researchers have attempted to theorize these issues over the past three decades.

Evolving Theories of Tourism and Development

It was in the 1970s and 1980s that tourism researchers first began to focus considerable attention on the broader context and outcomes of tourism development. The two approaches that dominated much of the discourse on tourism and development during this period were the dependency perspective and the life-cycle model.

While both emerged from quite different theoretical lineages (neo-marxism in the case of dependency, and modernisation theory in the case of the lifecycle approach) they are based on the shared premise that the industry's mass variant represents its crowning height. Companies minimize 'unit costs' by generating economies of scale, destinations receive increased visitor numbers, and tourists fulfill their wanderlust cheaply and efficiently.

As a new nation or region is initially incorporated into the global 'patchwork-quilt' of tourism destinations the emergent industry is characterised by relatively high levels of local involvement. As visitor numbers rise and incorporation into the global tourism system increases, local industry structures soon become characterised by overseas or local elite ownership. Locals end up receiving few economic benefits, while having to carry the inevitable costs of rapidly increasing tourist numbers. Unfortunately, the high costs associated with the inevitable rise of mass tourism provide both the communities and localities that rely on it with little prospect for local control and limited potential to achieve more sustainable forms of local development.

Both dependency and life-cycle approaches have been criticised on a number of common grounds. Dependency theory is often accused of being 'obsessed by the global level, and the world system', therefore ignoring the possibility that what occurs within a nation/region may be just as important as those influence that originate outside its boundaries. There is a failure, in the case of both approaches, to acknowledge the possibility that local government, industries and individuals can exert some degree of control over their own destinies. As

Preister notes: 'locally-affected people are not shaped passively by outside forces but react as well, at times even changing the conditions of the larger system'. Preister argues the development outcome is a 'negotiated process' between local groups or individuals and structural forces. Both frameworks fail to consider the possibility that by empowering locals to have input into development plans, the deteriorating cycle of evolution might be minimised or avoided.

These frameworks are equally limited in their ability to grapple with the changing nature of production and accumulation. Technological change and shifts in industrial organisation are not dealt with effectively. In particular there is an inability to incorporate notions of capital's ability (or otherwise) to cope with periodic episodes of profit down turn and crisis. As Lipietz notes: It (*dependency theory*) paid little attention to the concrete conditions of capitalist accumulation either in the centre or in the periphery. It therefore could not visualize that transformations in the logic of accumulation in the centre would modify the nature of centre–periphery relations. Another approach to emerge in the 1980s emphasised local agency, seeing communities and their constituent members playing an active role in determining tourism's outcomes. In dramatic contrast to the models just described the community approach views locals as being capable of planning and participating in tourism development, of making their voices heard when they are concerned, and of having the capability to control the outcomes of the industry to some degree. Murphy argues that if host communities can define the types of tourism they wish to attract and can accommodate over the long term, they can shape the type of industry that is most appropriate to their needs.

Unfortunately, proponents of community participation in the tourism development process have often ignored the tendency of local elites to appropriate the organs of participation for their own benefits. It is also often forgotten that factors such as gender relations and race will have an effect on power structures within communities, as will the ways in which these communities are embedded in broader socioeconomic, political and environmental structures.

Community participation can also be a double-edged sword. Such approaches promote mutual responsibility between the state and locals, incorporate vital local knowledge into projects, and provide outlets for the channelling of local political discontent. Nevertheless, local participation is often expensive to run, may generate expectations that far exceed eventual outcomes, and may create new conflicts as marginal groups become more articulate and elites are able to gain a greater slice of participatory benefits through their own networks. The counter-position of community and the tourism industry which is often inherent in the literature on local interaction with the industry is a form of reductionism found in a range of other settings. Given the profound and complex nature of the global social division of labour we should not assume that the interests of a specialist group of residents are always in accord with broader local wishes and desires. While localities depend heavily on their local economic base this does not mean that local interests can simply be defined in these terms and treated as unitary.

As Urry (1990) notes, the interests of people within a locality vary enormously in strength and kind, and it cannot be assumed that local attachments come first, so that people's interests can be represented territorially. Perhaps, most importantly, the community focused approach tends to ignore the local implications of the evolving nature of capitalist accumulation at broader scales of resolution.

Regulation Theory and 'New Tourism'

It has become a cliche to state that we are living in a globalised world, but whatever name is given to the present era (post-industrial, post-Fordist, 'new times') there is a widespread recognition that we are living in a world that has evolved considerably from a generation ago. This world needs new theoretical tools to enable us to understand our rapidly changing times. One response to these changes has been the emergence of the so called 'new' political economy and its gradual application to the study of the development process.

The flexible specialisation approach and the Regulation School have been particularly influential through much of the 1990s. As Peck notes, researchers have often been guilty of combining concepts from these two, conceptually different, approaches and, as a result, it sometimes becomes difficult to disentangle concepts that may have quite diverse theoretical and political lineages and implications. Our focus here is primarily on regulation theory – which has arguably had the greatest impact on the tourism literature. It is clear that the more production orientated flexible specialisation thesis has also influenced a number of tourism commentators. Proponents of the regulation approach argue that capitalism is an unstable, contradictory system that must restructure itself in order to resolve, albeit temporarily, its periodic crises. Each period of restructuring brings different regional and local economic impacts. Advocates of this approach maintain that a 'regime' of mass production and consumption, known as 'Fordism' dominated much of the past century. During the last quarter of the century, it is argued that Fordism has been yielding to a more 'flexible' and dynamic pattern of production and consumption, variously categorised as a 'post-Fordism', 'flexible accumulation' or 'flexible specialisation'. TEgulation theory introduces the concept of a 'regime of accumulation'– a social system linking production to consumption. The temporary stability of this system depends on a particular 'mode of social and political regulation' based on a 'set of internalised rules and social procedures, including state action, social institutions, behavioural norms and political practices.

The emerging production paradigm is based on achieving flexibility, both internally and externally. Internally, firms must be able to produce a greater variety of specialised products and to change product configurations rapidly in response to variations in market taste. Externally, these shifts are associated with vertical and horizontal disintegration and the emergence of down-sized specialised firms often organised into spatially proximate networks. Several tourism researchers have borrowed from these frameworks in their attempts to understand the changing structure of the industry and its evolving role in local, regional and national development processes. For example; utilising many of the basic tenets of flexible specialisation Poon sees the emergence of a new tourism 'best practice': The economics of new tourism is very different from the old profitability no longer rests solely on economies of scale and the exploitation of mass undifferentiated markets.

Economies of scope, systems gains, segmented markets, designed and customised holidays are becoming more and more important for profitability and competitiveness in tourism. The major characteristics of the new 'best' practice are its focus on product *flexibilility* and variety facilitated by the increased use of advanced technology. *Segmentation* results in the break-up of mass markets into cluster segments that display a diversity of needs and characteristics. At the same time, *diagonal integration* sees tourism firms move into new and different activities, seeking the tremendous energies, systems gains and scope economies that can potentially be derived from such integration.

Regulation and flexible specialisation approaches represent a major step forward in our attempts to theorize the complex links between tourism and economic development. Both approaches stress the need to understand broader processes of capitalist accumulation in order to understand the economic prospects facing regions and communities around the world. Another strength is the rejection of the fatalism inherent in the dependency/life-cycle frameworks described earlier. Thus commentators, such as Poon, view the emergence of new tourism as offering an opportunity for less developed regions and small firms to achieve a greater degree of self-determination than they have managed in the past.

There has, however, been concerted criticism and debate concerning the ability of these 'new' political economy theories to address the processes of change affecting contemporary capitalism, in general, and tourism, in particular. The first criticisms revolve around whether Fordism ever existed as a dominant regime of accumulation during the post-war period of the 1960s and 1970s. Indeed, it can be argued that, 'old' or mass tourism, characterised by ubiquitous 'sun, sand and sea'-based package tours, was in fact only ever dominant in parts of Europe, and was never as significant a mode of travel among, for example, North Americans.

A second set of criticisms concerns the 'crisis' of Fordism. Evidence of a relative decline in rates of output and productivity in mass production industries is inconclusive at best, with some classic mass production industries growing rapidly while others have been declining. The same can be argued for tourism. While we have seen rapid growth in the number of small tourism firms, archetypal mass tourism firms continue to prosper and thrive. Mass tourism's convenience, price and travel style remain attractive to many consumers, making it an important mainstay for the tourism industry. As Williams and Montanari attest, care must be taken not to over-simplify changes. While small firms may develop and thrive in this environment, we still know little about how they will interact with their larger counterparts, and what future exists for less flexible organisational structures. A further important shortcoming of these theories lies in their treatment of different spatial levels of analysis. Regulation theory focuses primarily on the underlying structures behind a regime of accumulation and modes of regulation at the national level, without providing a similar analysis at the regional level or theorising the relationship between scales. Thus it is unclear whether the mode of regulation which stabilises a particular regime of accumulation at the national level can be reproduced at a regional or local level. The difficulties that post-Fordist theories present, when attempts are made to move from a local level of analysis to the global level, are also attributable to the fact that empirical research has been carried out in only a few, usually developed countries. In addition, most sectoral research has focused on the manufacturing arena with little attention being paid to services, in general, and tourism, in particular.

It is also fair to say that in much of the 'new' political economy literature of the 1990s it is difficult to situate the role of culture and the environment. In the post-Fordist tourism literature, for example, one struggles to find detailed attention being paid to the impact of tourism on the condition of the natural environment, cultural attributes and people's broader quality of life. Despite these criticisms we argue that a regulationist approach provides a useful base from which to build a more complete understanding of the global–local relations that influence tourism's concrete development outcomes.

Embracing Complexity

Sayer argues that organisational forms are discoveries, worked out in specific historical and geographical contexts. This complexity must be addressed and embraced if we are really to gain an understanding of the links that exist between tourism and broader processes of development. Tourism must be viewed as a transaction process, incorporating both exogenous forces and the endogenous powers of local residents and entrepreneurs. There is a need to strive for a balance between structure and agency, rather than highlighting one at the expense of the other. There is also a sense that cultural and environmental dimensions must be more effectively grafted onto attempts to understand the development processes and outcomes associated with tourism. We also argue that we must acknowledge the impacts that rapidly evolving information and communication technologies have on the industry and those whose lives it influences. We now move on to address some of these issues focusing in particular on dimensions of culture, consumption and the rise of what Castells calls the network society.

Culture and Consumption

In recent years there have been growing attempts by economic, cultural and social geographers to reconceptualize their subdisciplines and embrace the 'de-differentiation of economy and culture'. Of particular relevance here is the rise of approaches that attempt to account for both the material condition and specific experience of individuals, while at the same time situating the individual within political and economic structures of power, conflict and resistance. The crossing of boundaries and the integration of cultural politics into the formation of knowledge have been marked as the 'cultural turn' in human geography. To accommodate these concerns, 'new' fields have begun to emerge that increasingly recognize the difficulties inherent in the separation of economic, cultural and social geographies, and which acknowledge the dialectics of structure and agency. Thus we have seen the emergence of the 'new' regional and economic geography and the 'new' geography of leisure.

The term 'new' does not imply creation of new sub-disciplines, but rather it is used as a label to ease the classification for a broad range and diversity of work that crosses the boundaries to improved knowledge construction. It is important to note that traditional issues of inquiry in economic geography (production, circulation and exchange) have not (and should not have) been abandoned, but rather reshaped to embrace the cultural and social construction of economic geographies. This combination of approaches has allowed us to take a fresh look at place and its role in shaping (and being shaped by) tourism. As Massey notes, space is: 'constructed out of interrelations, as the simultaneous coexistence of social interrelations and interactions at all spatial scales, from the most local level to the most global'. The collections of essays edited by Ringer and Rojek and Urry highlight the active role of tourism in the social construction of space through place. Place, therefore, is not just historically constructed in space, it is actively mediated upon and acts in conjunction with 'outside' and 'inside' factors at all times. In the same way, Oakes sees the social spaces of modernity as being as much cultural as economic constructs.

The emerging consensus is that tourism geography has to take both its economic and cultural dimensions seriously. It is vital that we transcend the boundaries between economic and cultural consumption if we are to understand the continuous recycling of commodities beyond the act of simple monetary exchange. It is essential that we delve 'into the social relations of production and forward into cycles of use and re-use'. Crang and Malbon suggest there are two ways of pursuing dedifferentiation between culture and economy: (1) the 'cultural regulation of the economic'; and (2) the 'cultural materialisation of the economic'. The former relates to the discursive construction of organisational identities and spaces of work (social relations of production) while the latter relate to social relations of consumption 'in which culturally meaningful goods and experiences become the objects and subjects to be provided and consumed'. There is a burgeoning geographical literature addressing issues of leisure, consumption and social identity. Tourism needs to be placed in the context of the contemporary cultural economy, within which groups and individuals increasingly attempt to construct their identities by certain consumption preferences and lifestyle practices which signal taste and position in society. As the 'culture of consumption' evolves in terms of 'you are what you buy' and 'where you go away', there will inevitably be impacts on the tourism industry. These trends have been widely related to the emerging 'new middle class' of so-called cultural producers.

The emerging cultural intermediaries of 'late' capitalism are the marketers, advertisers, public relations representatives, radio and television producers and presenters and magazine journalists. Bourdieu asserts that providers of symbolic goods and services shape consumption as an arena for social differentiation as they seek to associate more closely particular consumption preferences and lifestyle practices with class segments. The issue of consumption and identity becomes even more problematic when advertising begins to recognize 'multiple identities within the same individual'. Glennie and Thrift argue that individuals become 'increasingly fragmented, following particular lifestyles that may or may not chime with one another, but which require the adoption of particular persons to follow those'. In the same way, Jackson and Thrift seek 'to rethink conventional approaches to "identity", emphasising its fluid and dynamic nature rather than assuming identities to be in any way fixed or singular'.

The new cultural and economic geographies provide ways of re-conceptualising traditional views of tourism and providing alternative 'ways of seeing' the industry and broader patterns of leisure.

Space: Economic Development and the Global–local Nexus

It is from this era of post positivist geography that the new cultural geography has emerged and become merged with sociological and cultural studies analyses which are now combining to investigate the multiplicity of behaviours, meanings, consumption trends and identities constructed in and through leisure and tourism. Indeed, as Thrift notes, some of the most interesting work on the cultural geography of economies has begun to emerge from within the tourism arena. Crang's work on performativity in restaurants and the broader tourism industry, and Crain's analysis of performative aspects of women's role in the Ecuadorean tourist market, have provided us with new ways to view the role of culture in the shaping of and, in turn, being shaped by, touristic experiences. Perhaps, most importantly, given the global–local focus of this paper, we argue that the cultural analysis of economic relations gives us a new theoretical gaze through which to unpack the 'global' nature of tourism activity.

Ethnographic and case-based accounts of the way in which the tourism economy is embedded in cultural contexts allow us to move beyond some of the pessimistic and reductionist readings of globalisation effects. It is essential that we continue to evaluate the place and role of culture in our discussions of the economic development dimensions of tourism 'whether its cultural place be the individual (as representative of some wider spatial scale), the firm, the region or the nation-state'.

Networks and Information Technologies

In the newly evolving production environment the most ef.cient relationships are based on the creation of alliances, partnerships and networks between firms. These can be attained through a number of mechanisms including mutual dependency and adaptation, discussion and negotiation, honesty, long-term commitment, quality control and shared knowledge. Networks may also be created and enhanced by the emergence of new information and communication technologies (ICTs).The apparent association of growth in regions and of industries with conspicuous networking activity has encouraged suggestions that successful regional economies in the world economic system must be 'intelligent' or learning regions.

Networks are thus part of the dynamic of organisational creativity, directed towards building and maintaining competitive links to the global economy, and based on strengthening existing competitive activities. A central theme for future exploration is the degree to which networks play a role in influencing the structure, economic success and sustainability of the tourism industry. If networking and networks are, indeed, a general response to pressures in the global economy, increased knowledge of networking activity and network formation amongst key stakeholders within and between different scales of analysis is needed.

Destination communities and regions also rely on network formation (between businesses, between the private and public sectors) for the development of competitive tourist products. At the same time the sustainability of the industry may well be tied to creating effective alliances between the private and public sectors. One of the central questions that must be addressed by tourism researchers is to what extent does such activity translate into localities being able to engage more effectively and sustainably with the global economy and wrest more control over their economic destiny from outside forces? It is important to stress here that networks themselves are fundamentally based not on spatial proximity, or shared interests, but on notions of trust and reciprocity. The future competitiveness of destinations, and the development performance of tourism, will not simply depend on a destination's natural and cultural resource base, its ability to harness new technologies, or its depth of human capital. Success will also depend on the ill-defined attributes of trust and reciprocity. Given our focus on what kind of action is necessary for localities t o engage effectively with the global economy it is worthwhile examining what some commentators feel is the empowering potential of new information and communication technologies. In particular we want to explore two issues – how ICTs are likely to influence the structure and organisation of the tourism industry, and whether these technologies may assist localities to work more effectively within the bounds of the global–local nexus.

While there is plenty of 'hype' about what IT can do for various elements of the tourism industry, it is still not easy to find comprehensive accounts and reasoned analyses of the key issues associated with the adoption of ICTs. Online resources are proliferating and fewer and fewer components of tourism products are willing to risk being invisible in cyberspace. At the same time, numerous governments are implementing policy frameworks to foster ICT adoption by the industry, and tourists everywhere are beginning to see the potential for new technologies to improve their ability to make travel plans. The literature focuses on a number of ways in which the structure and performance of the tourism industry is being influenced by the adoption and development of IT. In addition to reducing communication and transaction costs the internet is also changing the shape and nature of traditional global distribution and destination marketing systems in the tourism industry.

Changing consumer behaviour: While it is difficult to quantify the internet's ability to shape consumer perceptions and decision-making, processes it is clear that the internet is already a force to be reckoned with in moulding visitor behaviour. The internet also provides a vital (and unparalleled) set of information to support consumer choice and skills development.

New product development: The internet offers the industry improved possibilities for price differentiation and also enables greater networking between disparate elements of the industry. In simple terms the Internet is said to improve the ability of the tourism industry to provide a flexible array of product choices. In effect the tourists themselves have a greater opportunity to create their own 'customised' packages. It can be argued, however, that online travel players will not see significant customer growth unless they create online product offerings that simplify the purchasing process and exceed the value of traditional offerings.

The empowerment of small and medium enterprises through IT: There is an expanding body of work dealing with the potential for e-commerce to 'level the playing field' for smaller businesses that have difficulty accessing traditional tourist distribution channels. It is also clear that the data-mining potential of e-commerce holds great benefits not just for larger firms but also their smaller counterparts. The internet has several key elements that make it an important alternative to traditional marketing approaches : web sites are flexible, the images and text they present can be readily changed; it decentralises and democratises access to the customer; there are cost savings in distribution, service, marketing and promotion.

Labour market impacts: Several commentators are now beginning to focus more closely on the impact that the adoption of the internet and e-commerce strategies can have on labour use, training regimes and service quality delivery in a broad range of tourism sectors.

Disintermediation: There is a growing interest in the impact of the internet on components of the tourism industry that have previously acted as intermediaries between the industry and the consumer (especially travel agents). Some commentators have predicted the demise of the travel agent unless skills are upgraded effectively. Nevertheless, despite falling commissions and increased competition, travel agents have conceded only one per cent of the US online travel market in the past two years. The increasing technological dependence of the industry and processes of industrial concentration are likely to lead to the further strengthening of large enterprises, while also potentially opening opportunities for small flexible firms. The use of networking and strategic alliances will become increasingly important. For small firms this will provide opportunities to overcome the disadvantages (most notably access to technology) associated with their size.

Extreme arguments suggest that cyberspace may even replace tourism as virtual travel technologies mature. What is of immediate concern, however, is how representation of tourist destinations in cyberspace will affect travel patterns. For some, virtual travel may be nothing more than a fancy digital travel brochure. For others, the post-modern virtual travel experience may not be that far off. Indeed we are now able to travel the globe in real-time visiting different locations via the web. The impact of virtual travel in this sense is powerful and some argue that by mixing real and virtual travel we may enhance the possibility of achieving sustainable tourism by replacing impacts on real environments and cultures with virtual experiences . At the same time there are potential dangers inherent in the ability to manipulate representations of tourist products to a greater extent than was possible in traditional travel brochures. The ultimate fear of the tourism industry in its traditional (non-cyber) guise must, however, be that: "Speed kills colour: the gyroscope when it spins quickly turns gray", wrote Paul Morand in 1937.

Thus 'traditional' localised communities have new tools through which to disseminate their concerns, and may, via global networks, gain new 'community members' that can represent their interests around the world. Other commentators argue that the very technologies that are being heralded by some as providing the basis for a resurgence of community life may, instead, simply reinforce existing power structures and inequalities, and lead to social discord and individual isolation.

While there are no clear answers to these debates, it is clear that tourism researchers ignore them at their peril. If we are to understand better the role of the local in the global we must grapple with ICTs impacts on the evolving notion of community and the seductive power of place. We need to be fully aware of the fact that these fundamental technological shifts will have profound impacts on the perception, consumption and construction of tourism spaces, and their local development outcomes.

Where do we go from here?

Tourism is a phenomenon that comprises a collage of producing and consuming moments. It is essentially a global process, which manifests itself locally and regionally, and explicitly involves the construction of place. As such, the study of tourism provides great potential to reveal the dialectics of production and consumption, the tensions between the global and the local, and core issues associated with social and spatial polarisation. The creation of meaning and experiences is becoming a key avenue for capital accumulation, with leisure and tourism at the forefront of this trend.

The identities of geographically defined places, namely tourist destinations, are endlessly re-invented, re-produced, re-captured and re-created by the simultaneous coexistence of global and local forces. Tourism activity not only gives shape to the land, and provides jobs and income to local peoples, but also produces meanings and representations. Tourism promotional material creates and projects powerful social, cultural and psychological meanings of place, in turn increasing and reproducing its value. For their part, consumers collect, read, interpret, compare and communicate these meanings re-producing processes of place re-construction. Over three decades our attempts to understand the links between tourism and local economic development have evolved considerably, from the development of largely 'top-down' theory, to attempts to conceptualize more fully the complexity and nuances of the tourism development process. This complexity is manifest in several dimensions. Consumers are increasingly viewed as 'a highly diverse set of actors who react in grounded and contextual ways'. At the same time it is increasingly apparent that we cannot, and should not, assume that shifts in industry structure and local development outcomes can be 'read off' from patterns predicted by conceptually 'neat' theories of global economic change.

From a geographical perspective, it can therefore be anticipated that institutions will routinely be associated with different (economic) effects in different places; that their forms – and certainly their effects will be difficult to replicate; and that they are unlikely to travel well. This inescapable spatial indeterminacy in institutional forms, dynamics and outcomes, coupled with the necessity for extra-economic regulation of market systems, means that uneven development and local differentiation will remain fundamental features of the real economy. This complexity and uncertainty is only enhanced by the fact that e-business may be about to transform consumer behaviour, value chains, business organisation, notions of community and resultant development outcomes. A new configuration of articulated economic spaces and scales of governance is emerging in the tourism industry. Our challenge as tourism researchers is to embrace this complexity, and not to shy away from dealing with a world of constant evolution and change. We cannot afford simply to view nations, regions and communities as being largely powerless in a globalised world and having to take the 'path of least resistance' in responding to processes of economic globalisation. As Amin and Thrift note so succinctly, the real question is 'not whether globalisation allows scope for national or local action, but what kind of action is necessary for positive engagement with the global economy'.

7

Economic Dimensions of International Tourism

In 1992 at the Rio Earth Summit, 178 governments approved Agenda 21 and the Rio Declaration. Agenda 21 offered a blueprint for sustainable development, while the Rio Declaration articulated the main principles for sustainable development in the 21st century. Both documents challenged organisations, governments and industries to work towards maximum levels of sustainability, defined by the Brundtland Commission in 1987 as 'development that meets the needs of the present without compromising the ability of future generations to meet their own needs'.

Since the summit, the social, political and economic world has developed at a rapid pace. The encroaching globalisation of the world, the increasing necessity and use of technology, and its inherent liberalisation, have altered the way business is conducted and in so doing have affected the relationships between people and the environment. The inevitable global shift towards 'globalisation' is transforming the workplace, the job market, lifestyles, communities, industries and markets.

The challenge for stakeholders involved in all industries is to find a balance between sustenance, prosperity and people's desire to improve their financial/material well-being, with the underlying need for identity, community, religion, home and family. Travel and tourism can play a vital role in balancing these forces.

Travel and tourism also plays a crucial role in encouraging governments to reduce their barriers to growth. Thomas Friedman in his book *The Lexus and the Olive Tree* suggests that governments need to don a 'golden straight jacket' in order to allow pure free market capitalism and enable both developed and developing countries to achieve full economic growth within a sustainable development framework.

The first step to achieving this balance between sustainable development and economic growth for travel and tourism was in 1996. The World Travel & Tourism Council (WTTC), the World Tourism Organisation (WTO/OMT) and the Earth Council, together launched *Agenda 21 for the Travel and Tourism Industry: Towards Environmentally Sustainable Development* a sectoral action plan for sustainable development based on the outcome of the Rio Earth Summit in 1992. At the time it was the only industry-specific adaptation of Agenda 21.

The following definition of tourism was officially adopted by the United Nations Statistical Commission in 1993: 'Tourism comprises the activities of persons travelling to and staying in places outside their usual environment for not more than one consecutive year for leisure, business and other purposes'.

Both the inter-governmental WTO/OMT and the private sector WTTC consider the travel and tourism sector to be one of the largest if not the largest in the world, particularly in terms of its contribution to the world economy. According to WTTC estimates, travel and tourism achieved the following economic impact directly and indirectly in 2001:

- USD3.3 trillion contribution to global GDP, almost 11% of total GDP;
- 207 million jobs worldwide, over 8% of all jobs;
- USD630 billion in capital investment, almost 9% of all capital investment.

This economic activity of the travel and tourism sector was generated by 698 million international tourist arrivals in

2000, representing an estimated 7.3% increase over 1999 according to preliminary estimates. This was the highest growth rate in nearly a decade and almost double the increase of 1999 with nearly 50 million more arrivals recorded, which is approximately what destinations such as Spain or the United States receive in the entire year. In less than a decade, international tourist arrivals are projected to reach one billion.

WTO/OMT submitted a concise report on *Sustainable Development of Tourism* to the United Nations (UN), in which it noted that 'the development of tourism has been characterised by continuing geographical spread and diversification of tourist destinations. While in 1950 the top 15 tourist destinations, all in western Europe and North America, attracted 97% of the world's total arrivals, by 1999 this figure had fallen to 62%, with market shares increasing for developing countries and economies in transition, particularly in south-east Asia, central and eastern Europe, and Latin America.'

The report also noted some of the main qualitative trends seen in the industry in the form of increased market segmentation, the development of new forms of tourism especially those related to nature and wildlife, rural areas and culture and how such programmes are influencing traditional package tours. Clearly, tourists are increasingly selective about destinations and are demanding higher quality products and services.

Tourism products and services that demonstrate 'greater sensitivity to the environment, traditional culture and local people at the destinations can create experience, whereas tourism in a context uncontrolled growth which puts increasing pressure on the natural, cultural and socioeconomic environment, risks diminishing visitor's experience. In short, increased market demand for experiences can contribute social, economic and environmental sustainability only if the resulting pressures from growth are properly planned and managed.

The travel and tourism industry is both receptive and conscious of the resulting pressures from economic growth and the need to protect our natural and social environment.

The preservation of the tourism product the environmental, social or cultural heritage specific to each country is the way to ensure a future for everyone. In response to this increase in recognition the need to safeguard natural resources, growing number of travel and tourism companies are seeking to create more responsible consumer behaviour by using products and services to educate and inform their customers. Many multinational companies such as Lusotur, British Airways, Japan Travel Bureau (JTB),Taj Hotels and Preussag have adopted 'corporate citizenship' programmes that have created dialogue between the community and the private sector, as well promoting sustainable development.

Economic Dimensions

Travel and tourism, if utilised effectively, can be a force for positive growth and economic success for both developed and developing countries. Markets have the potential to enhance lives in a sustainable framework through providing wealth creation, choice, innovation and competition. The travel and tourism industry contains these four elements that enable it to be a dynamic market force for sustainability in the future. It has the capacity to increase exports, bring in capital investment, boost an economies GDP and create employment.

Job Growth

Travel and tourism generates jobs throughout the economy, both in companies directly involved in the business and in related supplier industries such as retail, construction, manufacturing and telecommunications. WTTC estimated that travel and tourism generated 203 million jobs over 8% of all jobs worldwide in 2005, rising to over 207 million in 2007. Within a decade, this is estimated to increase to over 260 million jobs or 9% of all employment. These jobs employ a significant proportion of women, minorities and young people and are predominantly in small and medium-sized enterprises (SMEs). SMEs make up the majority of the travel and tourism sector, although the exact percentage is unknown. SMEs encourage entrepreneurs, provide many diverse job opportunities and enable low skills entry for emerging countries. Successful human resource management, in the shape of training and education, is crucial to achieve the economic prosperity, for both SMEs and the larger multinational companies that can be accrued through tourism. Highly competitive destinations are realising that quality of services and facilities are vital to ensure a consistency of tourists to the destination. On the other hand the fragmentation of the industry and the high proportion of SMEs has led to unconstructive training and protection for employees.

Given the number of low-skilled workers in the sector, the industry has been criticised for offering nothing more than 'hamburger flipping' jobs that contribute little to the sustainability of an economy or society. The travel and tourism industry is renowned for its high turnover, anti-social working hours, low pay, seasonal employment, instability and low job status. However, this does not tell the whole story. *Jobs for the Millennium – Mexico*, a report produced in 2000 by the WTTC and the Fundacitón Pro-Educación en Turismo, AC (FUTUR), paints a different picture of the hospitality workforce. While over 36% of the employees in over 200 companies surveyed were considered 'unskilled', almost a quarter of the jobs at these companies required professional or managerial competence, and over 45% required some level of skill.

Indeed, more than a third of employers surveyed reported serious shortages of skilled workers, which would suggest that real career opportunities do exist. This has met with industry recognition of the need for human resource development that raises the industry's profile, increases productivity and provides sustainable employment. One of the catalysts creating the urgency for trained, skilled workers within the industry is the increasing use of information technology. Travel and tourism is reliant on a human service, yet is increasingly using technology to facilitate the sector in competitive pricing. The growth in tourism forecast for the next ten years, will lead to a greater dependency on information technology, which will become more important in the future as the industry copes with rapid expansion and sophistication of the tourism and hospitality supply.

Tour Operators

While tour operators have a limited number of staff in some of their receiving countries, a huge network of activities and jobs across the economy depends upon delivering the demand for tourism. The tour operator industries reach many areas of the economy such as hotel and infrastructure development, transport services, agriculture, information technology, restaurants and entertainment and media, education and training, consumption of pharmaceutical products, clothing, equipment, and medical services.

Hospitality

The hospitality industry contributes to the important process of job creation. As a labour-intensive industry, it employs large numbers of wage earners, whose taxes and disposable income add to gross domestic output and help to create further employment opportunities. Given that each hotel room typically requires one member of staff, every hotel room built has the potential to create an additional job.

Cruise lines

The bulk of cruise line employees are from countries where employment opportunities are limited and training is scarce. The industry provides the opportunity to travel, free medical care and upward mobility, particularly for women from developing nations.

Tourism Contributions to the Economy

In order to achieve sustainable economic growth, the travel and tourism sector needs to reduce social, economic, environmental and cultural barriers. Some of the major obstacles to this growth are the lack of infrastructure, environmental degradation and fragile linkages that weaken a country's tourism potential. One way to address these barriers is for the sector to foster tourism investment through public-private sector partnerships that not only enable a country to grow economically, but retain the essential social, cultural and environmental assets that make each country a unique product.

Public-private sector co-operation and planning are also essential to creating sustainable employment in the tourism industry, and to this end the private sector has fought for recognition of its true contribution to job growth and economic development. Hitherto, the industry had been disadvantaged by a lack of data reflecting its full economic impact. Only recently has the methodology known as Tourism Satellite Accounting (TSA), pioneered by WTTC,WTO/OMT and others, been developed and accepted by governments as a means for fully measuring travel and tourism's contribution as an economic activity.

TSA is based on a 'demand-side' concept of economic activity (*i.e.,* the economic activities of visitors and travel companies), as tourism does not supply a homogenous product or service. Unlike traditional industries (agriculture, electronics, steel, *etc.*), travel and tourism is a diverse set of industries offering a multitude of products (consumer and capital durables and non-durables), and services ranging from airline and cruise ship fares and accommodations, to restaurant meals, entertainment, souvenirs and gifts, immigration and park services, recreational vehicles and automobiles, aircraft manufacturing and resort development.

By using input/output modelling, TSA is able to differentiate between travel and tourism industry supply and economy supply, including that portion of supply which it imports from abroad. Additionally, it breaks down the supply side accounts into direct and indirect impacts and the individual elements of GDP (wages and salaries, transaction taxes, operating surplus, depreciation and subsidies).These data ensure governments have a broader understanding of the impact of travel and tourism, in particular the implications of policy for the travel and tourism economy.

TSA data also reiterates the fact that travel and tourism has the potential to be a catalyst industry for emerging countries to kick-start their economies, offering many opportunities that are not available in other industries. For example, the rise in cultural, heritage and wildlife niche market tourism, in developing countries, is becoming a viable alternative for communities that want to move away from mono-culture farming, which can not only destroy sustainable patterns of agriculture and traditional fertility cycles but has been associated with negative changes in social structures and economic relationships.

Annual research undertaken by WTTC demonstrates that the impact of travel and tourism on the whole economy is much greater than the size of the industry itself. For every dollar spent on travel and tourism, a further dollar and a half is typically contributed to GDP in other sectors of the economy.

Tour Operators

Tour operators can have a significant impact upon economies. Whereas the Balearic Islands were the poorest province in the whole of Spain in 1950, by the year 2000 it was the richest almost entirely due to organised tourism. Other countries where travel and tourism has had a positive impact on the economy are the Maldives, Mexico and Turkey.

Hospitality

The hotel industry has considerable growth potential in those nations and regions that are just beginning to develop their economies and improve their performance, because the total output of the hotel industry is closely tied to the variables associated with economic development. These variables include basic infrastructure and levels of gross domestic output, employment, and education of the workforce. The hospitality industry also produces a 'multiplier effect' whereby money spent by hotel guests travels through a community generating further revenue.

Cruise lines

The cruise line industry is a significant economic contributor worldwide and particularly to the United States economy, leaking into industry, agriculture, airlines, travel agents, food and beverage suppliers and other service sectors. It is also a booming industry that is forecast to grow to 20.7 million passengers by 2010.

Social Dimensions

Tourism can be both a force for the preservation of or, conversely, a threat to a community's natural and cultural heritage. A 1999 report *Sustainable Tourism and Cultural Heritage* published by the World Bank underscores the symbiotic nature of the relationship. The mutual dependence that exists between tourism and cultural heritage is becoming more evident. While culture heritage creates a foundation for tourism's growth, tourism has the power to generate funds that make conservation possible. Cultural heritage loses much of its meaning without an audience, and a society participating in and benefiting from it. Without sustainable management, tourism loses its potential for growth. With the growing interest in culture and community, tourism is finally being recognised as an industry that can boost rural economies, create entrepreneurs and jobs and help preserve indigenous cultures. 'Above all, tourism offers a better life not just for those who make money, but for those who pay money to enjoy it'. For example, trekking tourism has led to the transformation of the traditional subsistence farming of the Sherpas of the Khumbu region into a cash economy that has generated income, jobs and a better standard of living. One of the main challenges, therefore, for all stakeholders involved in travel and tourism, including local authorities, NGOs and businesses, is to maintain an optimal balance to ensure sustainability. Otherwise, in destinations where the natural and cultural heritage deteriorates, the economy will be put at risk as tourists migrate to better-preserved destinations. The Addo Elephant National Park in

South Africa's Eastern Cape Province aimed to integrate community tourism initiatives with mainstream tourism. A multi-stakeholder dialogue process was adopted including all private and public sector voices. The outcome was that local groups have the potential to add diversification to a primarily wildlife destination and the private sector has the key for effective marketing and business development skills.

The business case and corporate citizenship have become joined in current debate about the changing role of business in society. Multinationals can help contribute to the wealth and welfare of us all, and increasingly leading players in the travel and tourism industry are recognising the importance of the contributions they can make to the communities within which they work. Corporate citizenship balances the interests of the economy with those of public policymakers, individuals and groups in civil society.

Tour Operators Initiative

The Tour Operators Initiative (TOI) launched in March 2007 is a network of tour operators that have joined forces to improve their practices, as well as raise the awareness of the industry. TOI acts as a platform to develop ideas and projects to address the environmental, social, economic and cultural aspects of sustainable development within the tourism sector.

Developed by tour operators, for tour operators, it has the support of UNEP, UNESCO and WTO/OMT. The members of TOI commit to:

- Adopt practices with regard to environmental, social-cultural and economic impacts of their activities internally and when forming business relationships with partners, suppliers and subcontractors;
- Encourage and seek co-operation with all stakeholders at destinations to develop integrated planning and management of destinations;
- Create awareness among their customers towards the natural, social and cultural environments they visit by promoting, in their communication and advertising,

behaviours and activities compatible with the principles of sustainable development.

Hospitality

As a major component of travel and tourism, the hospitality industry has a vested interest in protecting the environment its key resource and most hotels are likely to take a multitude of environmental actions that extend beyond the control of any single monitoring agency. Self-regulation appears to be the most viable course of action for this industry, whether in the form of in-house environmental audits, the adoption of an environmental management system, and/or application for co-certification.

Cruise Lines

ICCL members adhere to international conventions that have set a global benchmark for environmental and safety standards. In 1999, a forum on the situation of waste management and disposal practices led to a number of major initiatives being undertaken by the industry in potential problem areas. The cruise line industry has some of the strictest safety regulations and has one of the most enviable safety records. In July 2001, ICCL members adopted standards on environmental management.

Environmental Dimensions

The travel and tourism industry has come far since the Earth Summit in Rio de Janeiro,, when the impact of industries on the environment was high on the political agenda. The increasing numbers of travellers and the rise in package tours were causing a valid concern among environmentalists.

WTTC, with WTO/OMT and the Earth Council, in response to the scrutiny with which tourism was judged, collabourated and produced *Agenda 21 for the Travel & Tourism Industry*. This public-private sector effort was designed to ensure that as travel and tourism grew globally, its influence would not have an undesirable impact on the environment. Indeed all areas of travel and tourism have over the last decade implemented many individual environmental schemes and programmes, not for-pròfit funds and foundations all over the world.

Recently there has also been an increase in conferences on the environment hosted by governments and by private sector companies, which are highlighting the responsibility of both the public and private sector to protect natural and cultural heritage and emphasise the importance of environmental sustainability. If tourism is not planned and managed carefully, it can overwhelm the very assets with which it attracts visitors to the destination. Examples of tourism expansion, that have ignored the local environment, are well-known: tourism facilities built on pristine land without prior consultation with the local community; golf greens that use up scarce water supplies; water pipes and infrastructure that feed major developments but often ignore the local village. With the rise of mass tourism comes the threat of destruction of fragile eco-systems and coastal regions, local culture, and the depletion of natural resources. Conversely, tourism can generate the necessary revenue to protect and preserve biodiversity and act as a force for environmental protection especially in developing countries. Game parks and nature preserves are centres of institutional strength and can act as a focus for tourism development in rural areas.

The new concept of eco-tourism or nature tourism is experiencing faster-than-average growth. Eco-tourism alone contributed $154 billion in receipts in 2000 and is growing 20% annually compared with just 7% for tourism overall(31) in an already booming industry, and reflects those consumers who are aware of the issues facing travel and tourism. There are indications that consumers are also beginning to influence businesses, as they become more aware of the choices available to them, and of this rapid growth in the ecotourism niche market. However, eco-tourism alone is not the answer to addressing the environmental problems facing the industry.

It also remains to be seen how far consumers have the willingness to encourage businesses to adopt more sustainably-developed tourism, especially if it means paying higher prices.

How the industry has responded to sustainable tourism development Dialogue between stakeholders in both the private and public sectors, has led to the establishment of global voluntary initiatives throughout the last decade. These initiatives have taken various forms and represent all sectors of the travel and tourism industry.

Although there has been an encouraging explosion of such schemes, adoption of them by the industry is as yet limited. It has proved particularly difficult to encourage SMEs to participate in sustainable good practice. A small sample of examples of these initiatives are given in the following paragraphs.

Codes of Conduct

In 1992 the Pacific Asia Tourism Association (PATA) introduced its *Code for Environmentally Responsible Tourism* to strengthen the principles of conservation in the region, soliciting membership in its Green Leaf programme. Addressing one of the most sensitive social implications of tourism development, a multistakeholder, international public-private initiative has recently drafted the *Code of Conduct for the Protection of Children from Sexual Exploitation in Travel and Tourism.* The Africa Travel Association's *Responsible Traveller Guidelines* and the Japanese Association of Travel Agents' *Declaration of Earth Friendly Travellers* are just two examples of the many industry codes aimed at educating and influencing their customers.

Green Globe 21

As a follow-up to the Earth Summit, WTTC set up Green Globe. Now an independent private sector company, Green Globe 21 is an Agenda 21-based industry improvement programme, which provides guidance material and a certification process linked to both ISO standards and Agenda 21 principles, throughout the world.

Dodo

The CyberDodo programme, developed by CyberDodo Productions and supported by WTTC and by the United Nations High Commissioner for Human Rights, is designed to raise awareness among adults and children of important issues concerning the environment, human rights and children's rights. The programmes have already been shown in more than 60 countries.

Green Key

Green Key, Denmark, a scheme operated by the Hotel, Restaurant and Leisure Industry Association (HORESTA) in that country, applies 78 criteria to be met by properties seeking certification.

Eco-labels

UNEP's comprehensive publication on *Ecolabels in the Tourism Industry* examines this form of voluntary self-regulation in the tourism industry with the aim of helping applicants to understand the nature of eco-labelling schemes.

These private sector strategies are fast becoming an essential part of the process of sustaining natural and cultural heritage because the industry has a direct impact on local communities in which they operate. Some of these programmes not only provide valuable funds to support poorer host communities, but also help encourage protection of the environment and natural resources that often get depleted by the different sectors of the industry.

Future Challenges and Goals

To achieve the goals and challenges set for the travel and tourism industry as it continues to grow throughout the coming decades, will require a strong and co-operative partnership between government departments, national tourism authorities, international and national trade associations, trade unions and the travel and tourism private sector. All stakeholders now need to share the responsibility for travel and tourism's future and need to deliver the following to ensure its sustainability:

Governments need to:

- Integrate travel and tourism policy, especially the environment, into broader government policies;
- Set up realistic capacities within sustainability frameworks, which have been set in consultation with industry and other stakeholders;
- Create incentives for the travel and tourism industry backed up where necessary by effective regulation;
- Be committed to the controlled expansion, where appropriate, of infrastructure;
- Apply environmental taxes fairly and nondiscriminatorily, where needed. They should be carefully thought out to minimise their impact on economic development, and revenues should be allocated to travel and tourism-associated environment improvement programmes;
- Set up mechanisms to support SMEs in the adoption of sustainable good practice;
- Design policies creating incentives for corporate social responsibility in tourism, favouring a sensitive and engaging approach towards the local communities at the destinations, especially in the developing countries.

Public-private partnerships need to:

- Plan and develop infrastructure with a long-term view and within a reference framework based on Agenda 21;
- Implement indicators and environmental impact assessment tools to enable successful and effective local management and appropriate development;
- Agree on common standards and tools to enable the measurement of progress towards achieving sustainable development;

- Fund and develop contemporary research into sustainable tourism. Issues requiring attention include design, carrying capacity, tour operator activities, environmental reporting, and auditing and environmental impact assessments, socio-economic sustainability of the tourism businesses.

International bodies need to:

- Co-ordinate environmental action to be undertaken by all sectors of the travel and tourism industry, at an international level;
- Review existing voluntary initiatives to improve the quality of reporting, their transparency and credibility, and the assessment of their contribution to sustainability;
- Ensure that all funding, from international, national and local funding bodies, should be dependent on sound environmental practice;
- Encourage and support multi-stakeholder projects aiming for sustainable tourism development;
- Set up mechanisms to support the adoption of sustainable good practices by SMEs.

Private sector companies need to:

- Commit to place sustainable development issues at the core of the management structure;
- Develop and more widely apply certification criteria to industry initiatives;
- Innovate processes and applications through new technology;
- Make a commitment to the education and environmental training of staff;
- Encourage corporate citizenship as the standard for private sector companies;
- be willing to engage in multi-stakeholder dialogue.

The Way Forward

In recent years the UN has begun to make travel and tourism a priority in the sustainable development debate. In 1999,WTTC and IH&RA were designated by the United Nations Commission on Sustainable Development to represent the industry in a multi-stakeholder dialogue at its seventh session (UNCSD7). It was concluded that 'voluntary measures developed with multistakeholder participation, mutual trust and respect, transparency, monitoring, and assessment and verification were seen as most likely to generate confidence and support from all parties'.

The travel and tourism industry increasingly recognises the need for protecting culture, heritage and the environment and this responsibility must be shared by all stakeholders. It also needs to be balanced by a proportionate recognition that travel and tourism has the potential to bring social and environmental, as well as economic benefits. This would give developing countries the possibility to attain the full economic potential tourism can give. This must be coupled with sufficient training in management skills and education for local people. The human resources issue will be of much concern in the next few years because, without substantial and skilled human capital, the tourism industry cannot be productive in the future.

Adequate planning and development is also vital so that fragile eco-systems and scarce natural resources can be utilised effectively and protected for future generations. Moreover, the prevailing issues facing infrastructure are becoming more acute with the continuing increase in passenger travel. Governmental infrastructure constraints pose a critical barrier and can jeopardise anticipated economic growth and job creation with knock-on effects to all sectors of the community. The fundamental infrastructure issues such as airport congestion, air traffic management, sources of capital investment, regulation and political support, and institutional reform facing the sustainable development and growth of travel and tourism, concern both the private and public sectors. Governments are beginning to take a more dynamic role in developing sustainable and economically-successful tourism, but there urgentiy needs to be more proactive participation from government. With effective networking processes, legitimate policies, planning and development from government, tourism can alter its adverse environmental image to one of sustainability and stewardship. The many and varied voluntary industry initiatives, ranging from education to certification, are an important and imperative part of the ongoing process working towards sustainable development.

Tour Operators

Tour operators are looking at implementing strategies that combat both the indirect, as well as direct, impacts that tour operations have on the environment and the communities within which they operate. Direct issues that are being addressed include better information to consumers, ensuring that sustainable development concepts, procedures and practices are included in training programmes, and greater adherence to tour operator codes of conduct. Indirect impacts being addressed are the monitoring of subcontracted suppliers in environmental performance and having more involvement with other stakeholders in the sustainable development process.

Hospitality

Hotels from all geographic regions are successfully implementing strategies in favour of sustainable development. Key areas of progress include rising levels of awareness that using resources in an efficient and environmentally-sensible manner can positively impact the bottom line, and the recognition that transparency and reporting make for good business practice.

Cruise lines

As global leaders in the maritime industry, the members of ICCL strive to preserve local environments and cultural heritage, and work to generate and infuse local economies with sustainable income. Through public-private sector alliances ICCL devises solutions to all of the challenges facing the cruise lines sectors, and works in partnership with a number of public bodies and environmental agencies to find productive solutions to the issues that confront the industry on a daily basis. The need to maintain a sustainable travel and tourism sector is now becoming an urgency. WTTC wants to share a vision of the world where travel and tourism benefits everyone, making a positive, growing and sustainable contribution to the prosperity, understanding and well-being of people, shared by those who travel and the communities they visit, and their social, cultural and natural environments.

WTTC believes the way forward to achieving sustainable development for industry leaders is to lead by example and to practise corporate citizenship and responsible capitalism. For the industry sector to implement sustainable development initiatives successfully there needs to be a multi-stakeholder process whereby all stakeholders take responsibility for the future of travel and tourism. The industry is both willing and ready to undertake this dialogue and this report is one of the first steps to achieving this.

The Tour Operator Industry

Role and Influence of Tour Operators

The outbound tour operator has emerged in the past 50 years as a useful means of distributing leisure air travel and accommodation services to consumers. Consumers in one country wishing to visit another require information and want to book travel arrangements in advance. Tour operators obtain information, make contracts with suppliers of services, and publish their holiday offers in brochures, which are distributed directly to consumers or by travel agents.

Tour operators judge overall demand and the expected demand for each destination and seek to satisfy that demand if it can be accomplished profitably. Tour operators assemble the component parts of holidays. Another report covers air travel and other sections in this report cover the hospitality and cruise lines industry. There is limited value added as reflected in profit margins that represent 1% to 2% of turnover. Present in substantial numbers in Europe (approximately 5,000) and in the United States, Canada, Japan, South Korea, Russia, Australia, New Zealand, South and Latin America, tour operators remain small in number where tourism is less developed. Globally, they represent around 12% of international arrivals, while in Europe they account for 35% of leisure air holidays. There are five substantial European outbound tour operators, the remaining 4,995 being SMEs employing five to 100 people, which often cater for specialist interests or low volume destinations. The five large companies have integrated activities (travel agencies, tour operations, airlines, hotels, cruise ships and ground handling), but these are not exclusively used by the one integrated organisation. For example, owned airlines are used for some of the flight requirements, but large tour operators can have contracts with more than 150 airlines and owned airlines, and contract seats out to non-owned tour operators.

Economic Dimensions

Tour operating employs relatively few people across the world (a few tens of thousands), but their activities can stimulate hotel and infrastructure development. These include water, sewerage, airports, roads etc, transport services, agriculture, information technology, restaurants, entertainment and media, education and training, consumption of pharmaceutical products, clothing, equipment, medical services, excursion venues and public administration concerned with policy-making, marketing and management of tourism.

While tour operators have a limited number of staff in some of their receiving countries, a huge network of activities and jobs across the economy depend upon delivering the demand for tourism. The marketing efforts of tour operators are what the suppliers of services and governments look for.

The countries visited are 80% intra-regional (*e.g.*, Germany to Spain, Australia to Thailand) and 20% long-haul (*e.g.*, Europe to the Caribbean, Japan to Europe, the United States to Far

East). Tour operators can have a significant impact upon economies. Whereas the Balearic Islands were the poorest province in the whole of Spain in 1950, by the year 2000 it was the richest almost entirely due to organised tourism. The Maldives is no longer to be classified as a 'lesser developed country' thanks to the economic impact of tourism, particularly organised tourism. Cancun in Mexico had a local population of 600 before tourism arrived. It now provides income for 600,000 and support for ten times that number through organised tourism from North and South America, and Europe. In Turkey, tourism revenues reach 30% of total commodity exports, most attributed to organised tourism. Foreign exchange received by countries through tour operators takes the form of payments to hotels and ground handlers as well as taxes, duties and charges. In addition, consumers spend money outside the hotel on the 'complementary offer'. This amount can vary from 150% of the hotel cost in countries such as Spain to virtually zero in those developing countries that offer little to see, do or buy.

Outbound tourism demand is affected by confidence in economic conditions and security as well as perceptions of discretionary income. Leisure outbound travel has been growing at around one and a half times the growth in GDP and is not highly volatile, unless there are safety concerns. Fluctuations in tourism revenues in receiving countries are more marked due to consumer perceptions of the relative safety and attractiveness of destinations, as well as changes in relative price.

Social Dimensions

The ability to travel and to witness other cultures not only brings prosperity to the receiving country, but also fosters understanding and tolerance in the visitor. The tour operator offer based on high volumes, bulk buying and low prices has provided access to travel to millions of people. The tour operator's main contribution has been to increase tourism volume in many destinations that would otherwise have had little tourism development. However, the way in which different countries and destinations have dealt with the effects of this increase varies widely.

Influences of Increased Tourism on Citizens of Receiving Countries

By far the most positive influence of tourism has been on the citizens of the receiver countries, where the foreign influx has provided income for much greater social choices than have hitherto existed and accelerated the process of modernisation and openness. As local people have become richer through tourism, countries dependent on international tourism have found themselves generating a greater number of domestic tourists. The effect of this phenomenon in Spain, for example, has been the restoration of a strong Spanish identity both cultural and culinary which had been weakened. Tour operator distribution has created jobs in originating countries, particularly for women in travel agencies, airlines, airports and hotels as well as for tour operators themselves.

Negative social consequences have been felt in a number of different and significant ways. The 'homogenisation' of global products and services devoid of local identity has been exacerbated by tourism movements. There is no doubt that people brought for a short time to another country seek to retain their own habits and practices while host communities adapt to satisfy visitor tastes in order to make money from them. Those with vulnerable cultures are likely to suffer most and local disaffection is most keenly felt where there are high densities of tourists. Reaction tends to come from regional, religious or cultural entities attempting to preserve key features that provide a manifestation of a local identity.

Overall, the opportunity for jobs in tourism and tourism-related activities in receiving countries have been very positive, as has the opportunity for training and development. However, a major market failure has been the inability to develop and diversify the complementary offer (things to see, buy or do outside the hotel) that would provide extra jobs and income in the community and allow monies to be distributed more widely and deeply. This remains a significant opportunity to alleviate poverty in some developing countries. In countries where the money economy is limited and unemployment high, tourism can be seen to benefit the few who are directly involved in tourism, leaving workers in the informal economy marginalised and disaffected. In addition, children vulnerable to sexual exploitation have found themselves targeted by a small number of paedophiles.

The Role of Tour Operators in the Community

Tour operators have many sub-contracted suppliers that are expected to deliver quality services under some form of supervision. They rely upon close relationships with people working in the destinations at airports, hotels, restaurants, excursion venues, public administrations, medical authorities, *etc.* for without them, holidays could not be delivered.

Tour operators have resident staff, or those of their local agents that maintain these relationships and are expected to become familiar with concerns expressed by local communities. Where good quality accommodation for customers is in short supply, many tour operators co-finance developments on a short-term basis. Tour operators act as a bridge between suppliers, customers and the country visited, providing information about the destination, safety and cultural sensitivity (dress codes, etc). With smaller guided tours, customers often seek greater detailed interaction and are very aware of their social and cultural responsibilities.

The Role of the IFTO

The International Federation of Tour Operators (IFTO) acts as the spokesperson for tour operators (and their clients) with municipalities, regional and national governments and international organisations such as the WTO/OMT, UNCTAD, WHO, UNESCO, UNEP, and the EU. Issues range from the broadest level (*e.g.*, Code of Ethics of Tourism at WTO/OMT) to the narrowest (*e.g.*, provision of clean water to particular hotels or districts).

Its dealings with the public administration involve ministries of foreign affairs, home affairs, public works, environment, transport, tourism, education, health and finance.

In the private sector, all the actors in tourism and related to tourism are involved in discussions. As tourism is a horizontal activity, co-ordination, consultation and partnerships (public-public, private-private and public-private partnerships) are essential for it to be successful.

Environmental Dimensions

The direct environmental impact of tour operators is relatively limited, but there are ways in which they can have a positive influence. Tour operators communicate with customers mainly through paper-based media, therefore brochures need to be used efficiently and to be sourced from renewable forests and recycled whenever possible. Offices need to consume as little energy as possible and customers need to be encouraged to make choices and to behave in ways that are socially and environmentally acceptable. In considering the indirect effects of tour operators encouraging people to travel, a distinction needs to be made between developed and developing nations when considering environmental action. Developed nations have the technical and financial resources to monitor and enforce environmental standards in tourism development and, in many cases, the political will to act as well as a body of planning regulations. In these circumstances, should a problem arise (*e.g.*, an individual hotel failing to perform at the level required) a basis for negotiation exists between the governing authorities and the local tourism actors together with IFTO.

Developing countries may have priorities that are more pressing than sustainable development in tourism. There may be neither the political will nor the technical or financial resources to monitor environmental performance. In these situations it is important for the tour operator and other tourism actors to adopt self-regulation. For example, in the Antarctic where no legal framework exists and the environment is highly vulnerable, tour operators and cruise ships have signed up to a defined code of conduct. This is weaker than a legal solution as no effective sanctions can be applied to those not adhering to the code.

Energy Consumption/emissions

Tour operators encourage people to travel from their local airport, which usually means a taxi or a car journey. (A taxi journey is twice as long as that by the owner-driver, and doubles energy consumption/emissions). Airports have been extended as a result of consumer demand – larger aircraft are now used. Tour operators seek out the lowest seat mile costs – this requires in turn, high-density seating and fuel-efficient modern aircraft operating at high load factors. The resulting emissions of noise, CO_2 and NOx per passenger are lower than for other forms of aviation, but nonetheless would not have occurred had customers stayed at home.

Customers are usually transported from the destination airport to the hotel by modern diesel-engined or gas-powered coaches which can carry up to 58 people and have low seat/ mile CO2 emissions. These vehicles reduce the incidence of car traffic by more than 25 times. However, in many developing countries these are not available; LPG (liquid petroleum gas) or CNG (compressed nitrogen gas) distribution is extremely limited. While at the hotel, visitor energy consumption/ emissions due to air-conditioning is broadly equivalent to energy consumption/emissions through central heating at home unless, as in Cyprus, all tourist establishments are required to install solar panels, in which case energy consumption by tourists will be less than that by residents. In beach destinations where movement outside hotels is limited to excursions, consumption/emissions during a two-week stay are likely to be much less than staying at home.

Water Consumption?

The huge majority of tourists fly from colder to warmer climates in countries with beaches nearer the equator, which get less rain and have less available water. Although tourism uses very little water compared with agriculture, there is a significant increase in the consumption of water as a result of tourism. De-salination plants have been installed in some areas of high-density tourism where there are water shortages. Hotels pay for water consumption by volume and this is reflected in prices to consumers. Many hotels employ systems (including incentives for customers) to reduce consumption of water and energy consumption and waste, but this remains a major issue in much of the developed and developing world.

Waste Management

Sewerage systems are expensive and 'high tech' systems are required to avoid contamination of seawater. These may be funded through central/local government and through multi-lateral sources. Huge investments have taken place in coastal areas of high tourism density, but much remains to be done. Likewise, solid waste is a major issue for many municipalities operating in tourism areas.

Planning Regulations

Where construction of airports, roads, hotels and other infrastructure is concerned, planning regulations that determine maximum spread and density are required to maintain an appropriate balance. Where local governance is weak there are frequent examples of over development. The degradation of heritage sites that suffer from visitor congestion is another issue, which has yet to be dealt with satisfactorily.

Key Areas of Progress

In the past ten years, a lot of progress has been made. Firstly, information to consumers by tour operators has vastly improved although there are still no objective international measures to indicate to consumers the environmental performance of sub-contracted suppliers or destinations. A plethora of eco-labels exist, but none with global credibility. Secondly, tour operators have developed and attempt to comply with codes of conduct, with some success.

The response of tour operators to global warming issues relating to emissions has been to encourage zero emission engine manufacture and ensure that emissions per passenger are the lowest currently available economically by using modern fuel-efficient aircraft and coaches with high-density seating. In terms of indirect impact, where tour operators have been accepted as legitimate partners in tourism development in many countries and destinations, there is the opportunity for the tour operator to be influenced by, as well as to influence, the behaviour of various public and private sector actors in the destinations. However, results are very varied both between and within countries. It is in the area of tourism management that the large tour operators have sought to influence the public and private sectors. Many tour operators seek to monitor the environmental performance of sub-contracted suppliers and destinations. They support countries and regions in implementing the development processes of local 'Agenda 21s' and actively promote the harmonisation of local, communal and regional needs in tourism development plans. They support measures that help in visitor management and make their own staff aware of sustainable development needs.

Strong governance and institutional frameworks have helped to manage flows of tourism through tour operators in most developed nations, although more could be accomplished. In the developing world this has been less effective with the exception of low volume specialist destinations, which have benefited from responsible management policies of tour operators. It is in the few developing countries with volumes of tourists that are not appropriate for the habitat or current infrastructure that problems can arise. It should be emphasised that multi-stakeholder involvement in receiving countries/destinations can only be effective if tour operators are included as active partners. In the end it is for the country/destination to determine what role tourism should play in their community and what policies they want to follow. Attempts by outsiders (*e.g.*, tour operators or NGOs) to create solutions based on 'western criteria' are almost certain to fail.

Key Areas for Improvement

Key areas for improvement include:

- Tour operators need to develop a responsible tourism policy;
- Better information to consumers from tour operators, particularly on credible environmental standards applied to and monitored among sub-contracted suppliers;
- Stronger relationships with tour operators and local public-private sector actors in all significant tourism destinations to support destination management policies aimed at sustainable development. This should lead to constructive consultation as well as the emergence of true local partnerships;
- significant development of the 'complementary offer' to create jobs among women and the local community in developing countries, and greater development of local agriculture to provide specific foods for tourists;
- Encouragement of zero-emission terrestrial vehicles and aircraft;
- Management of water, waste and energy consumption and the protection of tourism sites (heritage and natural) from unmanaged tourism flows that degrade both the natural environment and the visitor experience;
- Encourage tour operators to adopt self regulation through appropriate codes of conduct specific to habitat and destination where there are insufficient governance and institutional frameworks;
- Raising tour operators' awareness of the social dimension of sustainable development and ensuring that policies and communications to consumers reflect local community concerns;
- Tour operators need to ensure those sustainable tourism development concepts, procedures and

practices are included in their management and representative training programmes;

- Tour operators need to set goals for sustainable development against which their performance can be measured and reported both internally and publicly.

Means of Implementation

Tour operators use a variety of tools to create feedback systems to alert the tour operators as well as public and private actors in the destinations.

- TUI, a part of Preussag, one of the largest tour operators in the world, with 23 million customers, and Scandinavian Leisure Group, part of MyTravel, track the environmental performance of destinations and sub-contracted suppliers;
- Many of the small tour operators have clear guidelines for their staff to follow and report back on adverse consequences of their tourism activity. Customers, too, are quick to bring to the attention of tour operators' adverse consequences. NGOs can also contribute their views; the issues raised are commonly dealt with through the local contacts of tour operators in the destination. Otherwise, in a destination with high volumes of tourists, IFTO is often used to communicate the adverse consequences and recommend remedial action; more recently, the Tour Operator Initiative has provided the beginnings of a network of tour operators large and small, to develop better policies and systems of implementation; IFTO has played an active and prominent role with WTO/OMT by chairing its Business Council. Sustainable development is a key part of WTO/OMT's programme of work.

Future Challenges and Goals

Tour operators should set the goal of introducing a comprehensive responsible tourism policy covering direct action and indirect impacts, within the next five years. Tour operators direct action: better information to consumers; more use of electronic communication; reduction in use of paper; better use of recycled paper and paper from renewable forests; eliminate use of toxic paper coating; aggregate performance data to support corporate annual reporting and year on year improvements,

- Ensure that sustainable development concepts, procedures and practices are included in management and representative training programmes;
- Ensure greater adherence to tour operator codes of conduct.

Success in the above areas will depend on:

- The development of agreed international criteria against which to measure the environmental performance of subcontracted suppliers in order to keep consumers better informed;
- The extent of the use of electronic means of communication;
- Technological innovation and progress that will allow the development of low cost, thin (low weight) shiny paper for brochures that have high levels of environmental performance.

Tour operators indirect impacts:

- Tour operators need to improve their monitoring of the social and environmental performance of sub-contracted suppliers and destinations;
- Tour operators should develop stronger relationships with local public and private sector actors in all significant tourism destinations, to support destination management policies and strategies aimed at sustainable development.

In addition, tour operators need to:

- Protect the natural environment and cultural heritage,

- Conserve plants and animals, protected areas and landscapes,
- Respect the integrity of local cultures and their social institutions.

Most international visitors are unfamiliar with the countries they visit. To assist them plan and operate their itineraries, hotels, visits and attractions, the role of the incoming tour operator, agent or ground handler has emerged. Many are simply organised as a service to customers, others have broadened the scope of their activities through backward integration by buying coach companies and hotels. With the emergence of outbound tour operators, the role of the incoming tour operator has been much enhanced. Contracts are made between the two to deliver transfers and excursions and (on occasions) hotels. The incoming tour operator provides all logistical support as well as providing local knowledge (commercial, legal, political and environmental) on what can and cannot be done.

Very few incoming tour operators have been acquired by outbound tour operators, and 99% remain as local independent businesses. Worldwide there are many thousands of incoming tour operators. In developing countries, in particular, these local businesses compete to represent tour operators and those that fail resent that all the business of the outbound tour operator goes through one local business. The incoming tour operator attempts to create a range of offers to attract consumers that are practical in terms of logistics and the environment and provide the right price/value to consumers and profits to themselves. From the perspective of the suppliers in the receiving destination, the incoming tour operator forms part of their destination network for which they are prepared to pay. The outbound tour operator can also play a role in that distribution to customers. The coach companies play a crucial role in the batch distribution of customers from airport to hotels and on tours to excursion venues. Their fleets are, in the main, very modern and well maintained. The rent-a-car companies usually provide new or nearly new vehicles for hire. The economic value of rent-a-cars for tourism is that customers can reach destinations not accessible without motorised transport.

The major attractions act as magnets to tourists providing the motivation for visits and leading to increased use of hotel rooms, roads, airports, rail transport as well as the land use for the attraction itself. They can provide a major drive for increased local employment. Major attractions depend on very high visitor throughput.

Social and Environmental Dimensions

The incoming tour operators can, and do, lay down clear policies and procedures for subcontracted suppliers to follow to protect the environment (for example, relating to driving on safari in Africa) and to support enlightened social policies, (portering in mountainous areas in south-east Asia). However, these local businesses are run on local labour law, regulations, custom and practice. In some developing countries, the custom and practice may not meet the standards demanded, for example, by International Labour Organisation (ILO). Outbound tour operators can have influence over how their passengers are handled by the incoming tour operators/ suppliers, however, they have no influence on how the incoming tour operator arranges for the majority of their work with their suppliers that takes place with individuals on independently organised groups. The incoming tour operators recognise that they have a significant role to play in tourism development. Their decisions on excursion venues and planning of trips can have strong impacts on particular communities. These communities are in competition with each other for offering attractions to tourists who have limited time (*e.g.*, craft markets).Tourists will often go to one craft market, but not two, so decisions by incoming tour operators count heavily.

The obligation of the coach companies is to ensure that the vehicles are safe and secure and emit the lowest emissions possible with the use of local fuels. Their social obligations relate to conditions of work, particularly drivers' hours, as well as driving and parking procedures.

The major attractions can be of cultural heritage *e.g.*, Karnak,Taj Mahal, or can be recently man-made *e.g.*, Disney or Universal Studios. The attractions of cultural heritage can lead to excessive use and congestion and to environmental degradation. The man-made attractions have imposed upon them a panoply of planning and social regulation with which to comply. This includes stringent environmental impact assessments before any project is finally approved.

The opportunities for incoming tour operators are to be recognised for the important and influential role they can play in tourism development. As small local enterprises, they are often not brought into policy discussions with government at the appropriate level. The challenges for incoming tour operators, agents and ground handlers are:

- To obtain from government recognition their influential role,
- To take a balanced and responsible approach to the provision of services that they provide within the context and possibilities of their local conditions,
- To influence their subcontracted suppliers to adopt a similar balanced responsible approach.

The coach and rent-a-car companies will adopt more fuel-efficient, and eventually, emission-free vehicles. What will then remain the question of congestion and the challenge of the measures taken by them, together with the authorities responsible for traffic management. Their objective should be to manage congestion, so that delays and disruption to the visitor experience are minimised. The challenge for attractions is to contribute to and obtain measures for access and subsequent distribution of very large numbers of customers, while complying with their social and environmental responsibilities. The hospitality sector (*i.e.*, hotels and restaurants) is an essential and dynamic component of the world's largest industry travel and tourism. The global hotel industry covers a wide range of accommodation services from full-service luxury hotels to bed and breakfast operations, inns, all-suite hotels, and limited service and economy properties. These establishments may be owned and/or managed by independent operators, multinational chains, insurance companies, pension funds, governments and other investors.

The International Hotel & Restaurant Association (IH&RA) as the sole trade association exclusively dedicated to representing the hospitality industry at the international level, is also the only body to have attempted to quantify the size and scale of the sector on a global basis. This research was published in 1995 and 2000 in the form of two White Papers on the Global Hospitality Industry. Their findings indicate that as of 1997 the industry comprised over 301,400 hotel properties worldwide, totalling 13 million rooms and generating over USD202 billion in revenues. It identifies the largest concentration of hotels in the European Economic Area (EEA) with 159,226 properties, followed by the North American region, with just over 65,000 hotels. This contrasts sharply, for instance, with South Asia, which, with 15,066 hotel properties, represents less than 1% of total world supply.

An industry of such magnitude inevitably has far-reaching impacts of a social, economic and environmental nature, as was confirmed by the second IH&RA White Paper (2000).This found that sustainable development and social issues had become key forces driving change in the multinational hospitality industry and an important yardstick against which the industry's development will be measured in the near future.

Economic Dimensions

Although industry consolidation is a continuing trend, the hospitality sector is still predominantly made up of small and mediumsised enterprises (SMEs). Research indicates that approximately 20% of hotels worldwide are branded (*i.e.*, have an affiliation to a national or international chain of hotels), and 80% are independent, although the ratio of branded to non-branded hotels in the United States is higher (70/30), a trend which Europe is likely to follow – albeit at a slower pace – given the existing low level of brand penetration and continued high volumes expected in international travel.

Given its size and scope, the international hospitality industry makes a major contribution to gross domestic output. In both developing nations (where tourism may be the primary industry) and developed countries, industry revenues constitute an important part of the local and national economy. They do so via four major activities, profits earned and distributed to owners, taxes paid on sales, wages and real estate, jobs created; and purchases of supplies and materials.

Industry taxation generates significant funding foı governments. This in turn, is used to provide services for citizens and travellers. As well as income tax, hotels pay business taxes, licence fees and real estate taxes, in addition to the social charges often imposed on employee wages. Being such an important source of tax revenue, hotels can be viewed as highly productive members of the economic community, compared with other property investments that do not provide this multiple taxing opportunity. Hotels and restaurants also contribute to the important process of job creation. As a labour-intensive industry, hospitality employs large numbers of wage earners, whose taxes and disposable income add to gross domestic output and help to create further employment opportunities. Given that each hotel room typically requires one member of staff, every hotel room built has the potential to create an additional job.

Furthermore, for every dollar spent by a guest in a hotel, one additional revenue dollar is generated for the community. Referred to as the 'multiplier effect', this concept is used by economists to explain how money spent by a hotel guest travels through a community to purchase the goods and services required to meet the guest's needs. In the United States, for example, the multiplier effect is approximately two; that is, for every dollar spent by a guest in a hotel, one additional revenue dollar is generated across a wide range of businesses.

The total output of the hotel industry is closely tied to the variables associated with economic development such as basic infrastructure and levels of Gross Domestic Product (GDP), employment and education of the workforce. This relationship is worth noting since it can be expected that the hotel industry has considerable growth potential in those nations and regions that are just beginning to fully develop their economies and improve their performance in each macroeconomic variable.

Labour Supply

Of particular concern to the hospitality industry in high-income countries are current demographic trends – notably declining birth rates and ageing populations – which put further pressure on an industry characterised by high turnover and a shortage of qualified labour in both developed and developing countries. These problems are exacerbated by constraints on the international mobility of workers as a result of visa restrictions and national immigration quotas.

Although no data is currently available as to the actual extent of the labour shortfall globally, it can be anticipated that trade associations will lobby for a more flexible job market on a global scale, and that in order to help combat the labour shortage hotels will have to embrace a training culture in their businesses and employ people from an increasingly wide cross-section of cultures and backgrounds.

Social Dimensions

By providing many young or unskilled people with their first job experience, the industry also effectively offers them an entry into the labour market. The industry's labour-intensive nature puts it in a prime position to draw upon all sectors of society to meet its workforce needs. It is worth noting that in some countries women account for up to 70% of all employees in the catering and accommodation sector, according to estimates by the International Labour Organisation (ILO). Given its key contribution to gross global output and employment generation, and the social consequences this may have, hospitality industry leaders are being challenged to demonstrate greater levels of social responsibility and will be increasingly called upon to address the gap between the so-called 'haves' and 'have-nots'.

In this spirit, some hotel companies have signed agreements with trade unions, which focus on issues of trade union rights, skills training and equality in the workplace. Noting that 'in the global economy, all social and economic progress is contingent upon the maintaining of a society based on democratic values and respect for human rights', the Accor Group and the International Union of Food, Agricultural, Hotel, Restaurant, Catering, Tobacco and Allied Workers' Associations (IUF) have undertaken to respect ILO conventions relating to:

- The right of employees to affiliate to the union of their choice,
- The protection of employees against all acts of discrimination that tend to violate freedom of association,
- The protection of employees against any measures that could harm them as a result of them being union representatives.

The Accor Group undertakes not to oppose efforts to unionise its employees and considers respect for union rights to be part of the good reputation of its brand names. There is also growing pressure on the multinational industry to plough more of its wealth back into those parts of the developing world where it operates. In an era when wealth sharing can be achieved through joint venture schemes or other forms of ownership, the expectation is that all stakeholders in a hotel project (be they investors, employees, or government) should have an equitable share in the profits. Increasingly, criticism is directed at governments that remove all forms of financial obstacles as an incentive to hotel companies to locate within their borders. The challenge of the shrinking labour pool is compounded by pandemic HIV/AIDS particularly for hotels located in high-risk areas where the disease is widespread. An actuarial study of South Africa, for example, revealed that the transport, catering and accommodation sectors are the most at risk from the epidemic with an estimated 26% of the region's hospitality workforce ultimately becoming infected.

Yet the problem is by no means exclusive to sub-Saharan Africa and its implications extend well beyond the labour supply. Hotels increasingly recognise the need for measures to protect 'frontline' employees given the higher-than-average extent of direct contact between customers and staff. One response to this need has been the publication of the *Guide for the Hospitality Industry on dealing with HIV/AIDS in the Workplace* produced by IH&RA in collabouration with UNAIDS. This gives guidance to hotels on introducing an AIDS policy and AIDS education in the workplace and details essential safety measures (treating injuries, disposing of syringes and razors *etc.*). The commercial sexual exploitation of children in tourism – commonly referred to as child sex tourism – is a further area of social concern with implications not just for hotels worldwide, but for the tourism industry as a whole. No matter how inadvertently, hotels along with other tourism operators may be implicated.

Experience in the field shows that this is one area where collabouration between the various private sector partners, national governments and their law-enforcing agencies is vital. IH&RA, for example, is an active member of the international steering committee on the *Code of Conduct for the Protection of Children from Sexual Exploitation in Travel and Tourism,* together with other stakeholders, including Interpol, TO, the Tourism Authority of Thailand (TAT), and other representatives from the tourism industry.

Environmental Dimensions

As a major component of travel and tourism, the hospitality industry (characteristically a private sector activity involving SMEs widely dispersed across the local environment) has a vested interest in protecting the environment -its key resource.

Individual operators and major hospitality chains alike are increasingly hearing this message as they implement environmentally friendly energy conservation and waste disposal measures tailored to their specific needs. Indeed, by the very nature of their operations, hotels are likely to take a multitude of environmental actions that extend beyond the control of any single monitoring agency. As a result, self-regulation appears to be the most viable course of action, whether in the form of in-house environmental audits, the adoption of an environmental management system, and/or application for eco-certification such as Green Leaf, Green Key or Green Globe issued by one of a number of recognised body. Indeed, the moral, social and political arguments for conducting business in an environmentally-sound manner are becoming more and more widely accepted. This is particularly noteworthy given the potential impacts the industry can have on air quality, energy and water consumption, land use and waste generation.

Although less 'polluting' than some other industries such as certain manufacturing processes, hospitality businesses, like most others, contribute to emissions into the atmosphere (through the use of fossil fuels and ozone-depleting substances and the transportation of supplies).The hospitality industry can also be considered a significant user of energy in the form of heat and power. As this directly involves the burning of fossil fuels and the emission of greenhouse gases, the hospitality industry is also an indirect contributor to global warming. As a result, industry bodies regularly draw attention to the importance of eliminating ozone-depleting substances in refrigeration, air-conditioning and fire-extinguishing appliances to avoid further contributing to this phenomenon.

Water is perhaps the hospitality industry's most important resource. Tourists typically consume considerably more water than local residents. A hotel can consume between 60m3 and 220m3 per guest room per year depending on the facilities provided and whether sound water conservation practices are in place, such as water flow restrictors and on-site waste water treatment facilities. Major efforts have been made by the industry to disseminate information and advice on these and other resource and energy-saving measures, including several produced jointly by IH&RA and partner organisations. Hotel developments can hasten the installation of much-needed water, power and transport infrastructure. Hospitality developers are well aware that poor siting, design, engineering and construction of tourism facilities run counter to their long-term interests by causing erosion, landslides and flooding. Much has been learnt from past experience, including the importance of preserving natural protective features such as dunes and vegetation cover when constructing hotel facilities on the waterfront in low-lying and coastal areas, and of harmoniously integrating hospitality facilities with the natural or architectural features of the surrounding area.

Constructing or refurbishing hotels can be an opportunity to apply traditional techniques and technologies, to rediscover local materials, and to consult with local communities to learn how best to construct buildings that respect a given landscape and suit a particular climate. The 2001 IH&RA Environmental Award Winner Chumbe Island Coral Park, Tanzania for example, employed local craftsmen for their knowledge and skills in the use of traditional building techniques. As a result, 14 'eco-bungalows' were constructed with materials that have close to zero impact on the environment. It should be remembered, however, that hospitality developers do not operate in a vacuum. The control of environmental impacts also depends on a strong local government capable of enforcing building and planning regulations. This is particularly important at a time when tourism and hospitality businesses continue to expand into remote areas.

Most hotels generate large quantities of solid waste including bottles and food packaging, kitchen and garden waste, old furniture and equipment and potentially hazardous wastes such as asbestos and solvents. Waste disposal costs money and for this reason, hotels are increasingly careful to reduce waste volumes because it makes sound business sense. They do so by minimising the materials used in the first place, recycling and reusing waste materials wherever possible, and by safely disposing of residual wastes. The Orchid Hotel in Mumbai, India, provides a particularly good example of innovative recycling and waste disposal. Virtually all in-room products are reusable or recyclable, paper usage is kept to a minimum and kitchen waste is composted in on-site vermiculture pits. As a major consumer of goods and services, the industry has a strong impact on the supply chain and can induce better environmental practices here. Through their collective efforts hospitality businesses can contribute to increasing recycling volumes, driving down recycling costs, increasing the profitability of local recycling markets and raising customer awareness.

Hospitality services people at leisure who offer a captive audience for environmental communication. Many tourists feel good knowing that they have spent a low-impact holiday and used the services of environment conscious operators. The feel-good factor is not limited to tourists it can also extend to employees. In fact, good environmental stewardship has been found to reduce employee turnover, and motivate employees to become environment-conscious citizens.

The 'triple bottom line' the consideration of ecological and social, as well as economic concerns is increasingly guiding business strategy. Since the introduction of Agenda 21 and its adaptation for travel and tourism in 1996, the hospitality industry has introduced numerous voluntary initiatives to reduce the negative and enhance the positive environmental impacts associated with its operations. This is particularly relevant given that shareholders, customers, employees, community groups and governments are increasingly showing an interest in the 'green' performance of their corporate citizens, including hospitality businesses. Most of the leading hospitality chains have introduced environmental policies and many have senior executives dedicated solely to environmental issues. In smaller hotels, environmentally-sound business practice is often driven by the individual general manager, resulting in both creative solutions and cost reductions. Clearly, the industry is progressing both in environmental awareness and concrete action, although opportunities for further improvement still abound.

As indicated, voluntary initiatives have been undertaken to help hotels deal effectively with HIV/AIDS in the workplace and the commercial sexual exploitation of children in tourism, but much remains to be done. To date, industry associations, such as IH&RA, have focused their efforts on raising awareness of the issues involved and formulating guidelines that can be incorporated into operating procedures. They have emphasised that the challenge for all hotels large or small, chain or independent is to address these problems proactively rather than be forced to comply with legislative requirements (by the government) on which they may not have been consulted.

Means of implementation Since the introduction of Agenda 21, the hospitality sector has adopted numerous strategies, approaches and measures in response to the challenge of sustainable development. These include:

- Environmental management systems and tools;
- Education, awareness creation, training and information dissemination;
- Voluntary initiatives;
- Multi-stakeholder communication and consultation;
- Environmental reporting;
- Implementation of the Rio principles.

Environmental Management Systems and Tools

Many multinational and independent hotel companies have introduced environmental management practices at the property level. Ideally, the framework for this involves defining an environmental policy and building a management system to measure environmental impacts and compliance both with corporate policy and with local regulations, as well as documenting the system's performance for inspection and auditing purposes.

One such system is Six Continents' (formerly Bass Hotels & Resorts) *Conserving for Tomorrow* programme, a worldwide initiative involving over 1,100 participating hotels. Such environmental management systems (EMS) help businesses to evaluate, manage and reduce their negative environmental impacts by providing a methodology to integrate environmental management into business operations in a systematic manner. Education, awareness creation, training and information dissemination IH&RA, in conjunction with partners such as UNEP-DTIE, the International Hotels Environment Initiative (IHEI), the UNAIDS programme and its member national hospitality associations, has sought to raise industry awareness of the social, economic and environmental dimensions of sustainable development through numerous educational programmes and publications.

As indicated above, in the social domain, IH&RA has collabourated with UNAIDS to produce a manual addressing the issue of HIV/AIDS in the workplace and has actively participated in WTO's campaign against Child Sex Tourism by publishing practical advice for hoteliers on how to deter this form of criminal activity and where to get help. At the corporate level, many global hospitaiity companies are also involved in a range of voluntary initiatives. Marriott International, for instance, has committed to assisting the communities in which it operates, believing that business enterprises should be active in supporting community concerns.

Voluntary Initiatives

Given the predominance of SMEs in the hospitality sector, legislative enforcement and verification of compliance with environmental measures is highly complex. Therefore, voluntary initiatives such as eco-labels, environment awards and codes of conduct are proving to be an effective method of encouraging environmental improvement across a large number of businesses. In response to growing consumer awareness of the environmental context when purchasing products, eco-labelling has been one of the most successful means for a hotel to gain environmental credibility and custom. Certification may originate within a national hotel association, such as the Hotel Association of Canada's Green Leaf programme, as a joint initiative between the national hotel association and other local tourism partners, such as HORESTA's Green Key programme in Denmark, and Green Globe 21 supported by WTTC and other key international players. Or, finally, it may be devised by a consulting firm such as the HVS Ecotel certification programme. In order to obtain an eco-label, a hotel must be independently audited on a regular basis to ensure it meets standards and policies relating to a general code of conduct or specific benchmark.

According to the Caribbean Alliance for Sustainable Tourism (CAST), an environmental initiative run by the Caribbean Hotel Association for the benefit of its member hotels, the eco-label certification process has not only created a competitive advantage for many hoteliers, but has also directly benefited the bottom line. Routine measures can reduce water consumption and related costs by up to 30%, provide significant savings in energy, solid waste haulage, chemical and maintenance costs, and have a typical payback period of less than two years. Other advantages frequently include a positive impact on corporate/hotel image, internal management, local community relations, client satisfaction (reported to be 90% under Costa Rica's Certification for Sustainable Tourism), and reduced environmental liability.

In terms of the hospitality industry's social contribution, one initiative particularly worth noting is the Singapore-based Pan Pacific Hotel & Resort's *Youth Career Initiative*. Launched with support from the United Nations Children's Fund (UNICEF) at the Pan Pacific Hotel in Bangkok in 1995, this IH&RA-endorsed programme offers severely under-privileged young people a 20-week training course in basic life skills along with an introduction to the hospitality industry. It seeks to open up genuine career opportunities that will lift them out of poverty and protect them from prostitution. The programme has now been set up in Manila (Philippines), Jakarta (Indonesia) and Dhaka (Bangladesh) and will be extended to other world regions such as Africa, Latin America and the Caribbean in the near future. To date, over 400 young people have benefited from the programme, some even using it as the stepping-stone to higher education. On the cultural side, IH&RA has partnered with the United Nations Educational, Scientific and Cultural Organisation (UNESCO) in a joint initiative encouraging hotel companies to invest in the archaeological and cultural heritage on which cultural tourism thrives. Major hotel chains participating in this 'Memories of the Future' programme have financially supported restoration and enhancement projects for UNESCO World Heritage Sites such as Prince Gong's Palace, Beijing and the Medina of Tunis (Accor) or the historic City of Krakow in Poland, the City of Tyre in Lebanon and the Bahla Fort in Oman (Radisson SAS).

Multi-stakeholder communication and consultation Hospitality companies, like all businesses, answer to a variety of stakeholders, including investors, customers, employees, suppliers and the local community. Increasingly, they are experiencing demand for greater participation in decision-making by representatives of the latter category, which may translate into a heightened need to obtain voter approval for planning and development, for example, by carrying-out an environmental impact assessment. In this new regulatory context, corporations are being pressured into making a higher community commitment through charitable involvement, a trend mirrored in the corporate marketing techniques increasingly used for the generation of brand awareness.

Exemplary instances of local community consultation can be found in both the independent and chain hotel sector. Facing the threat of becoming an island of conserved habitat in a sea of rural poverty, the Phinda Mountain & Forest Lodge, in South Africa, has made a commitment to ensure the local community draws sustained benefits from its natural resources. Radisson SAS has established its *Responsible Business Agenda* for key stakeholder groups (including suppliers, local communities, media and environmental representatives) to determine what they can rightfully expect from the company. Both companies recognise the role of key stakeholders in the decision-making process. Beyond these individual examples and others like them, however, further research must be conducted to track what the industry is doing as a whole in regard to communicating and consulting with its stakeholders.

Company environmental reports are considered an excellent means for self-assessment – by monitoring progress and measuring the results achieved. Indeed, environmental reporting is starting to evolve into 'sustainability reporting' which communicates the economic performance of the company, and its environmental and social impacts. Moreover, financial institutions have come to regard sustainable principles and practices as fundamental to sound business management, giving companies that wish to be considered 'responsible' an additional incentive to monitor, measure and report performance in the future. The passenger cruise industry is an exciting, modern and rapidly expanding global industry. During the current decade, it has continued to expand its capacity and to develop new cruising opportunities for vacationers. The growth and global reach has been exceptional for an industry with such high capital costs, and with such a complex regulatory and legal environment in which to operate.

With capacity projected to continue to increase each year, the future offers extraordinary opportunities for the industry, its customers and suppliers. This increase in capacity is driven by a record number of new ships coming into service. Among these will be mega-liners that can accommodate more than 3,000 passengers as well as smaller, more intimate luxury vessels. The industry has a history of growth approaching 8% per year for the past decade, and the outlook for the future seems extremely bright. According to a recent study conducted by analyst G.P. Wild, total cruise passengers are forecasted to grow from 9.8 million last year to 20.7 million by 2010. Within these figures, the North American market will go up from 6.8 million to 11.9 million and mainland Europe will grow from 1.3 million to 5.3 million. In sum, the passenger cruise industry is a dynamic sector of the global economy. ICCL is the leading trade association that represents the interests of the 16 largest passenger cruise lines that handle 95% of the North American vacation cruise market and approximately 85% worldwide. It also represents a growing number of over 73 strategic cruise industry business partners. In 2002, the member lines of ICCL will sail over 90 vessels and will carry more than seven million passengers.

The mission of ICCL is to participate in the international and United States regulatory and policy development process and ensure that all measures adopted provide for a safe, secure and healthy cruise ship environment. Under the direction of the chief executives of its member lines, ICCL advocates industry positions to key domestic and International regulatory organisations, policy-makers and other industry partners. ICCL actively monitors domestic and international shipping policy and regulations and develops recommendations for its membership on a wide variety of issues, including safety, public health, environmental protection, security, medical facilities, and passenger protection.

Conferred the status of a non-governmental consultative organisation to the International Maritime Organisation (IMO), ICCL actively participates in reviewing current maritime issues and developing conventions and treaties which, when adopted and ratified by member nations, become international law. Through IMO, maritime nations have developed consistent and uniform international standards that apply to all vessels engaged in international commerce. These standards are set forth in a number of conventions and codes such as:

- SOLAS (Safety of Life at Sea);
- STCW (Standards of Training, Certification and Watch keeping);
- MARPOL (Marine Prevention of Pollution from Ships);
- ISM (International Safety Management Code).

International conventions set the benchmark for environmental and safety standards throughout the world. As an NGO, ICCL actively contributes to the deliberations of the Maritime Safety Committee (MSC), the Marine Environment Protection Committee (MEPC) and the numerous sub-committees, working groups and correspondence groups through submission of reports and papers, participation in discussion, and correspondence groups. ICCL is an active participant in the development and fine-tuning of these important international regulatory regimes that apply throughout the world.

The countries where vessels are registered or 'flagged' have the responsibility to oversee compliance with the internationally agreed upon requirements established by these and other treaties. Additionally, a port state, such as the United States, provides additional oversight regarding compliance and exercises jurisdiction over vessels while they operate within the waters of that coastal nation. While operating within United States waters, laws such as the Resource Conservation and Recovery Act, the Clean Air Act, the Clean Water Act, the Refuse Act and the Federal Water Pollution Control Act apply. The United States Coast Guard enforces both international requirements and the United States domestic laws with regard to cruise ships operating within their jurisdiction. ICCL works with leading flag and port state administrations, international shipping associations and classification societies on safety, security and environmental issues. ICCL constantly strives to improve safety procedures, and the excellent safety record of ICCL member operators attests to the proactive steps taken by these operators to safeguard their passengers and crews, and their commitment to provide a safe, clean and fair work environment for their on-board personnel.

ICCL's commitment to excellence is also demonstrated by its readiness to work with, and to initiate partnerships with various United States government agencies. ICCL currently has a formal partnership agreement with the United States Coast Guard and a Memorandum of Understanding (MOU) with the Florida Department of Environmental Protection (FL DEP). ICCL also works closely with the United States EPA, other state and federal agencies and public advocacy groups to address safety, security, health and environmental protection concerns.

Economic Dimensions

During the last decade, the cruise ship business is a tourist industry that has grown rapidly. According to WTO, world demand reached 8.7 million passengers in 2006. The North American markets cover two-thirds of the global volume, this is primarily due to the renaissance of the cruising destinations in the Caribbean. Although the number is relatively small in the global holiday market, the industry has an enormous momentum and it is believed that North American and European demand will, by the end of 2010, surpass 12 million passengers.

In the North American market, the United States is the dominant source of cruise passengers. However, in recent years a growing percentage of passengers have come from Europe, Canada, and other areas. This expansion has led to cruise line employment of men and women in these markets both ashore and aboard ships. Comparing 1998 to 1990, cruise ship embarkation from North American ports increased by almost 70 %.The major United States ports of call are located in Florida, Alaska, California, Louisiana, New York, Texas and Massachusetts. In Florida alone, over 3.2 million passengers embarked from the ports of Miami, Everglades, Canaveral, Palm Beach and Tampa in 2001. An additional 1.1 million passengers also boarded in San Juan, Puerto Rico and non-US ports, primarily Vancouver and Montreal (Canada).

Globally, while the Caribbean region is the principal destination with 44.5% share of placement, a significant percentage of the global capacity is allocated to other markets. These include Alaska, 7.9%, the Mediterranean, 12.7%, Europe, 8.1%, the Trans-Canal (Panama), 4.0%, United States West Coast, 3.3%, Hawaii, 2.6%, and South America, 2.4%. Among the remaining destinations, the capacity for world, Transatlantic, Asia, Australia, Middle East and Antarctica cruises has more than doubled since 1990. The social, environmental and economic sectors of these emerging destinations will prove to be a challenge and an opportunity.

The cruise industry has developed into a significant economic contributor to the United States economy, including industry, agriculture, and the service sector. A study conducted in 2001 by the Business Research and Economic Advisors (BREA) concluded that in 2000, total economic benefit by the cruise industry and cruise-related activities was approximately USD17.9 billion. Of this, the cruise industry contributed USD9.4 billion in direct spending for the products and services of United States companies. The industry's extensive economic relationships include high-tech equipment, travel services, banking and insurance, textiles, technical services, dry-docking and shipyard repair. Other major United States industries that benefit from the cruise business are the airlines, travel agents, food and beverage suppliers and the business and service sectors. Total wages generated for United States employees was USD8.7 billion. As a result of these economic partnerships, the cruise industry is able to create employment for thousands of United States citizens and support for state and local economies in all 50 states. The BREA study estimates that in 2000, the cruise industry generated jobs for 257,067 Americans.

In the United States, capital expenditures by the cruise lines more than doubled between 1997 and 2000. According to BREA, this growth required significant investment in new cruise ships and upgrading of the existing fleet. Other purchases by the cruise lines rose 30%. In total, spending in the United States associated with the industry increased by nearly a third between 1997 and 2000, to USD9.4 billion.

While these economic benefits in the United States are substantial, there are also significant benefits worldwide in the industry's new emerging markets. By way of example, the cruise industry has significant impact in Germany, Finland and Italy due to the shipbuilding activities in those nations. In nations where tourism is encouraged, the cruise lines purchased services ashore (transportation, tour operations, supplies, etc) and many of the service sectors and local business benefit from cruise ship tourists spending ashore.

Moreover, tourism activity can lead to development of new markets for the products of local artisans, which not only has both the social and economic benefit of additional local income, but also helps preserve cultural tradition and identity. Although there has been some concern that these economic gains in tourist destinations are seasonal, it is clear that the markets involved are better off with the cruise industries financial input, and sufficient growth can more than compensate for the seasonal variation.

Economic Contributions

The cruise industry brings a burgeoning tourism economy to many ports around the world. The importance of the social and economic opportunities cannot be understated. It has an effect on all sectors in the port city and country. The cruise lines' presence, even on a seasonal basis, in port cities strengthens the economy for many local elements. In addition to local port user fees and head taxes and surcharges, cruise ships purchase supplies and services such as pilots, tugboats, waste disposal services, fuel and fresh water at ports of call worldwide. Visits by cruise ships generate hundreds of millions of dollars worth of business to attractions, restaurants, retail shops, shore tour operators and other businesses at ports of call. From local artisans and craftsmen to infrastructure development such as transportation, all benefit from the expenditures of the tourists that cruise ships provide. In some instances, foreign ports that the cruise industry decides to visit become an economic stimulus for host countries to develop tourism and destination evelopment programmes, involving local participation in providing goods and services.

A 2006 study conducted for the Florida- Caribbean Cruise Association (FCCA) by PricewaterhouseCoopers (PwC) and BREA(67) found that during the 2007/2008 cruise year in the Caribbean, a typical cruise ship carrying 2,000 passengers and 900 crew members generated an average of $260,000 in passenger and crew expenditures during an average port-of-call visit.

Other highlights of the PwC/BREA study include:

- FCCA member lines' passengers and crew accounted for a total economic impact of USD2.6 billion throughout the Caribbean;
- Cruise-related expenditures generated 60,136 jobs, paying USD285m in wage income to Caribbean residents;
- Average cruise passenger spending per port-of-call visit was USD103.83 and average spending by crew was USD72.06;
- Caribbean cruise passenger capacity grew by 21.8% in the year 2000;
- Almost 80% of cruise passengers reported a high degree of satisfaction with the destinations they visited, and many (51.6%) expressed an interest in returning to the ports of call on a land-based vacation because of their cruise visit.

Cruise lines are continuously reviewing existing ports of call for tour operation capabilities, investment opportunities for development and upgrades to passenger terminal facilities, and total customer satisfaction of the cruise experience. With the expectation that the high passenger growth in the last decade will continue, the industry actively seeks new destinations and often will contribute to the development of a new port facility seeking calls from cruise vessels.

One example of this is a new port of call in Mexico. Construction of that facility will be a joint venture between the owner of a Mexican nature park and a cruise line, and when constructed will be able to handle four 100,000 tonne ships simultaneously. The terminal design will feature Mayan motif relating to the local culture. An additional example is a recent investment by the industry in a Bahamian shipyard that will contribute skilled jobs into the local economy.

Social Dimensions

ICCL cruise line members demonstrate a commitment to environmental excellence that is embodied through their social responsibility. The industry promotes good stewardship of the marine environment through varying internal and external initiatives. They involve their crew members in reducing the number, volume and composition of chemicals used on ships and work with them to identify opportunities to reduce, reuse and recycle whenever possible.

Cruise guests are educated on the importance of using waste containers to ensure discarded items do not go over the side. Not only is recycling a part of the ships' day-to-day operating procedures, but passengers are also encouraged to assist in the effort by using special recycling bins located around the ships. The industry favours contracting with vendors, suppliers and service providers who have made their own commitment to similar standards for safety and health, as well as continuous improvement.

Social Contributions

Cruise lines generally donate to charitable causes throughout the world, including their local home ports and major ports of call. The following examples are just a brief overview of cruise line efforts to promote local environmental stewardship.

- In 2001, FCCA cruise line members partnered with St. Lucia, and Nassau, (Bahamas), to conduct the annual FCCA Caribbean Environmental Awareness Project. As part of their ongoing effort to spread environmental awareness, this project is staged every year throughout the Caribbean. In Nassau, more than 100 crew members teamed up, and were divided up into teams and given various tasks to beautify a section of Lighthouse Beach as follows:
    - o Removing sand that had been blown on to the walkway from past hurricanes,

- re-distributing the sand over the rocks that had been exposed,
- development of a native tree garden with rock formations,
- white-washing the exterior of the beach facilities,
- painting of concession stands for local vendors,
- construction of an obstacle course and play area for children.

- Grants have been awarded to the Centre for Marine Conservation and the World Wildlife Fund, the Alaska SeaLife Centre, Bahamas Reef Environment Educational Foundation, National Audubon Society and Earthwatch Institute.
    - The Centre for Marine Conservation is using the Ocean Fund grant to expand its Caribbean Model Communities programme, which aims to reduce marine pollution and improve waste management practices in Puerto Rico, the Bahamas, Bermuda and the United States Virgin Islands. Model communities, using education and citizen involvement to design local solutions, focuses on recreational boating and marina operations and curbing coastal littering.
    - The World Wildlife Fund's Marine Steward Council launched in March 2000 a public awareness campaign in the United States, Europe and Australia to promote long-term sustainable fishing, using the power of consumers and the certification of fisheries. Through global use of the Marine Steward Council logo, seafood companies and consumers will be encouraged to purchase fish only from those certified with environmentally responsible practices.

- Raised funds for flood relief efforts in Caracas, (Venezuela) after the country was hit by devastating floods.

Employment and Training

Cruise industry employment provides substantial opportunities for employees from developing nations. Approximately 85% to 90% of ICCL cruise industry employees are hired from the international workforce. Many of these employees are from developing nations where employment is often limited and difficult in terms of either opportunity or stability. Through cruise line employment, these men and women not only become economically independent, but in many cases direct a portion of their income back to their country of origin through contributions to family members. This way, the cruise industry not only provides a high level of economic opportunity for those who are employed, but also helps sustain these families in their home countries and feeds funds into local economies.

Moreover, a growing number of women across the globe are finding economic opportunities within the cruise industry. The devastating effects of poverty are particularly severe on women in nations struggling with a weak economy and oppressive social and cultural factors beyond their control. Women are relegated to either very low-paying wages or non-employment. Those women who are employed by the cruise industry enjoy personal autonomy from a sustained income that is not matched in their own country. In essence, the cruise industry has provided opportunity for women to achieve increased economic, social and cultural equality.

Another aspect of the benefits gained through cruise ship employment lies in the value of the skills acquired in the course of work aboard a ship. Training in new technologies, cross-cultural awareness, certification in management practices and hands-on experience brings added benefits to the employee. There are comprehensive education and training programmes in place for crew members, primarily to ensure that there are not inadvertent violations of environmental policies, and to heighten sensitivities to environmental issues.

When they return to their country of origin, the employees utilise their experiences, training and resources for the benefit of the local economy and fellow nationals. They also develop a sense of empowerment and leadership that comes from pride in position, economic autonomy and the development of contacts with nationals of other countries.

The working and living environment that the employee enjoys is clean, safe and controlled by international and United States laws. Room, board and medical care are provided by the industry, as well as the ability to experience international travel. The standard of medical care is excellent and usually far exceeds that of their country of origin.

Environmental Dimensions

ICCL member cruise lines are dedicated to preserving the marine environment, and the pristine condition of the waters upon which their vessels sail, and demonstrate this by a reduction of waste by over 50% over the past decade. As an industry that is based on carrying passengers to locations where they can experience and enjoy the beauties provided by nature or human achievements, ICCL members recognise that even a perception that the industry is not meeting relevant international and local environmental standards around the world is damaging to their image and therefore their business prospects. ICCL members have made a substantial investment in new building with over 32 ships scheduled for delivery between 2001 to 2005. With a capital cost of USD12 billion, the industry's investment in the future is substantial. With these realities in mind, ICCL member cruise lines have established standards regarding environmental practices and ship safety. In the past, initiatives such as ICCL's Waste Management Practices and Procedures were strictly voluntary guidelines.

The member lines of ICCL have agreed to adhere to these as standards, thus demonstrating the commitment of its members to protecting the safety and health of people on-board cruise ships, as well as the marine environment. ICCL members believe that these self-imposed voluntary industry standards meet or exceed all requirements of the law wherever ICCL ships operate throughout the world.

The goal of this initiative is to embrace the most advanced technology and procedures in order to establish a leadership position in environmental compliance and reduce the industry's environmental impact. This decision has far-reaching implications in sectors of the world where marine and shore environments are intricately linked to the social, commercial and economic status of its inhabitants.

The goals and objectives are set by the Environmental Committee of ICCL, which is comprised of representatives from all 16 member cruise lines. As a sign of their commitment, ICCL members continuously seek out and test new environmental and safety technologies. In keeping with this commitment, numerous ICCL members have invested millions of dollars to purchase and field test new advanced technology in graywater and blackwater (sewage) treatment.

These advanced treatment systems, when fully developed and proven, are expected to remove sediments and impurities from shipboard waste water streams to the point that the output is essentially clean water. This clean water may then be reused or discharged without fear of any environmental impact.

Additionally, ICCL member lines are investigating new technologies for dry-cleaning operations, photo processing, and digital imaging in order to reduce the production of hazardous waste. New on-board incineration systems are being investigated to improve the efficiency and cleanliness of on-board disposal of waste that cannot be recycled or reused.

The industry has also developed relationships with state and local officials in various communities on which it calls to establish co- operative relationships and to demonstrate its commitment to solving environmental challenges. For example, in Alaska, ICCL members have paid for waste water and air monitoring and have committed to discharging wastewater only when a vessel is underway at a speed of at least six knots, and away from port. ICCL members are committed to continuous improvement. Through this commitment, ICCL members have endorsed policy goals based upon the following fundamental principles:

- Full compliance with applicable international laws and regulations;
- Maintaining co-operative relationships with the regulatory community in the United States and internationally;
- Designing, constructing and operating vessels so as to minimise their impact on the environment;
- Embracing new technology;
- Eonserving resources through purchasing strategies and product management;
- Minimising waste generated and maximising reuse and recycling;
- Optimising energy efficiency through conservation and management;
- Managing water discharges;
- Educating staff, guests and the community.

The mechanism for accountability is established by placing the Mandatory Standards into each company and ship's Safety Management System (SMS).The requirement for a SMS is detailed in the ISM Code, which was mentioned previously. Additionally, the ISM Code requires annual internal audits of the SMS, as well as biannual third party audits conducted by a recognised auditor named by the vessel's flag state as acceptable for performing this task. The results of compliance audits for each vessel are archived and may be made available to appropriate enforcement entities upon request.

The ICCL's success has been based on continuing partnerships with government agencies and local communities. ICCL members have invested a large amount of time and resources to initiating and continuing the partnership with United States Coast Guard, joint environmental studies with

Florida Environmental protection Agency (EPA) and MOU with the Florida Department of Environmental protection (DEP) in order to contribute to the objective of sustainable tourism development. Additionally, ICCL has worked toward sustainable inter-relationships within the port cities visited by its members. The importance of a continued, open dialogue between the industry and the host countries cannot be overstated. In response to a petition from a number of environmental groups, United States EPA developed an action plan to evaluate cruise ship wastewater discharges as well as the industry's environmental operating practices.

Public meetings were held in Juneau, (Alaska), Los Angeles, (California) and Miami, (Florida) as a part of EPA's evaluation process. As a cooperative partnership issue, the United States Coast Guard together with ICCL, co-hosted a two-day workshop for United States EPA, other federal officials, cruise industry segments and public environmental advocacy groups. This forum focused on the practical application of the international regulatory regime and other aspects of environmental management practices adopted by ICCL vessel operators. In August 2001, United States EPA sampled waste water discharges from cruise ships and will utilise this research to determine dispersion patterns and, in turn, environmental impacts of cruise ship waste water discharges. This effort is being conducted with the full support and co-operation of ICCL members. ICCL welcomes the opportunity to demonstrate global adherence to these best practices, and responsibility to environmental preservation. ICCL knows of no other segment of maritime industry that will be willing or able to meet these types of standards. Indeed, ICCL is raising the bar for global environmental performance in maritime industry.

Health and Safety

In the 1970s, because of several gastrointestinal illness outbreaks on cruise vessels, the United States Centre for Disease Control (CDC) established the Vessel Sanitation Programme (VSP) as a co-operative activity with the cruise ship industry.

The programme assists the cruise ship industry in fulfilling its responsibility for developing and implementing comprehensive sanitation programmes, in order to minimise the risk for gastro-intestinal diseases. ICCL has embraced this programme to ensure health and safety on-board cruise ships.

Health and safety is built into every aspect of a cruise ship beginning at the vessel's design stage. CDC, in partnership with the cruise industry and the shipyards, developed construction guidelines for the various components of the vessel's facilities that are related to public health. These include food storage areas, refrigerators and freezers, food preparation service and serving areas, water bunkering, storage, disinfecting, and distribution systems, the construction of pools and spas, and many other aspects of ship construction. Experts from the CDC and the cruise industry completed the latest revision of the guidelines in August 2001.

Every vessel that has a foreign itinerary, carries 13 or more passengers, and calls on a United States port, is subject to unannounced biannual inspections and, when necessary, to reinspection by VSP staff. The vessel owner a fee, based on tonnage, for all inspections. Currently, over 140 cruise ships participate the programme. The inspections are conducted by Environmental Health Officers (EHO) of the United States VSP, and take place only in United States ports. The inspection focuses on the following: the ship's water supply, spas and pools, potential for or water contamination, practices and personal hygiene of employees, general cleanliness physical condition of the ship, and the environmental and public health practices training programmes. Since the programme began, the number disease illness outbreaks on ships has declined significantly despite substantial growth in the number of ships sailing and the number of passengers carried.

Cruise ship companies frequently ask the VSP staff to help them improve their on-board sanitation efforts. Since December 1989,VSP staff has offered sanitation seminars four times each year for shipboard personnel. These seminars bridge the communication gap between government regulators and shipboard personnel by explaining recommended standards, emphasising the reasons for them, and discussing how to comply with them. Topics covered are: the storage, distribution, protection and disinfecting of a ship's water supply, protection of food during storage, preparation, cooking, and service, employee practices and personal hygiene, general cleanliness, facility repair, vector control, and potential for contamination of food and water. This programme is also a global training environment for the shipboard employees from developing nations. Education, hands-on training and practical application in sanitation and the reduction of the risk of disease are skill sets that are applicable in their home countries. This training is often not available in the developing world or there are constraints due to the lack of trained professionals available. Often cruise ship staff attain leadership status in their communities as a direct result of being exposed to advanced training and practical experience opportunities.

Safety

Over the past two decades, an estimated 60 million passengers enjoyed a cruise vacation. During this period, not one passenger death due to a marine incident (such as a fire, collision, or grounding) occurred on any ICCL vessel operating from a United States port. This enviable safety record is the direct result of the important focus that is placed in this area. Of course, the cruise industry cannot be complacent; ICCL constantly investigates ways to improve its performance.

This excellent safety record demonstrates ICCL members' commitment to safety. In 1996, the United States Coast Guard published a comprehensive cruise ship safety study, which concluded that the industry was one of the safest modes of transportation available and that international safety initiatives coming into force would further improve its safety record.

As reported by this task force, many SOLAS requirements 'are now significantly more stringent than United States regulations. This is especially true with regard to fire protection. No other form of transportation (bus, train, or aeroplane) can claim to be as safe as a vacation cruise or provide as extensive fire emergency and life support systems. If a cruise ship sails from a United States port, the United States Coast Guard has conducted an in-depth examination of that ship for safety. The United States Coast Guard reviews the ship plans for compliance with construction requirements and then visits the vessel while under construction to assure it is properly built. The United States Coast Guard also verifies the adequacy of crew training through observation of drills, examination of documentation, and interviews with officers and crew.

To assure compliance with safety regulations, the United States Coast Guard exercises portstate control authority over foreign flag cruise ships operating from United States ports. Other maritime agencies exercise port-state control under similar programmes in the ports where they have jurisdiction. The United States Coast Guard, in accordance with its Control Verification Examination (CVE) programme, conducts quarterly inspections on all vessels embarking passengers at United States ports. The examinations focus on fire safety systems and life saving equipment and their safety and environmental protection items. Additionally, the United States Coast Guard witnesses fire and abandon ship drills to ensure crew proficiency. The average response time for an on-board emergency is within a matter of minutes – fire teams and trained emergency and medical crews are always only a few hundred feet away.

The formalised partnership with the United States Coast Guard has resulted in meetings on a regular basis both at the executive and technical levels to discuss emerging safety issues and recent passenger vessel initiatives adopted or under consideration at IMO. The partnership has planned and co-ordinated joint emergency preparedness exercises to ensure the effectiveness of response capabilities, has worked on methods to identify lessons learned from past marine casualties, and has instituted crew training policies in response to STCW.

ICCL believes this partnership is a productive way to exchange information on the operational impacts of proposed policies as well as identification of resources required to respond to various types of vessel emergencies. The partnership between ICCL and the United States Coast Guard has been a factor in the establishment of industry standards for lifejackets in excess of international requirements, infant personal flotation devices, and helicopter pick-up areas.

Passenger Security

The highest priority of the cruise industry is to provide a safe and secure vacation experience for our passengers. The cruise industry takes any and all cases of reported crimes on-board our ships seriously. Every person on-board a cruise ship, from the captain to the cleaning staff and all guests, is placed on an official manifest. Passengers and crew may embark or disembark only after passing through security.

Access is strictly limited to documented employees and fare-paying passengers. Most importantly, since 11 September 2001, the cruise industry has heightened its security measures both on and off the vessel in order to provide the most secure environment for its passengers and crew. Even though a cruise ship is inherently secure because it is a controlled environment with limited access, immediately following the terrorist attacks all ICCL members implemented Security Level III, even before the United States Coast Guard (USCG) ordered it.

Security Level III is the highest level of security set by Coast Guard Passenger Vessel Security regulations. At United States cruise terminals, passenger vessel security measures include passenger screening procedures similar to those found at airports. This includes 100% screening of all passenger baggage, carry-on luggage, ship stores and cargo, and also includes higher levels of screening of passenger identification. Official passenger lists are carefully reviewed and proper identification is ensured before anyone is allowed to board the vessel. Coast Guard regulations implemented in 1996 require ship operators to submit Comprehensive Security Plans to the USCG for review and acceptance. These regulations address both passenger ship and passenger terminal security and outline methods to deter unlawful activities on-board. All ICCL member lines have submitted security plans that have been accepted by USCG and these plans are audited annually.

Cruise lines operate within a very strict legal framework that gives international, federal and state authorities the right to investigate crimes on-board cruise ships. Unlike most instances crime ashore, the United States Federal Bureau of Investigation (FBI) has the authority to investigate alleged crimes in international waters when an American is involved. In July 1999, ICCL executives announced an industry wide position regarding the reporting of crimes committed on-board cruise ships. This statement of zero tolerance for any crime committed on-board ICCL vessels requires reporting of all serious crimes involving United States citizens to the FBI for further investigation. Incidents of criminal conduct are extremely low in comparison to similar incidents reported ashore. FBI and United States Census Bureau statistics indicate that the numbers of reported crimes in United States communities are at least 20 times greater than the number of reported shipboard assaults per capita. This level of security is carried on ICCL's ships as they travel around the world and visit the ports of many countries.

The cruise industry has taken a proactive role in addressing the provision of shipboard medical care. Over five years ago, members of ICCL began work on development of industry-wide guidelines for the medical facilities, staffing, equipment and procedures utilised on-board passenger vessels. Then, in 1996 it issued guidelines that represented the work of a group of experienced medical physicians and other medical experts knowledgeable about the unique needs and limitations of shipboard medical care.

Future Challenges and Goals

The international cruise industry has a remarkable story of success and achievement in a number of sectors, not the least of which has been our safety record, particularly for the 16 cruise line members of ICCL. This success could only have been achieved through the teamwork with industry partners and the innovation, energy and devotion of many very talented individuals. Moreover, because there is a mutual interdependence between the cruise line industry and the countries visited by its ships, there is a bright future. As the industry grows, so will the issues and challenges that it faces.

Issues that the industry will be focusing on in the future include safety, environmental management, and continued product enhancements. As the ships become more complex, and the locations visited become more distant, the sophistication of cruising operations will grow exponentially. Through private-public sector relationships, solutions can be devised for all issues and challenges. As global leaders in the maritime industry, the members of ICCL will always be at the cutting edge in the utilisation of new technologies.

As passenger demand increases and the cruise industry continues to grow, ICCL and its member lines will continue to participate in the development of new IMO safety initiatives that govern the operation of cruise vessels worldwide. Over the past several years, IMO has adopted several new international regulations that significantly enhance passenger vessel safety. These comprehensive IMO regulations established stringent new standards that require significant fire safety upgrades for new and existing vessels, adopted advanced crew safety training requirements, and required all vessels to implement a specified safety management system that delineates crew responsibilities and establishes mandatory codes of practice. These are internationally mandated by the United States government; both flag-state and port-state authorities closely monitor standards, and treaties are adopted throughout the world.

ICCL is dedicated to responsible environmental management and protection of global natural resources. Regulation by governments and international organisations is increasingly influenced by communities and local bodies directly participating in policy making. ICCL is committed to working in partnership with United States EPA, United States

Coast Guard, other international, federal and state environmental protection agencies and public environmental advocacy groups such as the United Nations, the Ocean Conservancy, and Ocean Advocates to find productive solutions to the very real issues that confront us on a daily basis. ICCL strives to inform the public that the cruise industry is dedicated to preserving the marine environment and the oceans upon which cruise vessels sail. Cruising is one of the most popular vacation options in large part because of its excellent safety record and the high level of quality service provided on-board cruise ships. ICCL will continue to work to ensure the safety and well-being of all passengers and crew on-board cruise vessels, as well as the pristine environments visited by ICCL's members' ships.

The World Summit on Sustainable Development (WSSD) will bring together representatives from governments, concerned citizens, UN agencies, multilateral financial institutions and other major groups. The purpose of the summit is to provide a forum to engage all stakeholders in sustainable development in a constructive and informative dialogue. The summit also provides an occasion to bridge the gap between these various stakeholders who are all ultimately responsible for the future of the planet. Tourism is one of the industry sectors UNEP was requested to report on at WSSD. The tourism industry agreed to be a part of the process and has written this tourism industry report charting the progress and priorities for the sustainable development of the industry.

To ensure the report offers an open, selfcritical assessment of the industry the authors agreed to be part of a multi-stakeholder dialogue. The authors of the tourism industry report participated in a consultative meeting on 3 October 2001, in Paris, with representatives from invited NGOs, trade unions, the International Labour Organisation (ILO), the WTO/OMT and other chosen groups. This provided an open forum for a frank and honest assessment of the report during which many suggestions were made to the industry partners. One of the criticisms from the stakeholders was the lack of case studies, statistics and hard data in the report. For every negative case study there is a positive one and the lack of hard data available makes examples very subjective. The authors therefore decided to reduce the amount of case studies and concentrate instead on the major issues facing the industry. The report has not mentioned the airline industry because they have co-ordinated their own report under ATAG that looks in detail at the impacts the airline industry makes and its specific contribution to sustainable development.

Many valid points were made during this process and many of these have now been incorporated into the main text. There are other avenues and processes that are looking at sustainable development topics in greater detail and other international bodies are conducting similar research. However, there are some areas that have been mentioned but have not been examined in more detail in this report. These issues include the following:

- NGOs are concerned that further work needs to be done to fully evaluate the impacts of tourism in developing countries. There are significant variations in the issues of sustainability between 'the north' and 'the south' and between developed and developing countries, which often require different approaches;
- Further attention has been requested towards issues such as human rights, labour rights, water rights, religious rights, child labour and indigenous people;
- Solutions to the shortage of skilled labour, training and human resources development are among the highest priorities for the industry, and are being explored further;
- There is disagreement as to whether tourism is a victim of the consequences of global warming or a contributor to it;
- Non-industry stakeholders urge the industry to set minimum and optimum levels of sustainable development that operators need to achieve using

specific performance indicators and to involve different stakeholders in this process;

- There is a need for clarity as to the extent to which the industry is committed to local partnerships for development and the empowerment of local communities;
- NGOs would welcome more detail on issues such as energy, water, sensitive ecosystems, and contributions to conservation of biological diversity and protected areas and international environmental regulations through the General Agreement on Trade in Services (GATS) and WTO;
- The question of transparency and monitoring of the tourism industry's activities is still open and needs to be further addressed.

This final report, however, cannot and will not satisfy all stakeholders' concerns. It was never designed to do so. It is an industry report, written and researched by industry representatives. Its purpose is not to reflect the many views of all the different stakeholders, who have other designated channels for expressing their views at WSSD. Nor does it provide perfect solutions for travel and tourism, or have all the answers to some of the pressing problems of real concern to the industry. The steering committee and the industry as a whole are well aware that there are still major challenges ahead to ensure preservation and protection of our natural resources and local and indigenous communities. However, this tourism industry report and the consultative process it went through demonstrates the industry's willingness to engage in an open, self-critical assessment with all groups involved in travel and tourism. It is now time for everyone to share in the responsibility of maintaining and sustaining the natural resources essential to tourism's very existence instead of each stakeholder blaming the other. Just as all should share the benefits that can be accrued from travel and tourism, so all, from consumers to governments, should start taking responsibility for their actions in this industry. The industry is aware and responsive to both the negative and positive impacts it makes on countries and destinations where it operates and sees this frank and open approach as a watershed for the way forward for travel and tourism. The industry stands ready and willing to take the initiative to work in partnership with all involved. It is now vital to engage all stakeholders, industry, governments, nongovernmental organisations, unions, consumers and UN organisations in constructive dialogue. The ultimate goal for the industry is for travel and tourism development to become fully sustainable and beneficial for everyone. Major progress towards this goal can be achieved during the next decade if all stakeholders work together in partnership. Moreover, practical and feasible sustainable development policies must be adopted by industry and governments alike – policies that can and will ensure the future of travel and tourism and thus sustain the natural resources and local communities of the planet.

8

International Tourism Market and the Organisations

Improving Competitiveness

In the present global and rapidly changing market the capacity to compete lies at the heart of national and industry efforts aimed to attract national and international visitors. The capacity to compete depends on the investments made to create an attractive and safe product, enhance its quality and provide for a friendly and encouraging competition environment. It brings into the picture the tourism enterprise and hence trade in tourism services, as well as tourism destinations whose quality " tourism product " is the sum of contributions and processes resulting from many stakeholders, both private and public.

The notion of quality of the tourism product includes assurance of safety and security as a basic factor. Quality also includes a professional approach to do things right at all times and meet legitimate expectations of consumers, thus helping to implement the principles contained in the Global Code of Ethics for Tourism. This programme recognises the fact that through trade and enterprise, tourism products and experiences are created and thus contribute to development goals such as reducing and eliminating poverty. However, it needs an appropriate and transparent regulatory framework, as well as the establishment and recognition of mandatory or voluntary standards, best practices and minimum requirements. In this way, tourism development can be linked to the achievement and measurement of progress towards social goals. The programme is also conceived from the consumer perspective which, on the supply side, contains a broad spectrum of enterprises and institutions, often going beyond the competence of NTAs and specific tourism businesses. It therefore requires different constituencies to be engaged at national level and international levels: economic actors, law enforcement and security bodies, health authorities, as well as public and industry standard- setting bodies.

WTO Position on Tourism Standards

The WTO Committee took note of the increasing role of standards in tourism activities responding to the needs of trade, consumer protection, promotion, marketing, communication and transparency and relating to terminology, management systems and technical specifications. It also took note of the search for international referents in the field and the variety of corresponding national and international activities and initiatives, particularly by the International Organisation for Standardisation (ISO) aiming to draft such standards.

The Committee welcomed the recent initiative undertaken by ISO, on the proposal of its Committee on Consumer Policy (COPOLCO) in which tourism sector organisations were represented, to create a new Technical Committee on tourism standards to deal with tourism terminology and technical specifications, and to develop the already existing quality management standards with a view to adapting them to the specificity of tourism activities.

The Committee considered that the already existing ISO standard on tourism terminology should be revised in order to achieve a broader international consensus. With respect to future standards on specifications of services offered by tourism service suppliers, the Committee took note that the principal aim of standardisation would be to address primarily the aspects of safety, security, hygiene and accessibility and recommended that the future standards, whenever touching upon other aspects, provide for the protection of cultural identity and cultural differences.

It further recommended that:

- the future ISO Technical Committee on tourism standards provide for a facility to allow representatives of consumer organisations to be permanently involved in the drafting procedure and that the Technical Committee terms of reference would encourage equitable participation from all world regions;
- the first areas for standard development include the activities in which there already exists more substantial national experience.

Economic and Social Phenomenon

Over the decades, tourism has experienced continued growth and deepening diversification to become one of the fastest growing economic sectors in the world. Modern tourism is closely linked to development and encompasses a growing number of new destinations. These dynamics have turned tourism into a key driver for socio-ýeconomic progress.

Today, the business volume of tourism equals or even surpasses that of oil exports,food products or automobiles. Tourism has become one of the major players ininternational commerce, and represents at the same time one of the main incomesources for many developing countries. This growth goes hand in hand with an increasing diversification and competition among destinations.

This global spread of tourism in industrialised and developed states has produced economic and employment benefits in many related sectors from construction to agriculture or telecommunications. The contribution of tourism to economic well-being depends on the quality and therevenues of the tourism offer. UNWTO assists destinations in their sustainablepositioning in ever more complex national and international markets. As the UN agencydedicated to tourism, UNWTO points out that particularly developing countries stand tobenefit from sustainable tourism and acts to help make this a reality.

Key numbers:

- From 1950 to 2005, international tourism arrivals expanded at an annual rate ofý 6.5%, growing from 25 million to 806 million travellers.
- The income generated by these arrivals grew at an even stronger rate reachingý11.2% during the same period, outgrowing the world economy, reaching aroundUS$ 680 billion in 2005.
- While in 1950 the top 15 destinations absorbed 88% of international arrivals, iný1970 the proportion was 75% and decreased to 57% in 2005, reflecting the emergence of new destinations, many of them in developing countries.

Current developments & forecasts:

- Worldwide arrivals reached 842 million in 2006, representing a 4.6% year onyear growth.
- 2008 looks set to be the fourth consecutive year of sustained growth for aglobal tourism industry that continues to show its resilience to any natural orman-made crises.
- UNWTO predicts a 4% growth of international tourist arrivals in 2007, in linewith its long-term forecast growth rate through to 2020 of 4.1%.

By 2020 international arrivals are expected to surpass 1.5 billion people.

Travel Advisories and Trade Liberalisation High on UNWTO Quality Support Committee Agenda

The World Tourism Organisation's (UNWTO) Quality support and trade committee met for the first time under the new chairmanship of Portugal and addressed the issues of travel advisories, trade liberalisation and health in international travel. The challenge is to manage travel advisories in such a way as to maximize the protection of travellers and minimize the impact on travel, trade and development. While this is an issue in the hands of industrial countries today, the potential flow of travellers from developing markets indicates two-way trading considerations, the Committee stressed.

UNWTO Secretary-General Mr. Francesco Frangialli underlined that the governments in cooperation with the international tourism industry "have to make a step forward in implementing travel advisories in accordance with the Global Code of Ethics". While the quality of cautionary travel advisories is undoubtedly improving with experience, there are currently a number of continuing concerns, for example lack of geographical specificity and the nature of the threat, consultation with the affected State, updating and review of the advisory, and inconsistencies amongst advisories issued by different states. Portugal as Chairman of Committee suggested that the UNWTO Secretariat prepares a code of conduct, if possible in cooperation with the International Civil Aviation Organisation (ICAO) and the World Health Organisation (WHO). The issue of travel advisories will be raised again end of April at the meeting of UNWTO regional commission for the Middle East and North Africa in Damascus, Syria. Furthermore, the Committee assessed the findings of a recent International symposium on liberalisation and trade in tourism services, showing that trade and specifically tourism-related policies at national level are poorly coordinated and that groups of countries, generators and recipients of visitor flows, are not equitably equipped with consumer protection, competition and "sustainability" laws, thus making it difficult for countries not enjoying an adequate regulatory structure to reap the benefits of liberalisation.

It is now expected that negotiators become more aware of the importance of tourism, including various modes of supply of tourism services and other factors, such as the sector's versatility and ubiquity, the mutual dependence between air transport and access to services at destinations, and the need to provide for non-discriminatory standards attached to commitments and anchored in domestic regulation.

The Role of UNWTO

UNWTO is committed to Tourism, Travel and the Millennium Development Goals. It is fair to assume that this growth scenario will suffer from the economic downturn and more than fair to say that massive prolonged increases in fuel price, with few short term options (at least for airlines), as well as other "mega crises" will have a fundamental depressant effect. But the numbers of potential travellers are so huge and the logic of targeting tourism for development so pervasive that the long term growth prospects will remain substantial by any measure. Before UNWTO becoming the UN tourism Agency; in a world where mega disasters – man made and natural and are proliferating and the UN is increasingly the default response system.

- UNWTO has a seat at the top UN table and the decisive and central role in representing the interests of the sector be it pandemics: Tsunamis: earthquakes, floods or terrorism.
- We have a proud track record in areas like statistics, market and brand support, crisis response, local level poverty reduction, climate solutions and sustainable development.

UN Promotes Sustainable Tourism at World Heritage Sites

UNESCO World Heritage Sites must be treated as an integral part of the tourism product as they face up to future challenges. The ever-growing number of international and domestic tourists who are attracted to these emblematic destinations can also be a threat to their conservation. This was one of the key messages emerged from the conference

Sustainable Tourism Management at World Heritage Sites, jointly organised by UNWTO and the UNESCO (United Nations Educational, Scientific and Cultural Organisation) World Heritage Centre. The need for effective public-private partnerships to ensure the sustainable management of such diverse sites, which represent complex systems of cultural and natural heritage values, was underscored.

Mainstreaming World Heritage Sites

Heritage sites need to be integrated in the management of destinations and regions, taking into consideration the complete tourism supply chain. Heritage sites cannot be managed in isolation. Tourism functions through a long supply chain and there is a range of transportation, accommodation, information and tour operation services that are delivered before a tourist actually arrives at the gate of a heritage site; tourism can be influenced at any of these points.

One UN

Art Pederson, tourism specialist at the UNESCO World Heritage Centre, highlighted the relevance of the meeting for enhancing United Nations coordination on key tourism-related conservation and economic development issues. "Cooperation must take place to combine forces, so as to build capacity to deal with the growing visitor management pressures in China and in other countries. The ongoing collabouration of the UNESCO World Heritage Tourism Programme with UNWTO facilitates this and will help us meet current and future tourism challenges and utilize the industry's benefits for site conservation and local communities."

Tourism and the World Economy

International tourism receipts represented in 2006 approximately 6 per cent of worldwide exports of goods and services (as expressed in US$). When considering service exports exclusively, the share of tourism exports increases to nearly 30 per cent.

2006

World Exports of Merchandise and commercial services (Balance of Payments, Goods and Services Credit)

US$ billion	Share (%)	Share (%)	
Total		**9,089**	**100**
Merchandise exports	**9,089**	**100**	
Agricultural products	674	7	
Mining products	960	11	
Manufactures	5,437	60	
Other	223	2	
Commercial services	**1,795**	**20**	**100**
Transportation	405	4	23
Travel	525	6	29
Other	885	10	48

Source: World Trade Organisation, World Tourism Organisation

Tourism demand depends above all strongly on the economic conditions in major generating markets. When economies grow, levels of disposable income will usually also rise. A relatively large part of discretionary income will typically be spent on tourism, in particular in the case of emerging economies. A tightening of the economic situation on the other hand, will often result in a decrease or trading down of tourism spending. In general, the growth of international tourism arrivals significantly outpaces growth of economic output as measured in Gross Domestic Product (GDP). In years when world economic growth exceeds 4 per cent, the growth of tourism volume tends to be higher. When GDP growth falls below 2 per cent, tourism growth tends to be even lower. In and GDP at 3.5 per cent, *i.e.,* tourism grew on average 1.3 times faster than GDP. the period 1975-2000 tourism increased at an average rate of 4.6 per cent a year. With 846 million international tourist arrivals, corresponding to an increase of 5.4% over the previous year, 2006 exceeded expectations. The tourism sector continued to enjoy above average results and recorded a third year of sustained growth. One notable feature of 2006 was the continuing healthy performance of emerging destinations, backed up by one of the longest periods of sustained economic expansion. All regions and subregions succeeded in achieving positive growth, although the regional averages mask some fairly mixed performances across different subregions and countries.

The 846 million international arrivals currently estimated represent an additional 43 million over 2005's level marking a new record year for the industry. Of these 43 million, 22 million were for Europe, 12 million for Asia and the Pacific, and 3 million for each of the remaining regions the Americas, Africa and the Middle East.

Africa (+9%) was again the star performer in 2006, continuing to record growth at almost twice the global rate. Subsaharan Africa (+10%) was the major contributor to this rise, while North Africa (+7%) also ended the year above the world average. Asia and the Pacific (+8%) maintained its positive growth level of the previous year – due in no small part to the full recovery of Thailand and the Maldives from the impact of the December 2004 tsunami, as well as to excellent performances from other emerging destinations in the region.

Europe (+5%) performed well above target while, in the Middle East, international tourist arrivals are estimated to have risen by 9%, in spite of the overall geopolitical situation and the Israel-Lebanon crisis, which marked the summer months in the region. The weakest region was the Americas, whose 2% estimated growth was well below target, largely as a result of a stagnation in arrivals in Canada and Mexico and despite excellent results for Central America and healthy performances from the Caribbean and South America.

In 2006, just over half of all international tourist arrivals were motivated by leisure, recreation and holidays (51%) a total of 430 million. Business travel accounted for some 16% (131 million), and 27% represented travel for other purposes, such as visiting friends and relatives (VFR), religious reasons/ pilgrimages, health treatment, etc (225 million). The purpose of visit for the remaining 6% of arrivals was not specified.

Air transport (46%) and transport over land – whether by road (43%) or rail (4%) generate roughly equal shares of all arrivals, while arrivals over water accounted for 7% in 2006. For the past three years, the trend has been for air transport to grow at a faster pace than ground and water transport.

US$ 57 billion more in receipts from international tourism worldwide

For many destinations, visitor expenditure on accommodation, food and drink, local transport, entertainment, shopping, *etc.* is an important pillar of their economies, creating much needed employment and opportunities for development. Some 75 countries earned more than US$ 1 billion from international tourism in 2006. UNWTO estimates that worldwide receipts from international tourism reached US$ 733 billion (584 billion euros) in 2006. In absolute terms, international tourism receipts increased by US$ 57 billion (40 billion euros) in 2006 an amount well above the receipts of the world's second biggest tourism earner, Spain, or the combined receipts of the Middle East and Africa.

Asia and the Pacific improved results by US$ 18 billion to US$ 153 billion, while the Americas recorded an absolute increase of US$ 9 billion to US$ 154 billion. In 2002, Asia and the Pacific surpassed the Americas in terms of international tourist arrivals, becoming the second most visited region in the world after Europe. As international tourism in Asia and the Pacific tends to grow at a faster pace than it does in the Americas both in terms of arrivals and receipts the region is firmly on track to overtake the Americas in terms of tourism receipts as well in the coming years.

In absolute volume of receipts, the biggest winner last year was still Europe, which gained an additional US$ 26 billion, lifting its total to US$ 374 billion, or 298 billion euros

(51% of the world total). Africa added US$ 3 billion, raising to US$ 24 billion (3% share). Meanwhile, estimates based on available data point to an increase of US$ 1 billion to US$ 27 billion for the Middle East (4% share).

Although all regions and subregions shared in last year's absolute increase, growth rates varied. In relative terms, and as expressed in local currencies at constant prices (*i.e.*, taking out the effect of exchange rates and inflation), international tourism receipts worldwide grew by 4.3% in 2006, following a 3.2% rise in 2005. By comparison, international tourist arrivals worldwide increased by around 5.5% in both 2006 and 2005. As was the case with arrivals, the relative growth in receipts was strongest in Africa (+10%) and Asia and the Pacific (+9%). Europe's receipts increased by 4% well above the 2.5% growth recorded in 2005 while growth in the Americas (+2%) fell to less than half its 2005 level. The only region to show a negative growth trend in relative terms in 2006 was the Middle East (-1.4%), since its growth in absolute terms was not sufficient to keep up with inflation. The relative growth reached double-digit rates in a number of subregions, such as North Africa (+17%), South Asia (+14%), North-East Asia (+11%), Central America and South-East Asia (each at around +10%).

For destination countries, receipts from international tourism count as exports and cover transactions generated by same-day as well as overnight visitors. However, these do not include receipts from international passenger transport contracted from companies outside the travellers' countries of residence, which are reported in a separate category, 'international passenger transport'. Although the availability of comparable international data is somewhat limited, the export value of international passenger transport has in recent years been estimated at around 17% of the combined receipts from international tourism and passenger transport, corresponding in 2006 to some US$ 148 billion.

This takes receipts from international tourism, including international passenger transport, to over US$ 880 billion in 2006. In other words, around US$ 2.4 billion is earned every day by international tourism. European tourism was boosted by a whole host of events in 2006, from the Winter Olympic Games in Turin to the FIFA World Football Cup in Germany, the Ryder Cup in Ireland, and numerous cultural events – such as the 400th anniversary of Rembrandt's birth, Mozart's 250th and Picasso's 125th. The continuing expansion and spread of low-cost carriers (LCCs) across the region also contributed to stimulating demand. The estimated 5% growth in international tourist arrivals may seem modest by comparison with other world regions. But the growth, which comes on top of an already very large base (since Europe attracts over half the world's tourist arrivals), represents 22 million additional international tourists in just one year. Moreover, Europe has been one of the regions turning in a steady performance over recent years without large peaks and troughs.

The 5% growth for international tourist arrivals marks some variations from one subregion to another. Both Central and Eastern Europe (+4%) and Western Europe (+5%) recovered in 2006 from their lower-than average growth of the previous year, while arrivals in Southern and Mediterranean Europe (+5%) averaged one percentage point less than in 2005. Nevertheless, this was still an excellent result for a subregion that receives 165 million tourists annually. But all three subregions lagged behind the star performer of the last three years – Northern Europe (+8% in 2006).

Tourism demand for the traditional sun and sea destinations of Southern and Mediterranean Europe remained buoyant, as is reflected in the results for Italy (+12%), Greece (+9%), Spain (+4%) and Portugal (+6%). Among Europe's main destinations, Italy was by far the best performer in 2006, after a number of weaker years. Arrivals were up 12%, following an excellent winter season at the start of the year, thanks in part to Turin's hosting of the Winter Olympics. Greece (+9%) also performed above average. The post- Olympics effect has reportedly had a very positive impact on city tourism and on the meetings industry, as a result of the improved infrastructure and quality of hotels. By contrast, arrivals fell 7% in Turkey.

This can of course be attributed in part to increased political tension as a result of the Israel-Lebanon crisis, although Turkey has also suffered from terrorist attacks and threats.

In Northern Europe, the UK achieved a healthy 9% increase, following its already strong performances of 2004 and 2005, while Ireland (+9%) saw continued healthy growth from all major markets. In Western Europe, Germany's hosting of the FIFA Football World Cup brought significant gains – international arrivals were up 10%. The Netherlands (+7%) had an excellent year with celebrations surrounding the 400th anniversary of Rembrandt making a major contribution to growth. Switzerland (+9%) saw growth from emerging long- and short-haul markets, but LCCs also boosted short-break business. Meanwhile, France (+4%) finally overcame its arrivals stagnation of recent years. In Central and Eastern Europe, Ukraine and Bulgaria (+7% each) did particularly well.

Asia and the Pacific

Asia and the Pacific was, after Africa, the second best performing region in the world in 2006, recording an estimated 8% increase in arrivals. Both South Asia (+11%) and South-East Asia (+9%) performed above average. North-East Asia is estimated to have finished the year 7% above 2005's level, while data for Oceania (+0.4%) points to stagnation for the subregion. Asia and the Pacific's healthy performance is all the more remarkable as it reflects sustained growth achieved by the region over the past few years. 2004 was a record year in terms of growth (+27%), but it was followed by another two strong years – +8% in 2005 and 2006 even after the December 2004 tsunami. In North-East Asia, Macao (China) (+18%) was the subregion's star performer in 2006, thanks in no small part to the development of new hotels and casinos and to increased LCC access. Japan (+9%) also enjoyed a very good year. Inbound tourism to China (+6%) and Hong Kong (China) (+7%) slowed somewhat in 2006, as demand was comparatively weak from neighbouring Korea (Republic of) and Japan. Nevertheless, growth was still significant, in particular since it followed the extraordinary growth rates of the previous two years. The Republic of Korea's lower than average 2% rise is attributed to its strong won, which has made the destination less competitive. Growth for Taiwan (province of China) (+4%) was also below average.

Meanwhile, in South-East Asia, several destinations recorded 10% or higher growth Thailand and Cambodia achieved +20% each. Thailand's strong performance is largely attributable to its recovery from the December 2004 tsunami. As for many of its neighbours, LCCs have helped boost tourism demand for Malaysia (+7%), as well as opening up new regional source markets and destinations. 2006 was another good year for tourism to the Philippines (+8%), following its upbeat performance over the previous two years, but also for Singapore, where arrivals were up by 7%. In South Asia, the Maldives (+52%) made a full recovery from the December 2004 tsunami, thanks mainly to increased airline access and enhanced marketing and promotion, and India's tourism (+13%) goes from strength to strength as greater awareness of the country and increased promotion boost demand. Among Oceania's main destinations, a decline from Japan is to blame in part for Australia's disappointing performance (+0.9%). Australia, as well as New Zealand (+1.8%), suffered from increased oil prices and, consequently, higher airfares – a factor contributing to the erosion of both destinations' competitiveness in international markets as they depend heavily on longhaul airline traffic. In 2006, Africa was the leading region in terms of growth in international tourist arrivals – for the second consecutive year with the full year at a 9% increase (+7% for North Africa and +10% for Subsaharan Africa).

North Africa's growth is primarily due to Morocco's stellar performance (+12%), attributable among other factors to dedicated investment in tourism infrastructure and to the liberalisation of air transport and the subsequent entry of low-cost airlines. Tunisia, on the other hand, had a slightly lower than average results (+3%) due to market volatility and problems with air transport. Among the major Subsaharan

African destinations that have provided data for 2006, Cape Verde (+22%), Kenya (+15% in visitor arrivals), Lesotho (+18%), Madagascar (+13%), South Africa (+14%), Sudan (+33%), Uganda (+15%) and Zimbabwe (+47%) turned in some of the best results.

Demand for Long-haul Travel Keeps Growing

While as much as 80% of international travel takes place within the same region, travel between different regions tends to grow at a faster rate than intraregional travel. This was not the case between 2001 and 2003, due to events such as SARS, terrorism and the Iraq war in fact, long-haul travel demand declined over the three years.

However, and since 2004, interregional travel has been growing faster than intraregional travel again. In 2006, interregional travel increased by 8% as against a growth of 5% for intraregional traffic. In terms of source markets, international tourism is still largely concentrated in the industrialised countries of Europe, the Americas and Asia and the Pacific. However, with rising levels of disposable income, many emerging economies have shown fast growth over recent years, in particular markets in North-East and South-East Asia, Central and Eastern Europe, the Middle East and Southern Africa. In 2006, most markets maintained the growth levels regained in 2004, when they rebounded from the depressed results of the preceding years. By region, Africa recorded the biggest gain in relative terms in 2006 (+12%), followed by the Middle East (+9%) and Asia and the Pacific (+8%). The Americas continued its recovery (+4%), while arrivals originating from Europe (+5%) grew in line with their performance of the previous two years. Most interestingly, the Middle East was the fastest growing source region over the last six years, recording an average annual increase of 10%, followed by Africa (+7%) and Asia and the Pacific (+6%).

International Tourism Top Spenders

In 2006, there were almost no changes in the leaders'

ranking of the world's biggest spenders on international tourism. Two major exceptions China continued to rise up the ranking, overtaking Italy to take sixth place, and the Netherlands was ousted from the top ten by the Republic of Korea, thanks to an 18% increase in spending on tourism abroad by Koreans in 2006.

Among the top ten world source markets, which accounted for over half of all international tourism spending worldwide, the best performers in 2006, apart from the Republic of Korea, were China (+12%), Canada and the Russian Federation (+6% each). Among the top five major source markets, it is worth noting the 4% to 5% increase for the USA, the UK and Japan, as well as the stagnation in expenditure by German travellers abroad (-0.3%) and France's more modest rise (+2%) compared with its 9% growth in 2005.

Long-term prospects

Tourism 2020 Vision is the World Tourism Organisation's long-term forecast and assessment of the development of tourism up to the first 20 years of the new millennium. An essential outcome of the *Tourism 2020 Vision* are quantitative forecasts covering a 25 years period, with 1995 as base year and forecasts for 2010 and 2020. Although the evolution of tourism in the last years has been irregular, UNWTO maintains its long-term forecast for the moment. The underlying structural trends of the forecast are believed not to have significantly changed. Experience shows that in the short-term, periods of faster growth (1995, 1996, 2000, 2004 to 2006) alternate with periods of slow growth (2001 to 2003). And, the actual pace of growth is in reality in line with the *Tourism 2020 Vision* forecast as international tourist arrivals show an average growth of 4.2% between 1995 and 2006.

Tourism

UNWTO's *Tourism 2020 Vision* forecasts that international arrivals are expected to reach nearly 1.6 billion by the year 2020. Of these worldwide arrivals in 2020, 1.2 billion will be intraregional and 378 million will be long-haul travellers.

The total tourist arrivals by region shows that by 2020 the top three receiving regions will be Europe (717 million tourists), East Asia and the Pacific (397 million) and Americas (282 million), followed by Africa, the Middle East and South Asia. East Asia and the Pacific, South Asia, the Middle East and Africa are forecasted to record growth at rates of over 5% per year, compared to the world average of 4.1%. The more mature regions, Europe and Americas, are anticipated to show lower than average growth rates. Europe will maintain the highest share of world arrivals, although there will be a decline from 60% in 1995 to 46% in 2020.

Tourism demand depends above all strongly on the economic conditions in major generating markets. When economies grow, levels of disposable income will usually also rise. A relatively large part of discretionary income will typically be spent on tourism, in particular in the case of emerging economies. A tightening of the economic situation on the other hand, will often result in a decrease or trading down of tourism spending.

In general, the growth of international tourism arrivals significantly outpaces growth of economic output as measured in Gross Domestic Product (GDP). In years when world economic growth exceeds 4 per cent, the growth of tourism volume tends to be higher. When GDP growth falls below 2 per cent, tourism growth tends to be even lower. In and GDP at 3.5 per cent, *i.e.*, tourism grew on average 1.3 times faster than GDP. the period 1975-2000 tourism increased at an average rate of 4.6 per cent a year.

Bibliography

A.J. Burkart and S. Medlik, *Tourism: Past, Present, and Future*, 2nd ed. London: Heinemann, p.189, 1981.

Baaijens, S.R., Nijkamp, P. and K.V. Montfort. Explanatory meta-analysis for the comparison and transfer of regional tourist income multipliers. *Regional Studies,* 32: 839-849, 1998.

Barff, R. and Knight III, P.L. Dynamic Shift Share Analysis , *Growth and Change*, 19 (1), pp.1-11, 1988.

Beaver, Allan. *A Dictionary of Travel and Tourism Terminology.* Wallingford: CAB International. p. 313, 2002.

Beynon, J. & Dunkerkey, D. *Globalization: The Reader.* New York: Routledge, 2001.

Communicate at the Interregional Conference at United Nations regarding the arrangement of the territory according to the tourism development, Dubrovnik, 2002,

Cooper, Chris; et al. *Tourism: Principles and Practice* (3rd ed.). Harlow: Pearson Education, 2005.

Escobar, A. Gender, Place and Networks: A Political Ecology of Cyberculture. In *Women @ Internet: Creating New Cultures in Cyberspace* W. Harcourt (Ed.). London: Zed Books, 1999.

Frechtling, D. C. Assessing the impacts of travel and tourism — Introduction to travel impact estimation. Chapter 27 in Ritchie, J.R.B. & Goeldner, C.R. *Travel Tourism and Hospitality Research: A Handbook for Managers*. New York: John Wiley, 1987.

Gummesson, E. *Total Relationship Marketing*. Oxford: Butterworth-Heinemann, 1999.

Guy Montford, *Tourism and Conservation*, Wildlife, London, 1975.

Haynes, K.E. and Machunda, Z.B. Considerations in Extending Shift Share Analysis: Note , *Growth and Change*, 18 (2), pp. 69-78, 1987.

Horner, S. & Swarbrooke, J. *International Cases in Tourism Management.* Oxford: Elsevier Butterworth-Heinemann, 2004.

J. Hannigan, *Fantasy City: Pleasure and Profit in the Postmodern Metropolis,* D. Judd and S. Fainstein (eds), *The Tourist City*, New Haven: Yale University Press, 1999.

J. Kotkin, *The New Geography* (New York: Random House); A.J. Scott, 'The Cultural Economy: Geography and the Creative Field', *Media, Culture, and Society* 21, pp.807–17, 2000.

Lennon, J. John; Foley, Malcolm. *Dark Tourism*. London: Continuum, 2000.

Maturana, H.R. & Varela, F.J. *Autopoiesis and Congnition: The Realization of the Living.* Dordrecht, Netherlands: D. Reidel, 1980.

Mirela Mazilu, *Eco-tourism and touristic arrangements*, Ed. Scrisul Romanesc, 2004.

Mirela Mazilu, Geography of Tourism, Ed.Didactica –Pedagogica, Bucharest, 2007.

Mirela Mazilu, Le Tourisme roumain dans le contexte du tourisme europeen, Ed.Universitaria, Craiova,2007.

Morrison, A., Rimmington, M. & Williams, C. *Entrepreneurship in the Hospitality, Tourism and Leisure Industries*. Oxford: Butterworth-Heinemann, 1999.

Nunnally, J.O, Psychometric Theory , New York: McGraw-Hill, 1978.

Pallant, J. SPSS Survival Manual , Sydney: Allen and Unwin, 2001.

Quinion, Michael. "Dark Tourism". *World Wide Words*, 2010.

Recommendations on Tourism Statistics". *Statistical Papers*. M; New York: United Nations, (83): 5. 1994,

Robertson, R. Glocalization:Time-Space and Homogeneity-Heterogeneity'. In *Global Modernities.* M. Featherstone, S. Lash and R. Robertson (Eds.), London: Sage, 1995.

S. Negut, *Tourism Geography*, Ed. Meteor Press, Bucuresti, 2003.

See R. Stock, 'Political and Social Contributions of International Tourism to the Development of Israel', *Annals of Tourism Research* 5, pp.30–42; L.K. Richter, *The Politics of Tourism in Asia,* Honolulu, HI: University of Hawaii Press. 1989.

Stokes, H.K. Shift Share Once Again , *Regional and Urban Economics*, Vol. 4, pp. 57-60, 1974.

Tabachnick, L.L. and Fidell, L.S. Using Multivariate Statistics , New York: Harper Collins, 1996.

Theobald, W. *Global Tourism: The Next Decade*. Oxford: Butterworth-Heinemann, 1998.

Toh, R.S., Khan, H. and Lim, L. Two-Stage Shift-Share Analyses of Tourism Arrivals and Arrivals by Purpose of Visit: The Singapore Experience , *Journal of Travel Research*, Vol.43, August, pp.57-66, 2004.

Translated by Ministry of Tourism – Prognoses on Tourism. Ministry of Tourism Center of Studies and Projects for the promotion of the tourism, 2007.

Tsuchiko, T. *The New Generation of Japanese Swordsmiths*. London: Kodansha Europea, 2002.

Turner and J. Ash, *The Golden Hordes: International Tourism and the Plcasure Periphery,* London: Constable, 1975.

UNWTO technical manual: Collection of Tourism Expenditure Statistics" (PDF). World Tourism Organization. 1995.

UNWTO Tourism Highlights, 2009 Edition". World Tourism Organization. 2009.

Wagner, J. E. Estimating the economic impacts of tourism. *Annals of Tourism Research*, 24 (3): 592-608, 1997.

Wahab, S. & Cooper, C. *Tourism in the Globalisation Age.* London: Routledge, 2001.

Wang, G. *The New Communications Landscape: Demystifying Media Globalization* London: Routledge, 2000.

Wilson, S. and Mei, W.Y. The Export Competitiveness of ASEAN Economies *Asian Economic Bulletin*, Vol.16, No.2, pp. 208-229, 1999.

Wood, R. E. Last Access, 2004.

WTO Compendium of Tourism Statistics , Madrid, Spain. World Bank Little Data Book, 2007.

Zhou, D., Yanagida, J. F., Chakravorty, U., and Leung, P. Estimating economic impacts from tourism. *Annals of Tourism Research*, 24 (1): 76-89, 1997.